★ TOO MUCH

HOPELESS ™

SAVAGES

★ TOO MUCH ★ HOPELESS SAVAGES

Written
by
JEN VAN METER

Illustrated
by
CHRISTINE NORRIE

Flashbacks & Chapter 4
by
ROSS CAMPBELL

Pencil Breakdowns
by
CHYNNA CLUGSTON-MAJ
(Chapter 3)
&
CHRISTINE NORRIE
(Chapter 4)

Cover
by
CHRISTINE NORRIE
&
GUY MAJOR

Lettered
by
CHRISTINE NORRIE & ANDY LIS,
AMIE MCKELVIE, TOM ORZECHOWSKI,
& BRYAN LEE O'MALLEY

Introduction & Afterword
by
JAMIE S. RICH
&
CHRISTINE NORRIE

Hopless Savages logo based
on logo designed
by
ANDI WATSON

Designed
by
KEITH WOOD

Original Series Edited
by
JAMIE S. RICH

Collection Edited
by
RANDAL C. JARRELL

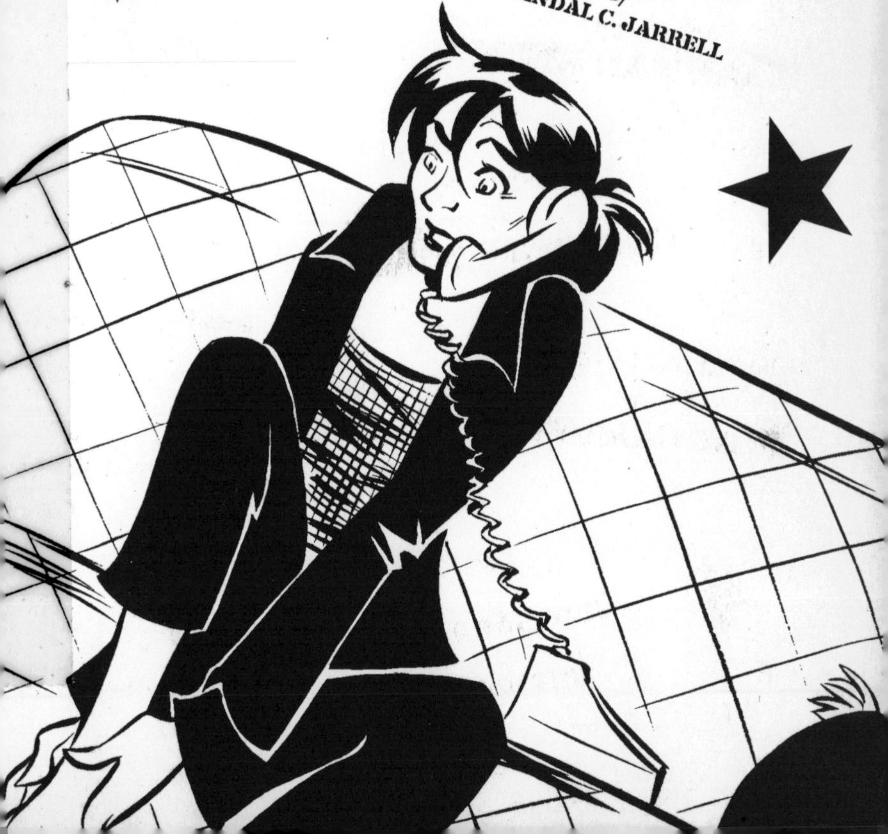

Published
by
Oni Press, Inc.

Joe Nozemack, publisher
James Lucas Jones, senior editor
Randal C. Jarrell, managing editor
Ian Shaughnessy, series editorial assistant

This collects issues 1-4 of the miniseries
Too Much Hopeless Savages.

ONI PRESS, INC.
6336 SE Milwaukie Avenue, PMB 30
Portland, OR 97202
USA

www.onipress.com
www.spookoo.com
www.greenoblivion.com

First edition: August 2004
ISBN 1-929998-85-6

1 3 5 7 9 10 8 6 4 2

PRINTED IN CANADA.

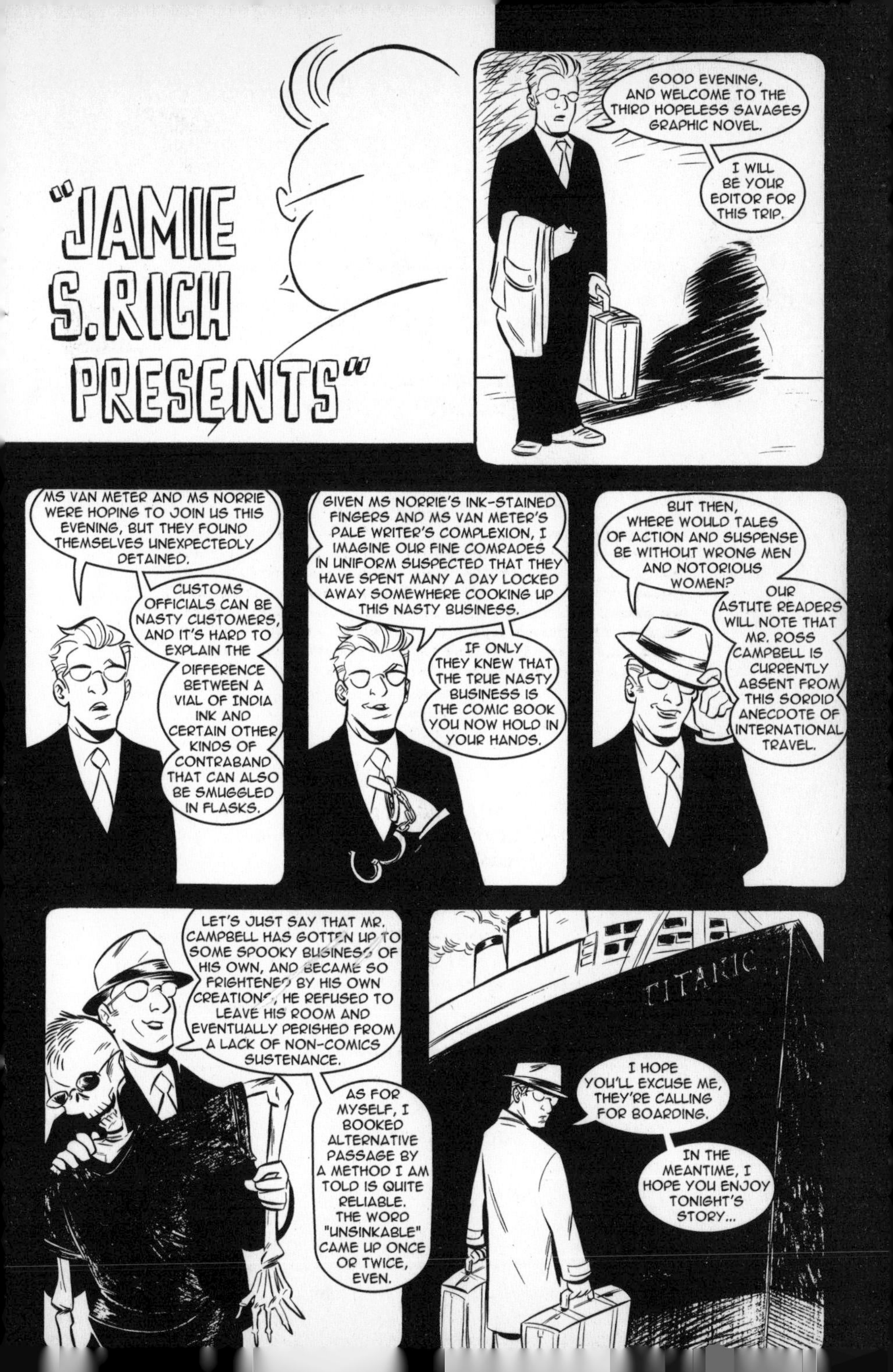
"JAMIE S.RICH PRESENTS"
GOOD EVENING, AND WELCOME TO THE THIRD HOPELESS SAVAGES GRAPHIC NOVEL.
I WILL BE YOUR EDITOR FOR THIS TRIP.
MS VAN METER AND MS NORRIE WERE HOPING TO JOIN US THIS EVENING, BUT THEY FOUND THEMSELVES UNEXPECTEDLY DETAINED.
CUSTOMS OFFICIALS CAN BE NASTY CUSTOMERS, AND IT'S HARD TO EXPLAIN THE DIFFERENCE BETWEEN A VIAL OF INDIA INK AND CERTAIN OTHER KINDS OF CONTRABAND THAT CAN ALSO BE SMUGGLED IN FLASKS.
GIVEN MS NORRIE'S INK-STAINED FINGERS AND MS VAN METER'S PALE WRITER'S COMPLEXION, I IMAGINE OUR FINE COMRADES IN UNIFORM SUSPECTED THAT THEY HAVE SPENT MANY A DAY LOCKED AWAY SOMEWHERE COOKING UP THIS NASTY BUSINESS.
IF ONLY THEY KNEW THAT THE TRUE NASTY BUSINESS IS THE COMIC BOOK YOU NOW HOLD IN YOUR HANDS.
BUT THEN, WHERE WOULD TALES OF ACTION AND SUSPENSE BE WITHOUT WRONG MEN AND NOTORIOUS WOMEN?
OUR ASTUTE READERS WILL NOTE THAT MR. ROSS CAMPBELL IS CURRENTLY ABSENT FROM THIS SORDID ANECDOTE OF INTERNATIONAL TRAVEL.
LET'S JUST SAY THAT MR. CAMPBELL HAS GOTTEN UP TO SOME SPOOKY BUSINESS OF HIS OWN, AND BECAME SO FRIGHTENED BY HIS OWN CREATIONS, HE REFUSED TO LEAVE HIS ROOM AND EVENTUALLY PERISHED FROM A LACK OF NON-COMICS SUSTENANCE.
AS FOR MYSELF, I BOOKED ALTERNATIVE PASSAGE BY A METHOD I AM TOLD IS QUITE RELIABLE. THE WORD "UNSINKABLE" CAME UP ONCE OR TWICE, EVEN.
TITANIC
I HOPE YOU'LL EXCUSE ME, THEY'RE CALLING FOR BOARDING.
IN THE MEANTIME, I HOPE YOU ENJOY TONIGHT'S STORY...

THE HOPELESS-SAVAGE FAMILY

Dirk Hopeless
a.k.a. David Sterling

Nikki Savage

Rat Bastard
Hopeless-Savage

Arsenal Fierce
Hopeless-Savage

Twitch Strummer
Hopeless-Savage

Skank Zero
Hopeless-Savage

Claude Shi
Arsenal's Boyfriend

EXTENDED FAMILY

Henry Shi
Twitch's Boyfriend

Vera Savage
Nikki's mother

Grandma Shi
The eldest matriarch of the Shi family, rumored to be a witch

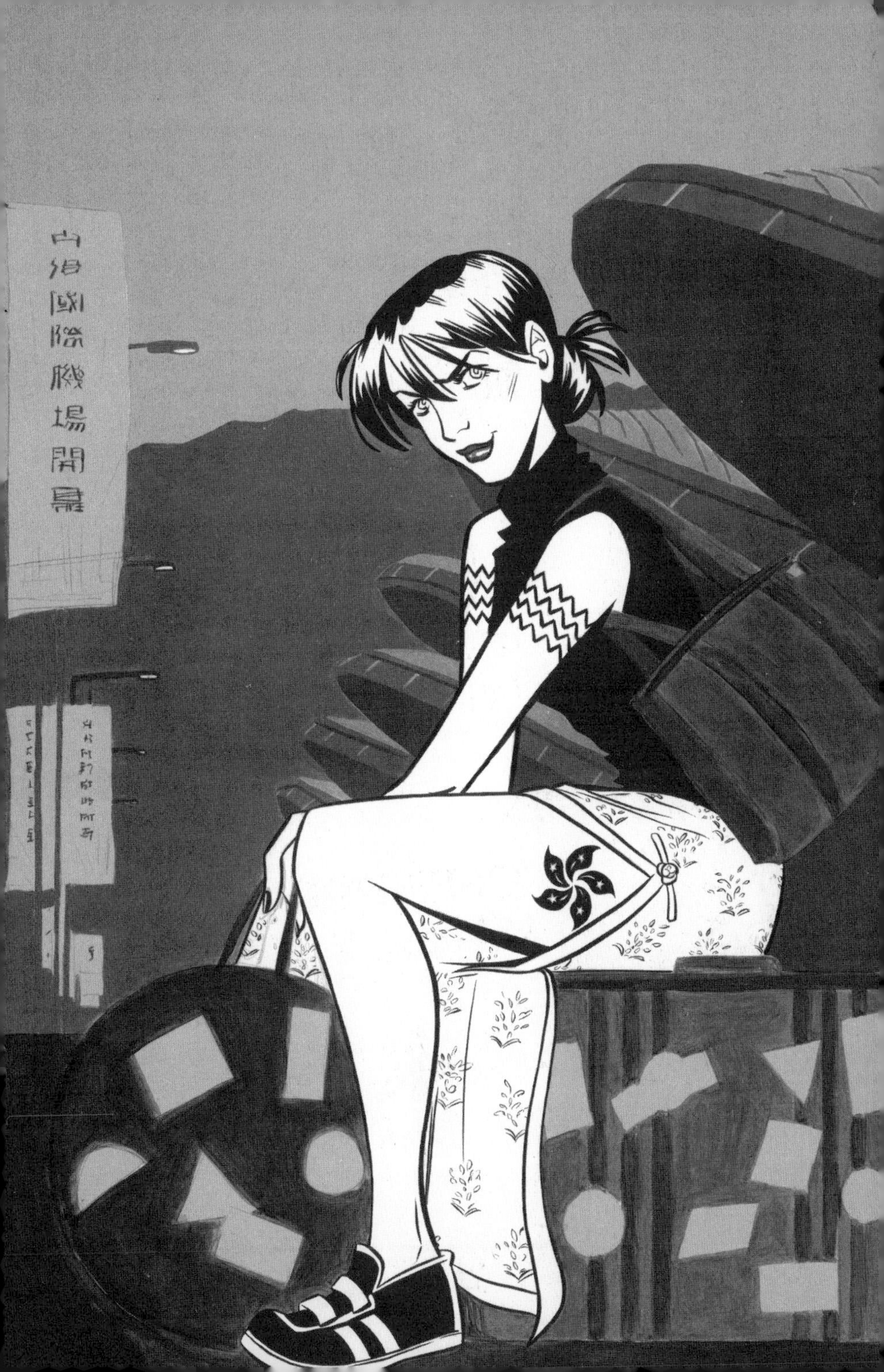
國際機場開幕

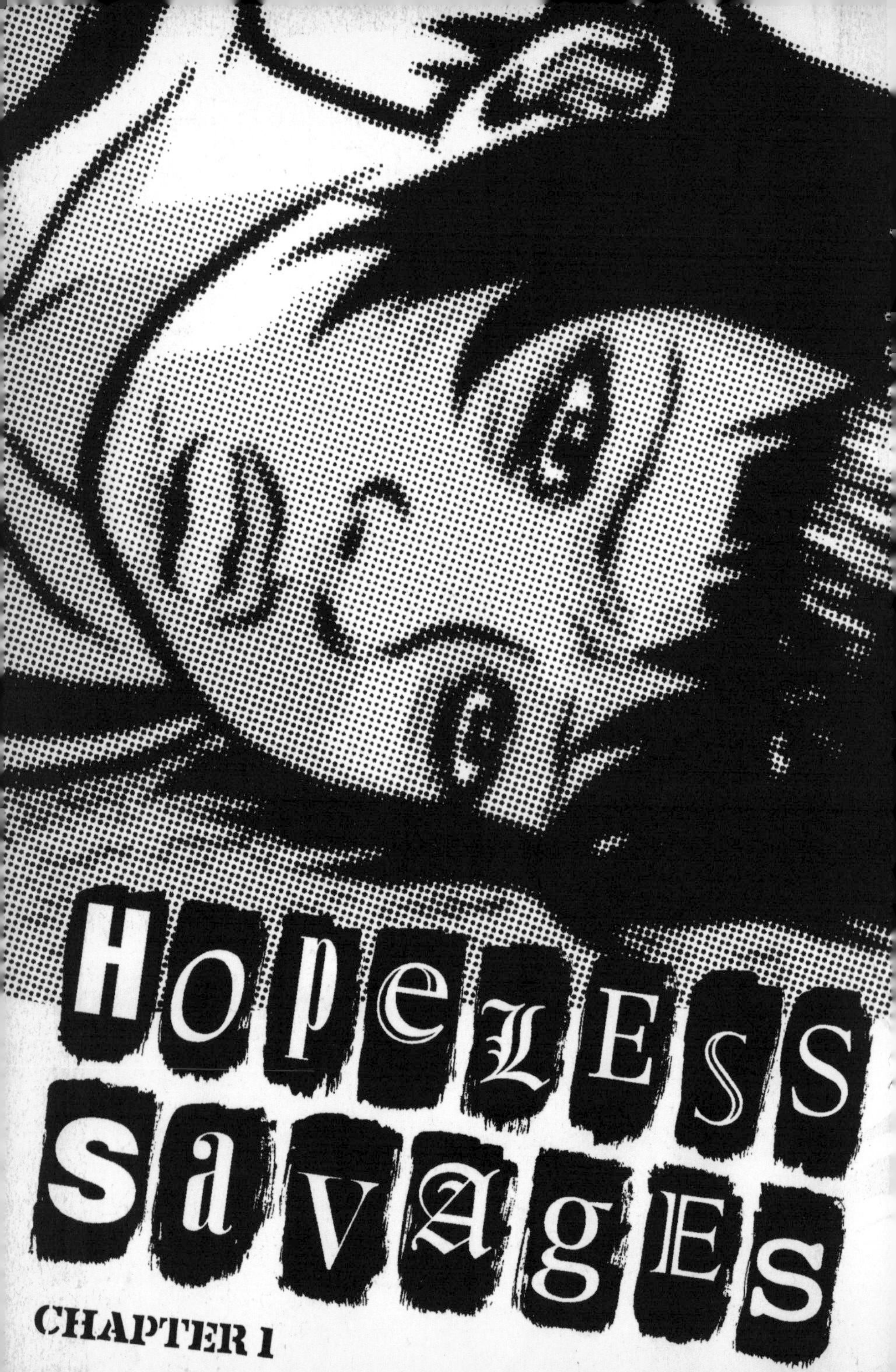

HOPELESS SAVAGES

CHAPTER 1

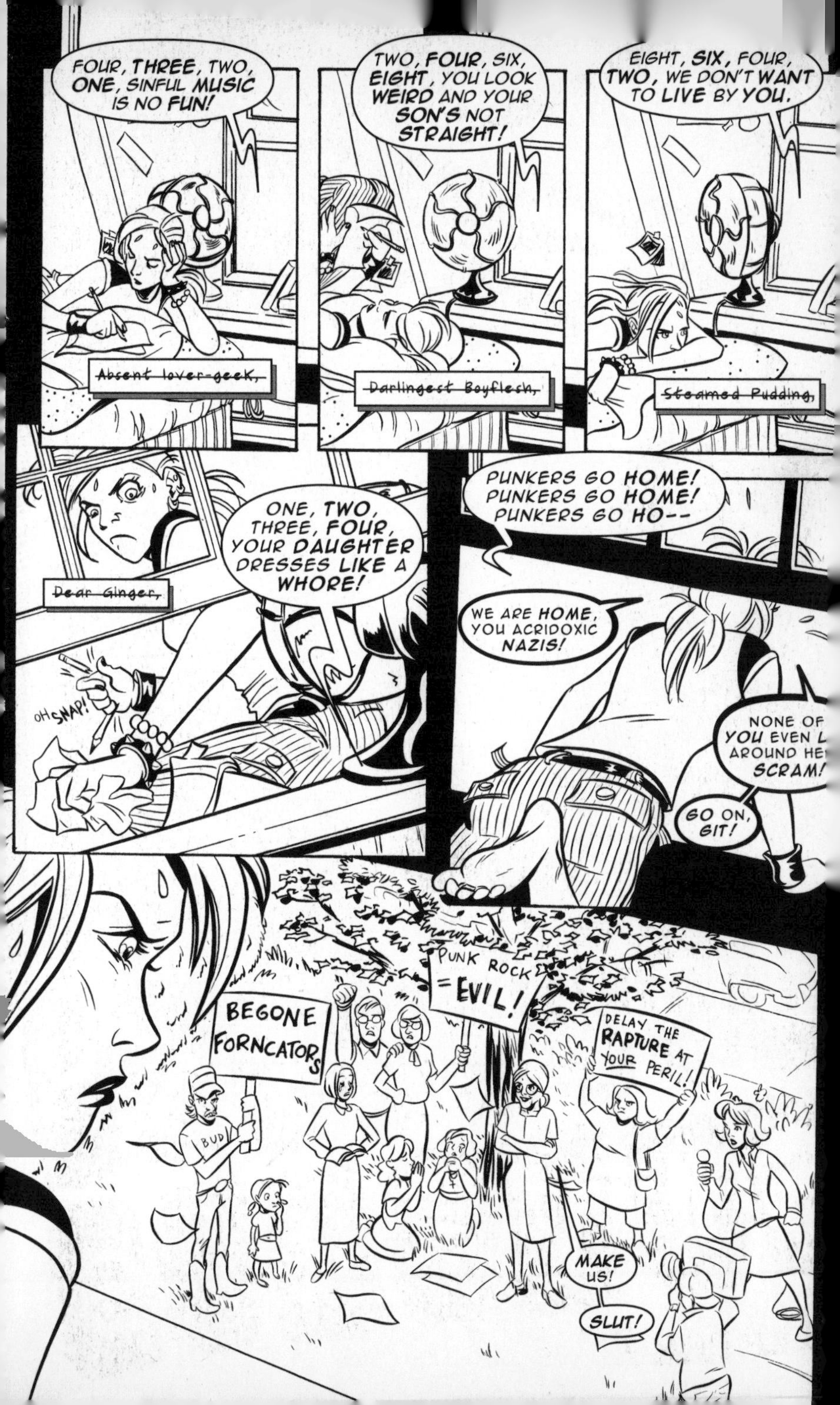
FOUR, THREE, TWO, ONE, SINFUL MUSIC IS NO FUN!
Absent lover-geek,
TWO, FOUR, SIX, EIGHT, YOU LOOK WEIRD AND YOUR SON'S NOT STRAIGHT!
Darlingest Boyflesh,
EIGHT, SIX, FOUR, TWO, WE DON'T WANT TO LIVE BY YOU.
Steamed Pudding,
Dear Ginger,
ONE, TWO, THREE, FOUR, YOUR DAUGHTER DRESSES LIKE A WHORE!
OH SNAP!
PUNKERS GO HOME! PUNKERS GO HOME! PUNKERS GO HO--
WE ARE HOME, YOU ACRIDOXIC NAZIS!
NONE OF YOU EVEN L AROUND HE SCRAM!
GO ON, GIT!
BEGONE FORNCATORS
PUNK ROCK = EVIL!
DELAY THE RAPTURE AT YOUR PERIL!
BUD
MAKE US!
SLUT!

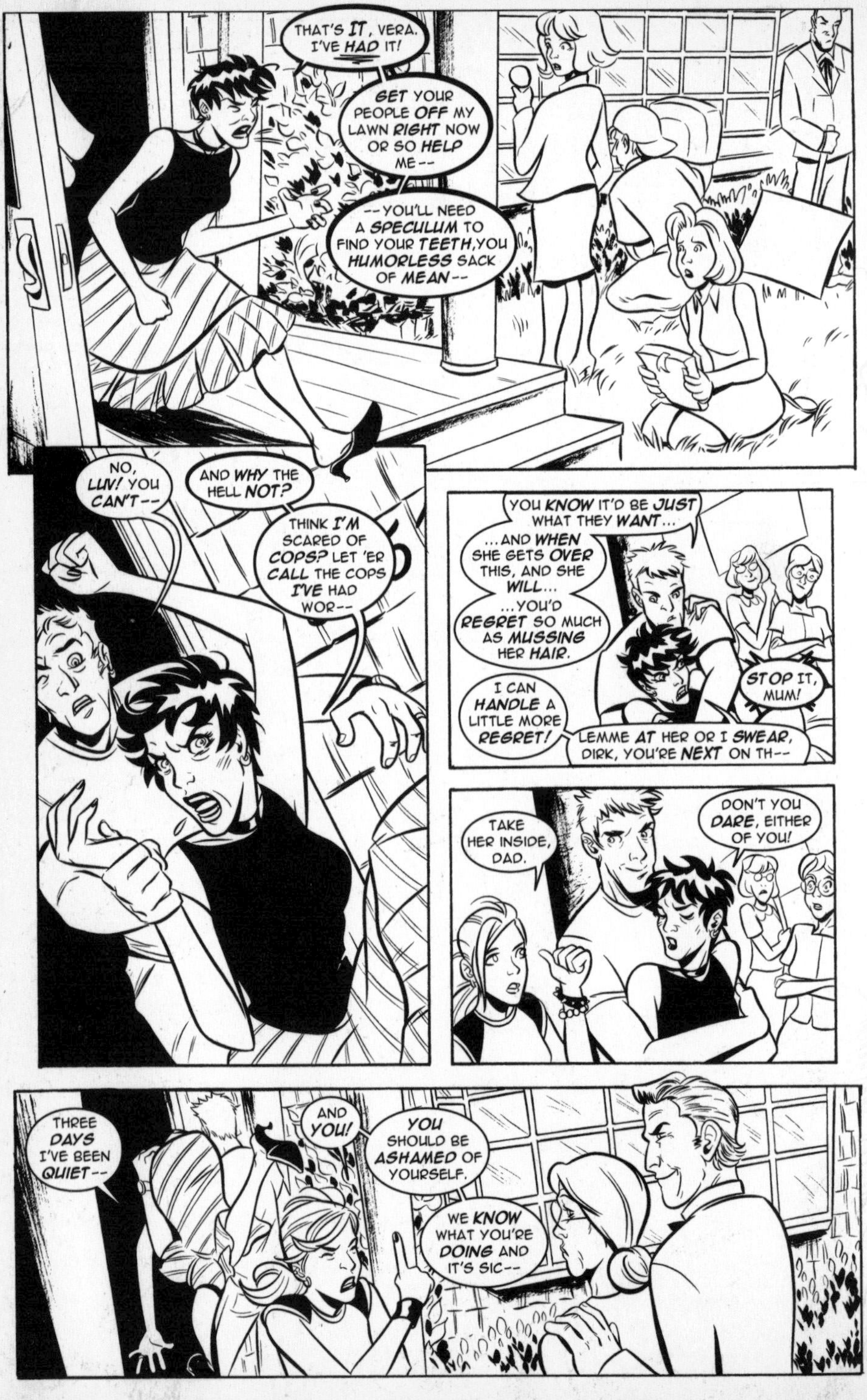
THAT'S IT, VERA. I'VE HAD IT!
GET YOUR PEOPLE OFF MY LAWN RIGHT NOW OR SO HELP ME--
--YOU'LL NEED A SPECULUM TO FIND YOUR TEETH, YOU HUMORLESS SACK OF MEAN--
NO, LUV! YOU CAN'T--
AND WHY THE HELL NOT?
THINK I'M SCARED OF COPS? LET 'ER CALL THE COPS I'VE HAD WOR--
YOU KNOW IT'D BE JUST WHAT THEY WANT...
...AND WHEN SHE GETS OVER THIS, AND SHE WILL...
...YOU'D REGRET SO MUCH AS MUSSING HER HAIR.
I CAN HANDLE A LITTLE MORE REGRET!
STOP IT, MUM!
LEMME AT HER OR I SWEAR, DIRK, YOU'RE NEXT ON TH--
TAKE HER INSIDE, DAD.
DON'T YOU DARE, EITHER OF YOU!
THREE DAYS I'VE BEEN QUIET--
AND YOU!
YOU SHOULD BE ASHAMED OF YOURSELF.
WE KNOW WHAT YOU'RE DOING AND IT'S SIC--

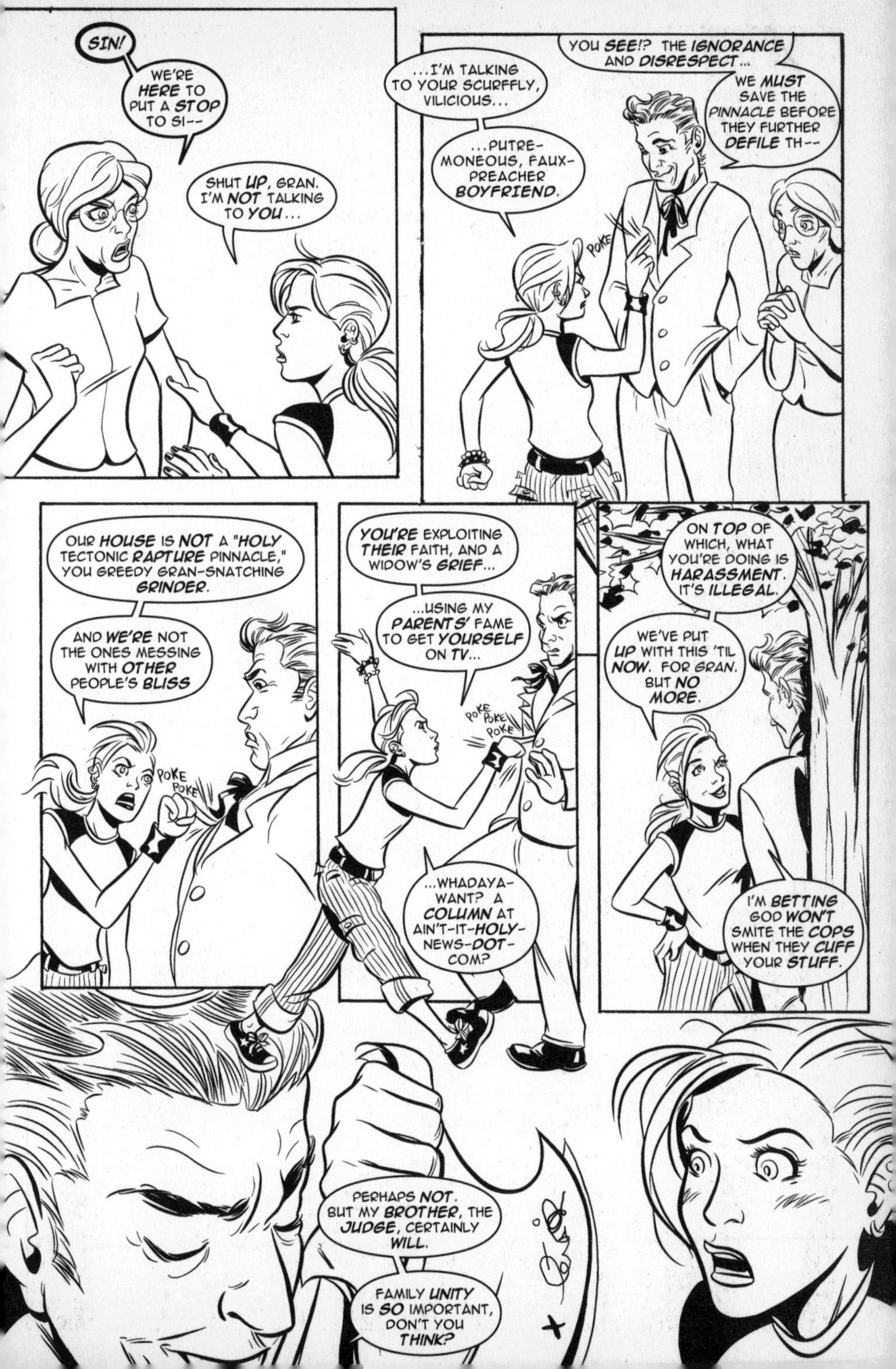
SIN!
WE'RE HERE TO PUT A STOP TO SI--
SHUT UP, GRAN. I'M NOT TALKING TO YOU...
...I'M TALKING TO YOUR SCURFFLY, VILICIOUS...
...PUTRE-MONEOUS, FAUX-PREACHER BOYFRIEND.
POKE
YOU SEE!? THE IGNORANCE AND DISRESPECT...
WE MUST SAVE THE PINNACLE BEFORE THEY FURTHER DEFILE TH--
OUR HOUSE IS NOT A "HOLY TECTONIC RAPTURE PINNACLE," YOU GREEDY GRAN-SNATCHING GRINDER.
AND WE'RE NOT THE ONES MESSING WITH OTHER PEOPLE'S BLISS
POKE POKE
YOU'RE EXPLOITING THEIR FAITH, AND A WIDOW'S GRIEF...
...USING MY PARENTS' FAME TO GET YOURSELF ON TV...
POKE POKE POKE
...WHADAYA-WANT? A COLUMN AT AIN'T-IT-HOLY-NEWS-DOT-COM?
ON TOP OF WHICH, WHAT YOU'RE DOING IS HARASSMENT. IT'S ILLEGAL.
WE'VE PUT UP WITH THIS 'TIL NOW. FOR GRAN. BUT NO MORE.
I'M BETTING GOD WON'T SMITE THE COPS WHEN THEY CUFF YOUR STUFF.
PERHAPS NOT. BUT MY BROTHER, THE JUDGE, CERTAINLY WILL.
FAMILY UNITY IS SO IMPORTANT, DON'T YOU THINK?

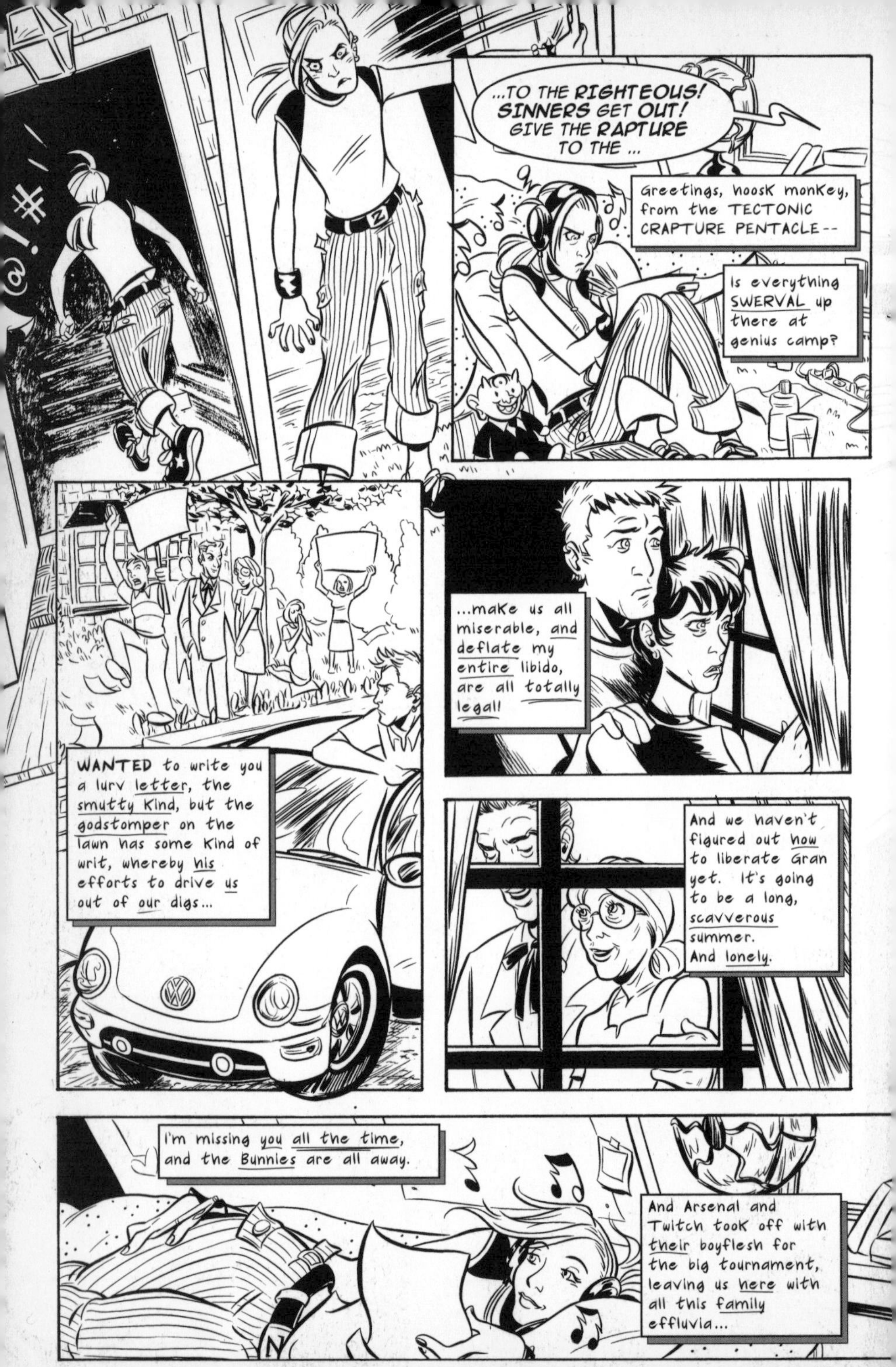

@!#!
...TO THE RIGHTEOUS! SINNERS GET OUT! GIVE THE RAPTURE TO THE ...
Greetings, hoosk monkey, from the TECTONIC CRAPTURE PENTACLE--
Is everything SWERVAL up there at genius camp?
WANTED to write you a lurv letter, the smutty kind, but the godstomper on the lawn has some kind of writ, whereby his efforts to drive us out of our digs...
...make us all miserable, and deflate my entire libido, are all totally legal!
And we haven't figured out how to liberate Gran yet. It's going to be a long, scavverous summer.
And lonely.
I'm missing you all the time, and the Bunnies are all away.
And Arsenal and Twitch took off with their boyflesh for the big tournament, leaving us here with all this family effluvia...

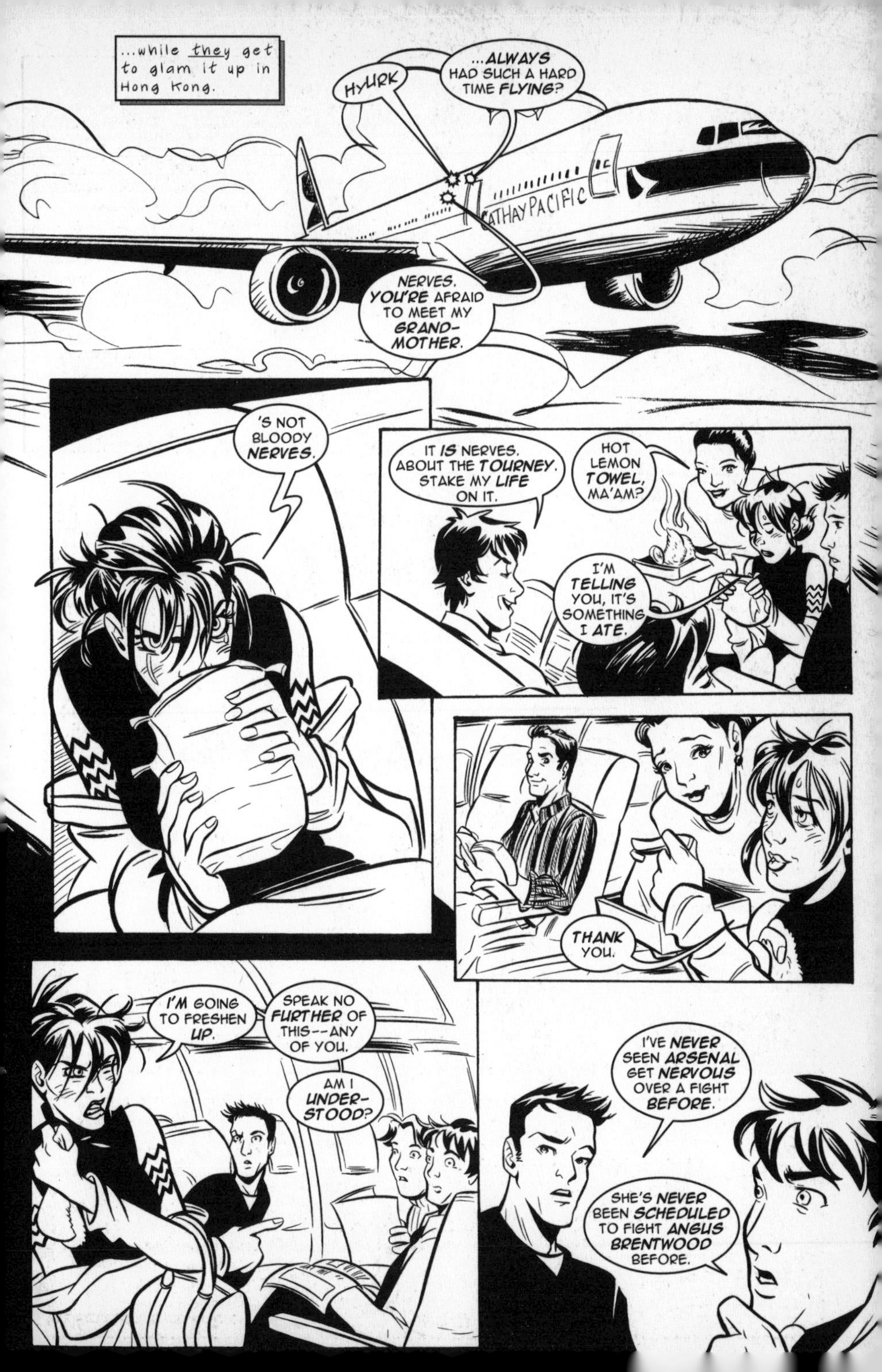
...while they get to glam it up in Hong Kong.
HYURK
...ALWAYS HAD SUCH A HARD TIME FLYING?
CATHAY PACIFIC
NERVES. YOU'RE AFRAID TO MEET MY GRAND-MOTHER.
'S NOT BLOODY NERVES.
IT IS NERVES. ABOUT THE TOURNEY. STAKE MY LIFE ON IT.
HOT LEMON TOWEL, MA'AM?
I'M TELLING YOU, IT'S SOMETHING I ATE.
THANK YOU.
I'M GOING TO FRESHEN UP.
SPEAK NO FURTHER OF THIS--ANY OF YOU.
AM I UNDER-STOOD?
I'VE NEVER SEEN ARSENAL GET NERVOUS OVER A FIGHT BEFORE.
SHE'S NEVER BEEN SCHEDULED TO FIGHT ANGUS BRENTWOOD BEFORE.

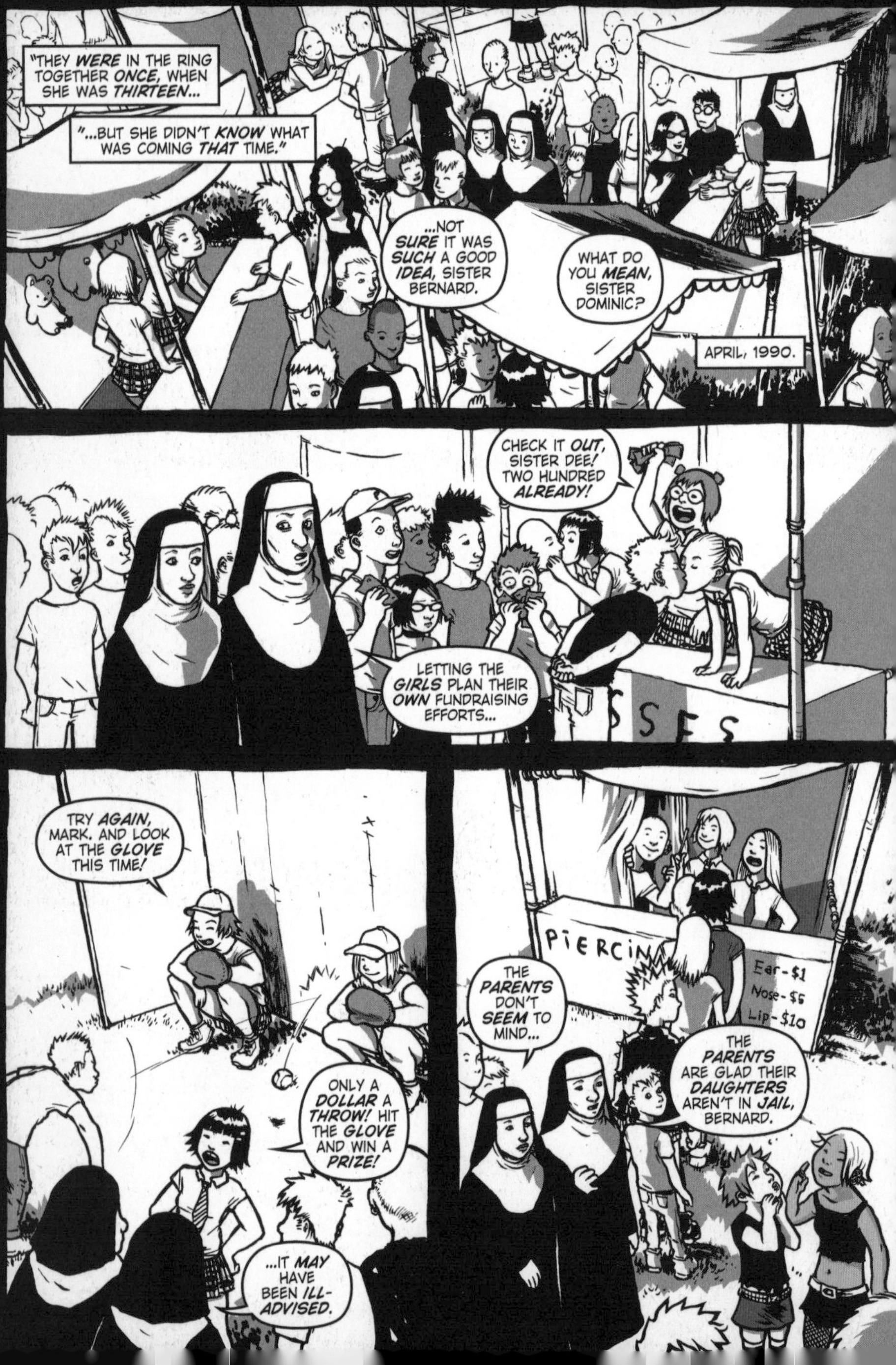
"THEY WERE IN THE RING TOGETHER ONCE, WHEN SHE WAS THIRTEEN...
"...BUT SHE DIDN'T KNOW WHAT WAS COMING THAT TIME."
...NOT SURE IT WAS SUCH A GOOD IDEA, SISTER BERNARD.
WHAT DO YOU MEAN, SISTER DOMINIC?
APRIL, 1990.
CHECK IT OUT, SISTER DEE! TWO HUNDRED ALREADY!
LETTING THE GIRLS PLAN THEIR OWN FUNDRAISING EFFORTS...
SSES
TRY AGAIN, MARK. AND LOOK AT THE GLOVE THIS TIME!
ONLY A DOLLAR A THROW! HIT THE GLOVE AND WIN A PRIZE!
...IT MAY HAVE BEEN ILL-ADVISED.
PIERCIN
Ear-$1
Nose-$5
Lip-$10
THE PARENTS DON'T SEEM TO MIND...
THE PARENTS ARE GLAD THEIR DAUGHTERS AREN'T IN JAIL, BERNARD.

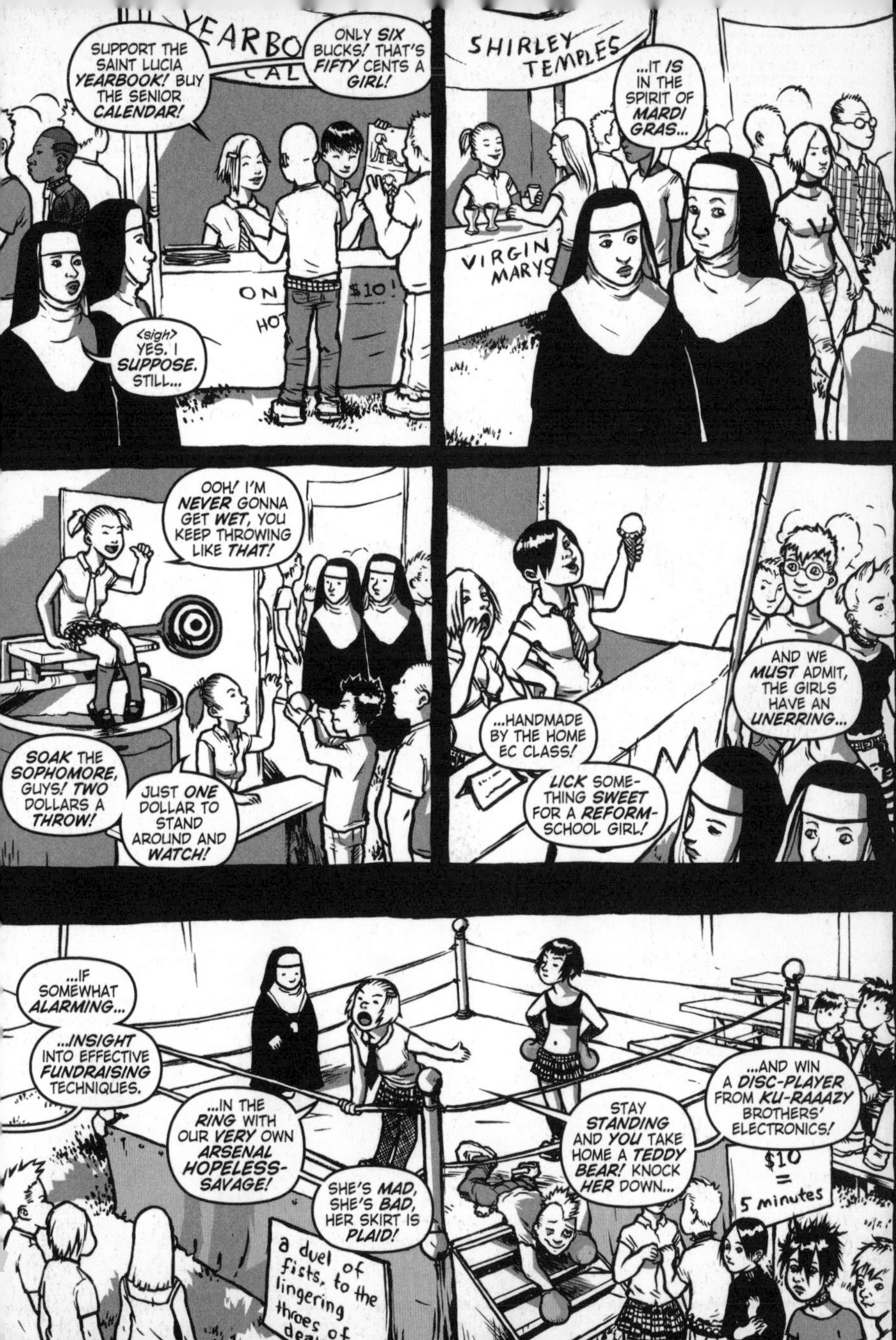
YEARBO
CAL
SUPPORT THE SAINT LUCIA YEARBOOK! BUY THE SENIOR CALENDAR!
ONLY SIX BUCKS! THAT'S FIFTY CENTS A GIRL!
ON $10!
HOT
<sigh> YES. I SUPPOSE. STILL...
SHIRLEY TEMPLES
...IT IS IN THE SPIRIT OF MARDI GRAS...
VIRGIN MARYS
OOH! I'M NEVER GONNA GET WET, YOU KEEP THROWING LIKE THAT!
SOAK THE SOPHOMORE, GUYS! TWO DOLLARS A THROW!
JUST ONE DOLLAR TO STAND AROUND AND WATCH!
AND WE MUST ADMIT, THE GIRLS HAVE AN UNERRING...
...HANDMADE BY THE HOME EC CLASS!
LICK SOMETHING SWEET FOR A REFORM-SCHOOL GIRL!
...IF SOMEWHAT ALARMING...
...INSIGHT INTO EFFECTIVE FUNDRAISING TECHNIQUES.
...IN THE RING WITH OUR VERY OWN ARSENAL HOPELESS-SAVAGE!
SHE'S MAD, SHE'S BAD, HER SKIRT IS PLAID!
STAY STANDING AND YOU TAKE HOME A TEDDY BEAR! KNOCK HER DOWN...
...AND WIN A DISC-PLAYER FROM KU-RAAAZY BROTHERS' ELECTRONICS!
$10 = 5 minutes
a duel of fists, to the lingering throes of death

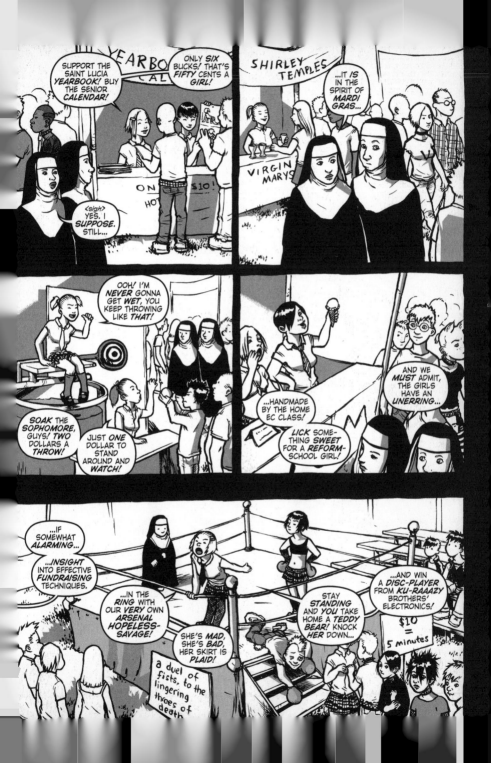

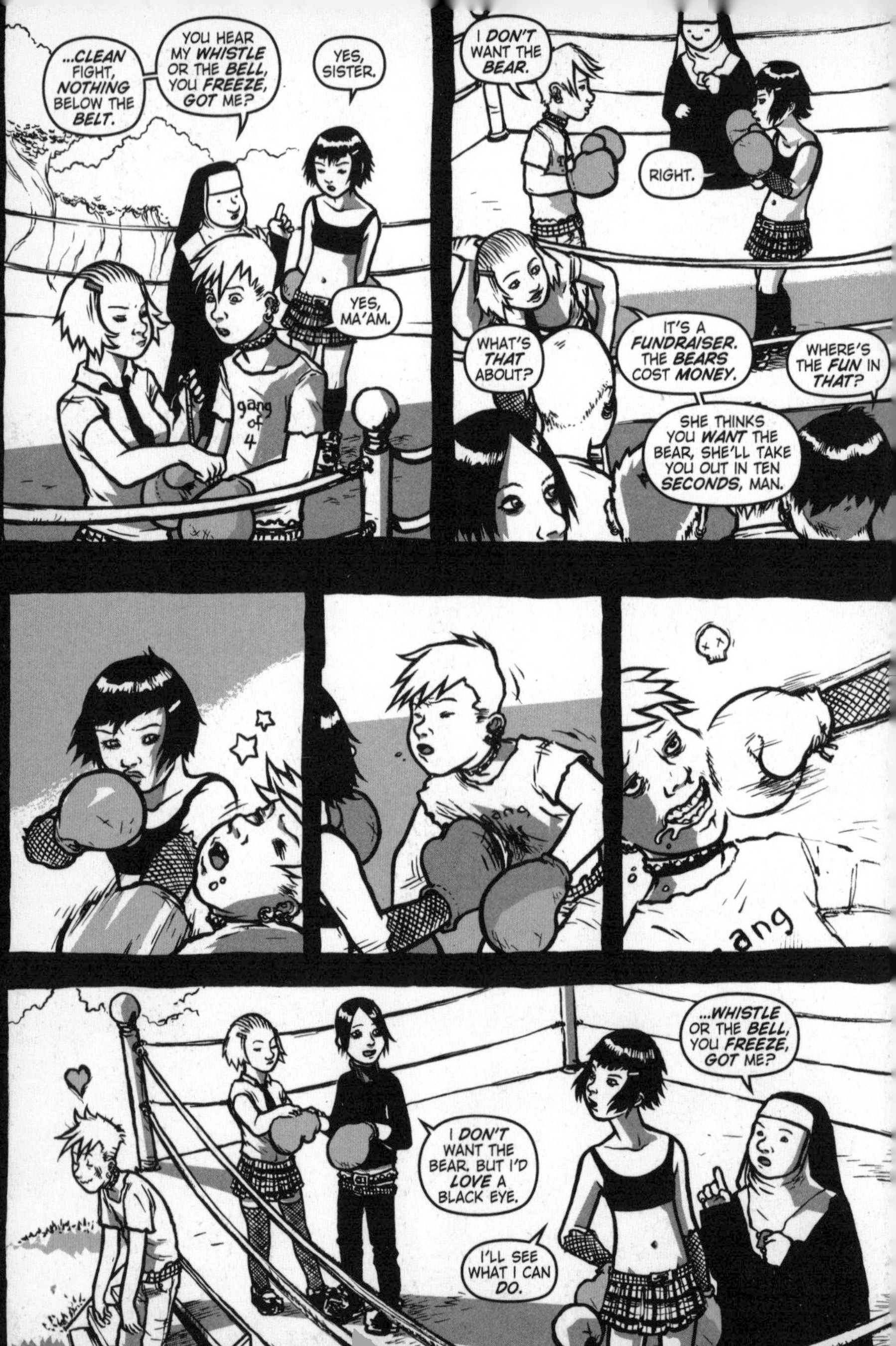
...CLEAN FIGHT, NOTHING BELOW THE BELT.
YOU HEAR MY WHISTLE OR THE BELL, YOU FREEZE, GOT ME?
YES, SISTER.
YES, MA'AM.
gang of 4
I DON'T WANT THE BEAR.
RIGHT.
WHAT'S THAT ABOUT?
IT'S A FUNDRAISER. THE BEARS COST MONEY.
WHERE'S THE FUN IN THAT?
SHE THINKS YOU WANT THE BEAR, SHE'LL TAKE YOU OUT IN TEN SECONDS, MAN.
...WHISTLE OR THE BELL, YOU FREEZE, GOT ME?
I DON'T WANT THE BEAR. BUT I'D LOVE A BLACK EYE.
I'LL SEE WHAT I CAN DO.

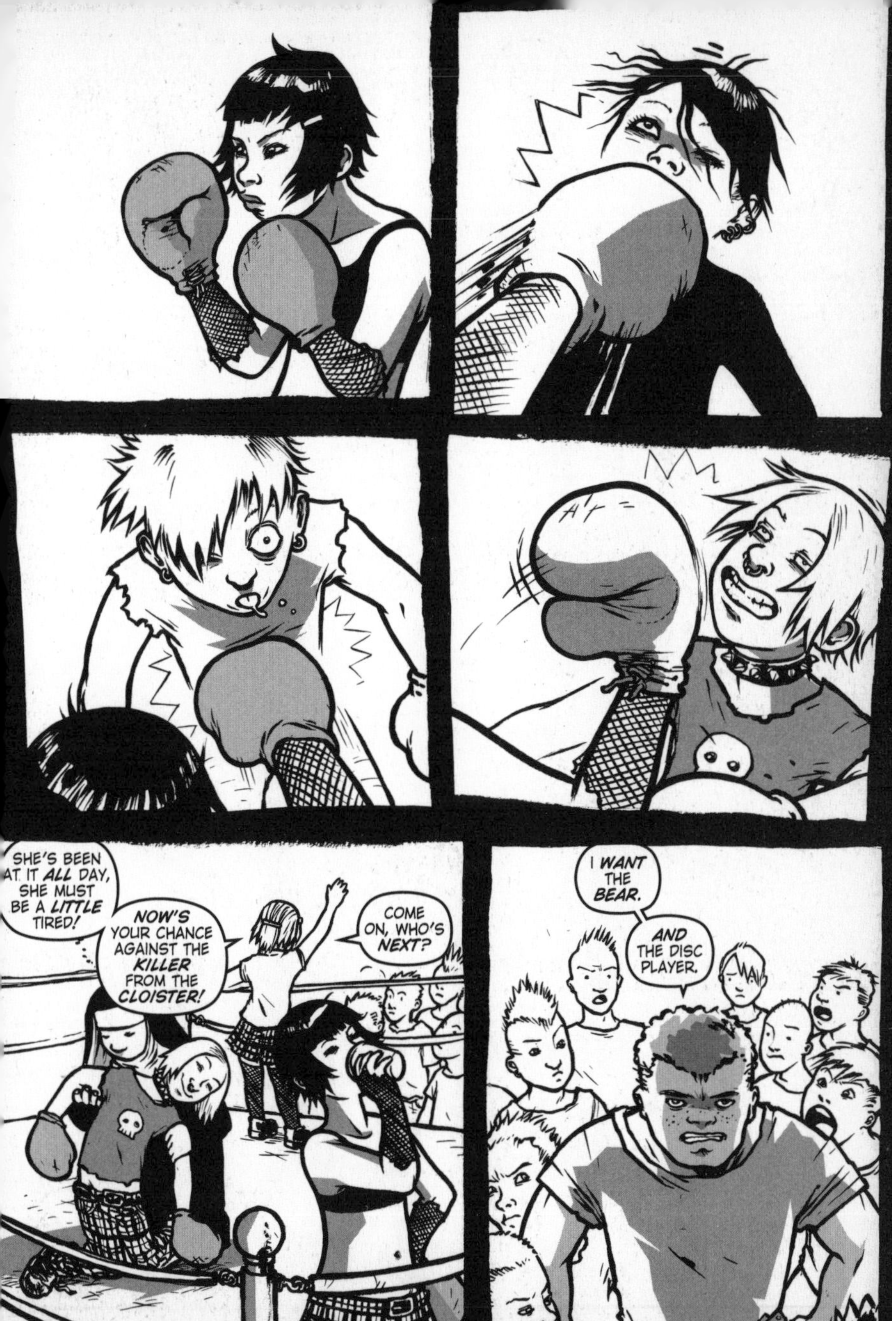
SHE'S BEEN AT IT ALL DAY, SHE MUST BE A LITTLE TIRED!
NOW'S YOUR CHANCE AGAINST THE KILLER FROM THE CLOISTER!
COME ON, WHO'S NEXT?
I WANT THE BEAR.
AND THE DISC PLAYER.

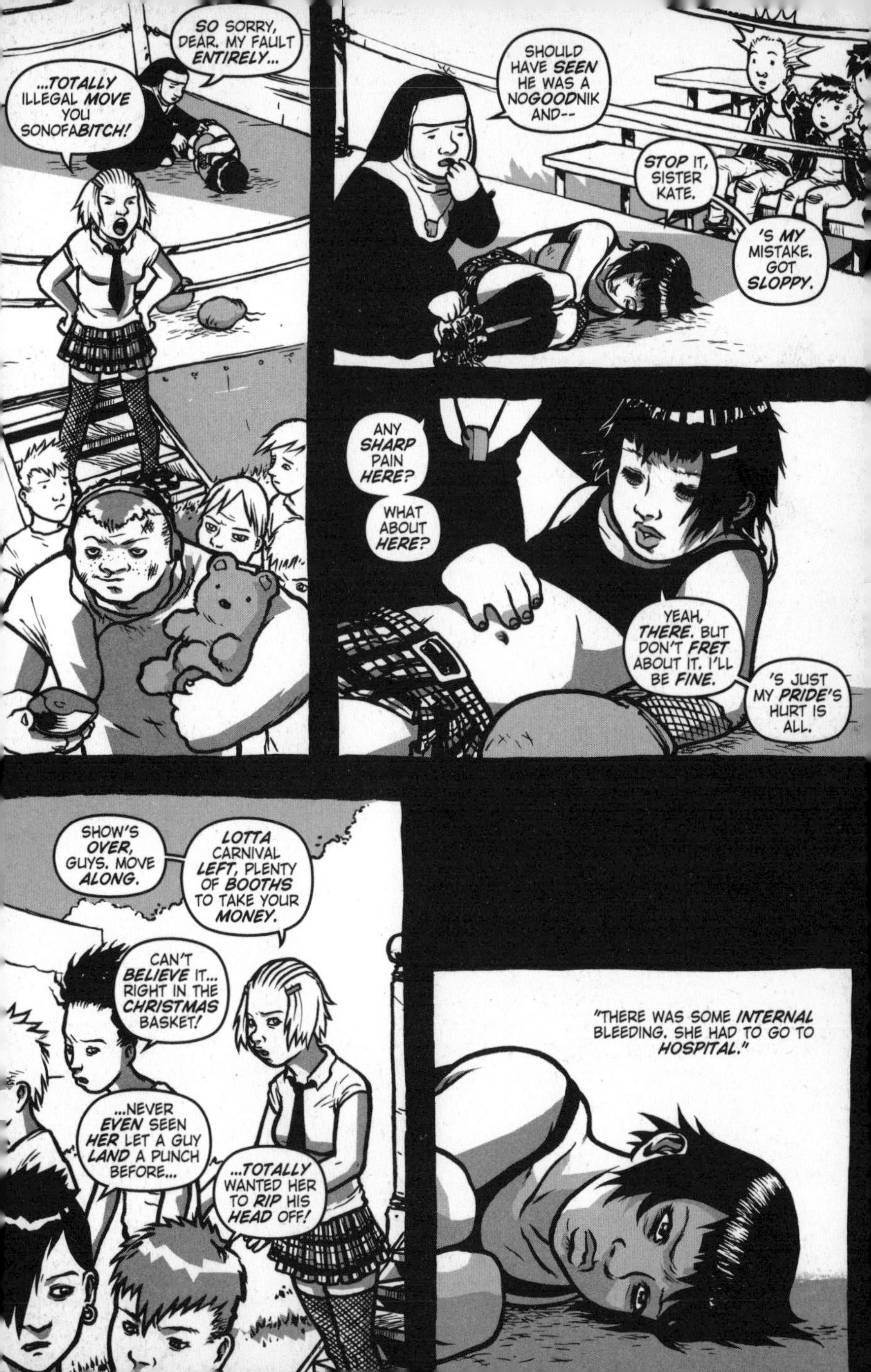
...TOTALLY ILLEGAL MOVE YOU SONOFABITCH!
SO SORRY, DEAR. MY FAULT ENTIRELY...
SHOULD HAVE SEEN HE WAS A NOGOODNIK AND--
STOP IT, SISTER KATE.
'S MY MISTAKE. GOT SLOPPY.
ANY SHARP PAIN HERE?
WHAT ABOUT HERE?
YEAH, THERE. BUT DON'T FRET ABOUT IT. I'LL BE FINE.
'S JUST MY PRIDE'S HURT IS ALL.
SHOW'S OVER, GUYS. MOVE ALONG.
LOTTA CARNIVAL LEFT, PLENTY OF BOOTHS TO TAKE YOUR MONEY.
CAN'T BELIEVE IT... RIGHT IN THE CHRISTMAS BASKET!
...NEVER EVEN SEEN HER LET A GUY LAND A PUNCH BEFORE...
...TOTALLY WANTED HER TO RIP HIS HEAD OFF!
"THERE WAS SOME INTERNAL BLEEDING. SHE HAD TO GO TO HOSPITAL."

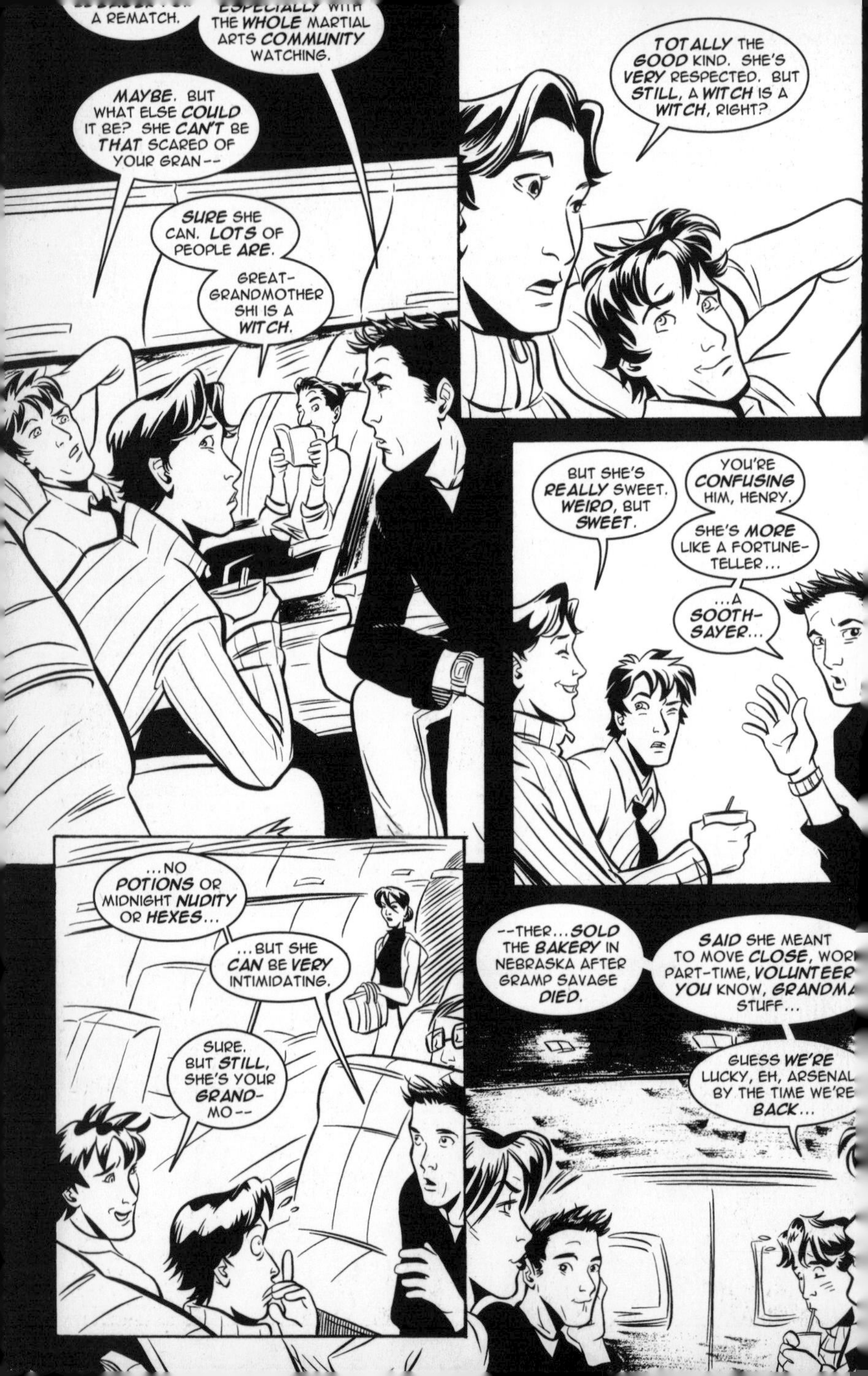

A REMATCH.
ESPECIALLY WITH THE WHOLE MARTIAL ARTS COMMUNITY WATCHING.
MAYBE. BUT WHAT ELSE COULD IT BE? SHE CAN'T BE THAT SCARED OF YOUR GRAN--
SURE SHE CAN. LOTS OF PEOPLE ARE.
GREAT-GRANDMOTHER SHI IS A WITCH.
TOTALLY THE GOOD KIND. SHE'S VERY RESPECTED. BUT STILL, A WITCH IS A WITCH, RIGHT?
BUT SHE'S REALLY SWEET. WEIRD, BUT SWEET.
YOU'RE CONFUSING HIM, HENRY.
SHE'S MORE LIKE A FORTUNE-TELLER...
...A SOOTH-SAYER...
...NO POTIONS OR MIDNIGHT NUDITY OR HEXES...
...BUT SHE CAN BE VERY INTIMIDATING.
SURE. BUT STILL, SHE'S YOUR GRAND-MO--
--THER...SOLD THE BAKERY IN NEBRASKA AFTER GRAMP SAVAGE DIED.
SAID SHE MEANT TO MOVE CLOSE, WOR PART-TIME, VOLUNTEER YOU KNOW, GRANDMA STUFF...
GUESS WE'RE LUCKY, EH, ARSENAL BY THE TIME WE'RE BACK...

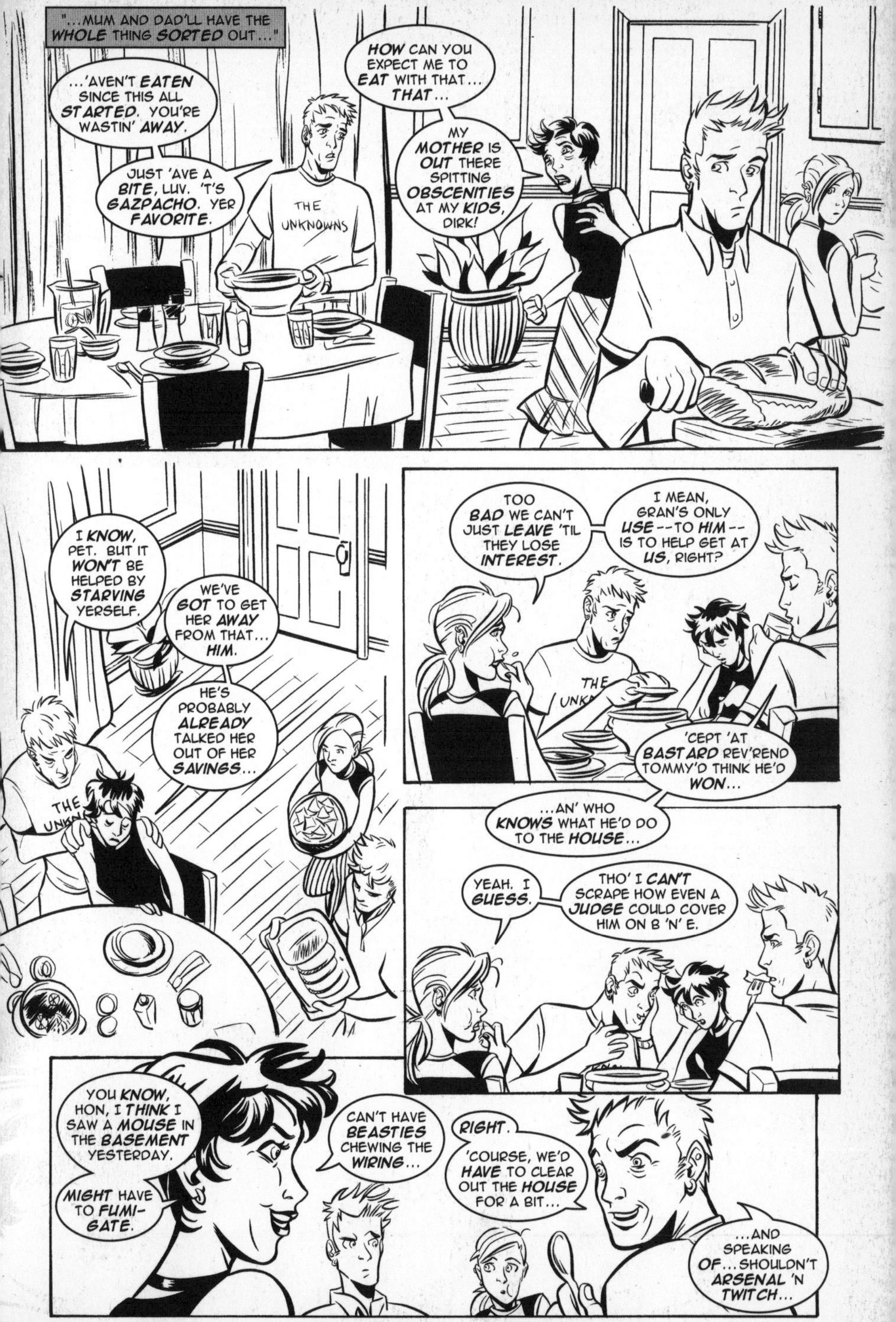
"...MUM AND DAD'LL HAVE THE WHOLE THING SORTED OUT..."
...'AVEN'T EATEN SINCE THIS ALL STARTED. YOU'RE WASTIN' AWAY.
JUST 'AVE A BITE, LUV. 'T'S GAZPACHO. YER FAVORITE.
THE UNKNOWNS
HOW CAN YOU EXPECT ME TO EAT WITH THAT... THAT...
MY MOTHER IS OUT THERE SPITTING OBSCENITIES AT MY KIDS, DIRK!
I KNOW, PET. BUT IT WON'T BE HELPED BY STARVING YERSELF.
WE'VE GOT TO GET HER AWAY FROM THAT... HIM.
HE'S PROBABLY ALREADY TALKED HER OUT OF HER SAVINGS...
TOO BAD WE CAN'T JUST LEAVE 'TIL THEY LOSE INTEREST.
I MEAN, GRAN'S ONLY USE--TO HIM--IS TO HELP GET AT US, RIGHT?
'CEPT 'AT BASTARD REV'REND TOMMY'D THINK HE'D WON...
...AN' WHO KNOWS WHAT HE'D DO TO THE HOUSE...
YEAH. I GUESS.
THO' I CAN'T SCRAPE HOW EVEN A JUDGE COULD COVER HIM ON B 'N' E.
YOU KNOW, HON, I THINK I SAW A MOUSE IN THE BASEMENT YESTERDAY.
MIGHT HAVE TO FUMI-GATE.
CAN'T HAVE BEASTIES CHEWING THE WIRING...
RIGHT.
'COURSE, WE'D HAVE TO CLEAR OUT THE HOUSE FOR A BIT...
...AND SPEAKING OF... SHOULDN'T ARSENAL 'N TWITCH...

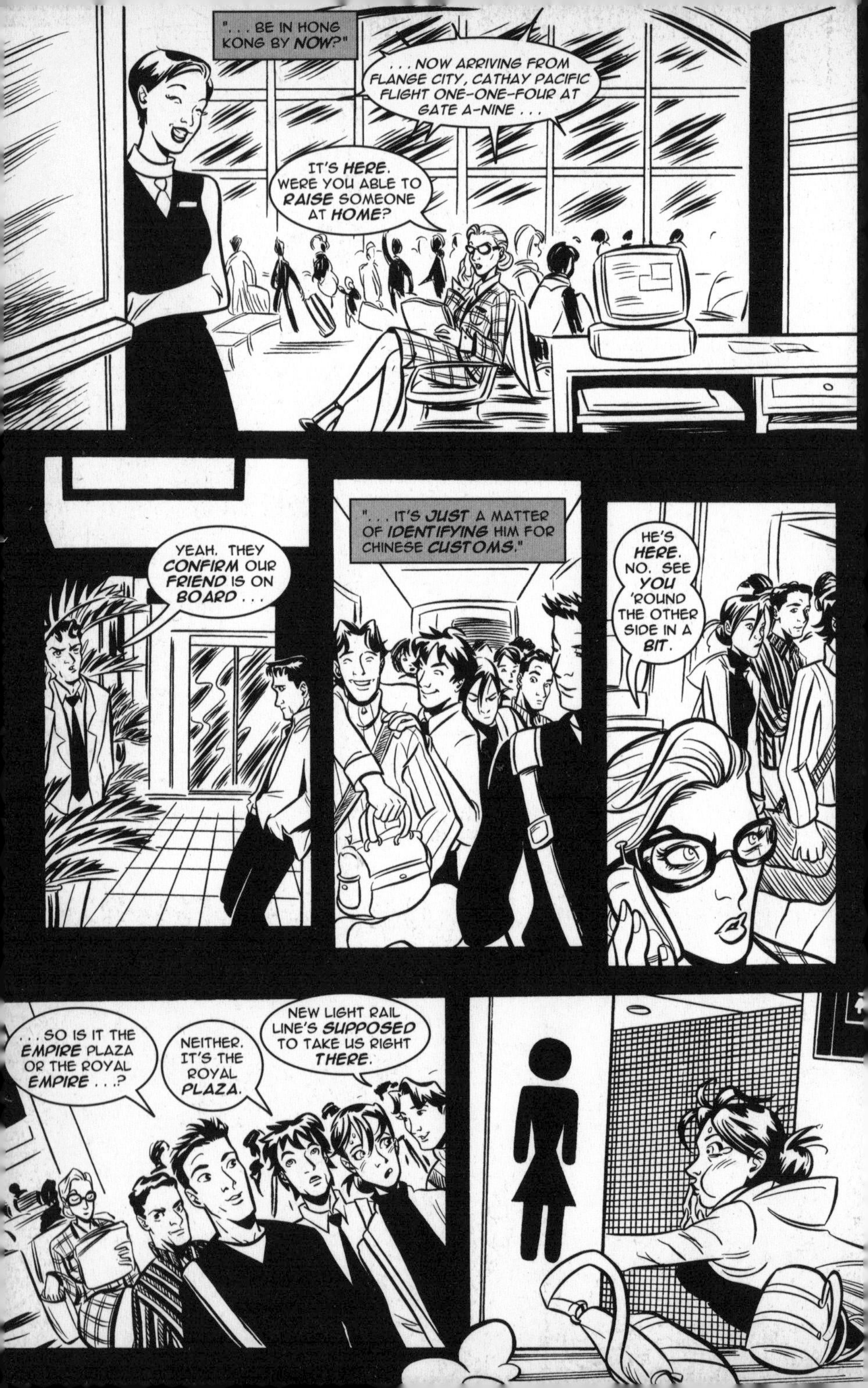
"... BE IN HONG KONG BY NOW?"
...NOW ARRIVING FROM FLANGE CITY, CATHAY PACIFIC FLIGHT ONE-ONE-FOUR AT GATE A-NINE...
IT'S HERE. WERE YOU ABLE TO RAISE SOMEONE AT HOME?
YEAH. THEY CONFIRM OUR FRIEND IS ON BOARD...
"...IT'S JUST A MATTER OF IDENTIFYING HIM FOR CHINESE CUSTOMS."
HE'S HERE. NO. SEE YOU 'ROUND THE OTHER SIDE IN A BIT.
...SO IS IT THE EMPIRE PLAZA OR THE ROYAL EMPIRE...?
NEITHER. IT'S THE ROYAL PLAZA.
NEW LIGHT RAIL LINE'S SUPPOSED TO TAKE US RIGHT THERE.

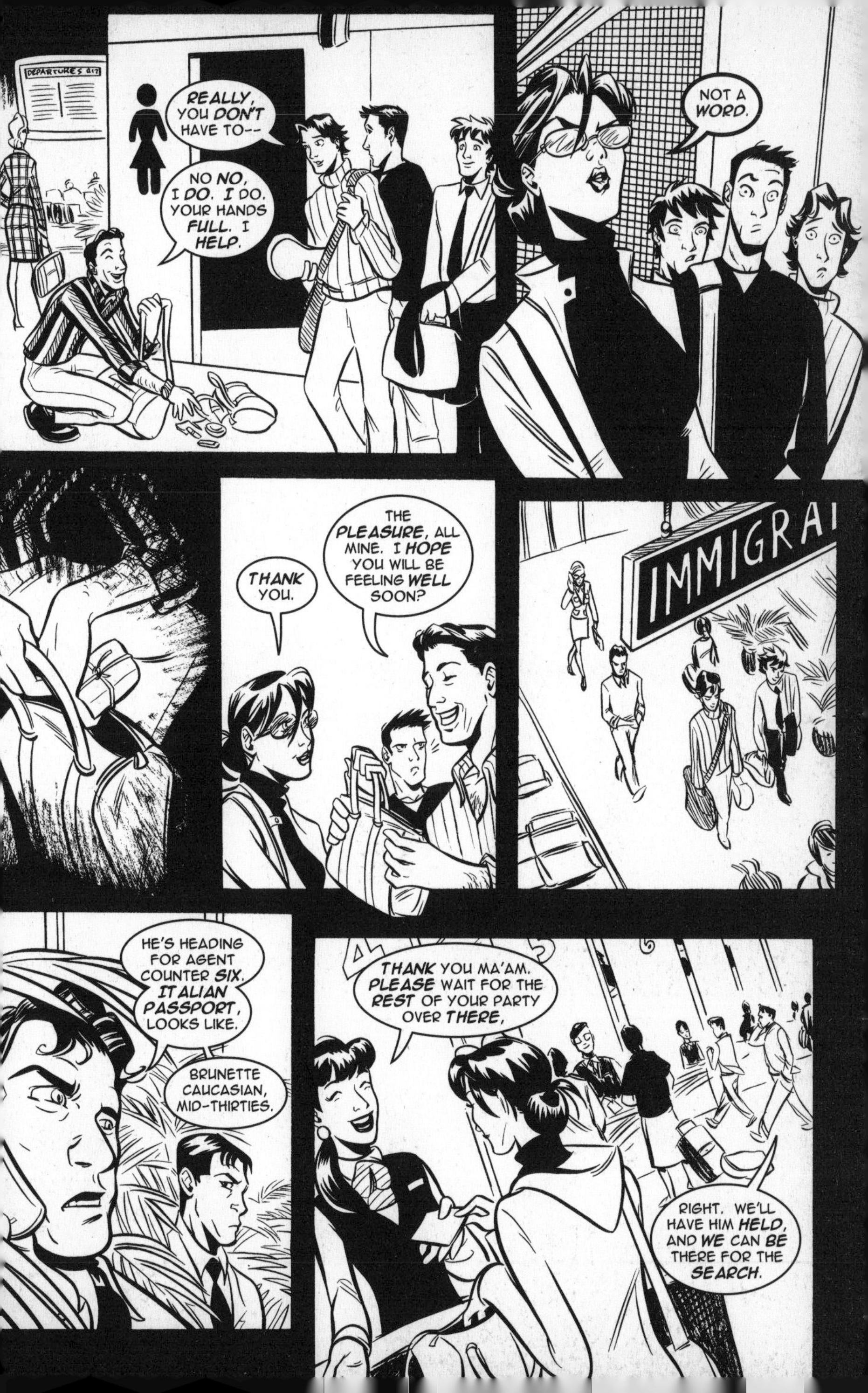
DEPARTURES
REALLY, YOU DON'T HAVE TO--
NO NO, I DO. I DO. YOUR HANDS FULL. I HELP.
NOT A WORD.
THANK YOU.
THE PLEASURE, ALL MINE. I HOPE YOU WILL BE FEELING WELL SOON?
IMMIGRA
HE'S HEADING FOR AGENT COUNTER SIX. ITALIAN PASSPORT, LOOKS LIKE.
BRUNETTE CAUCASIAN, MID-THIRTIES.
THANK YOU MA'AM. PLEASE WAIT FOR THE REST OF YOUR PARTY OVER THERE.
RIGHT. WE'LL HAVE HIM HELD, AND WE CAN BE THERE FOR THE SEARCH.

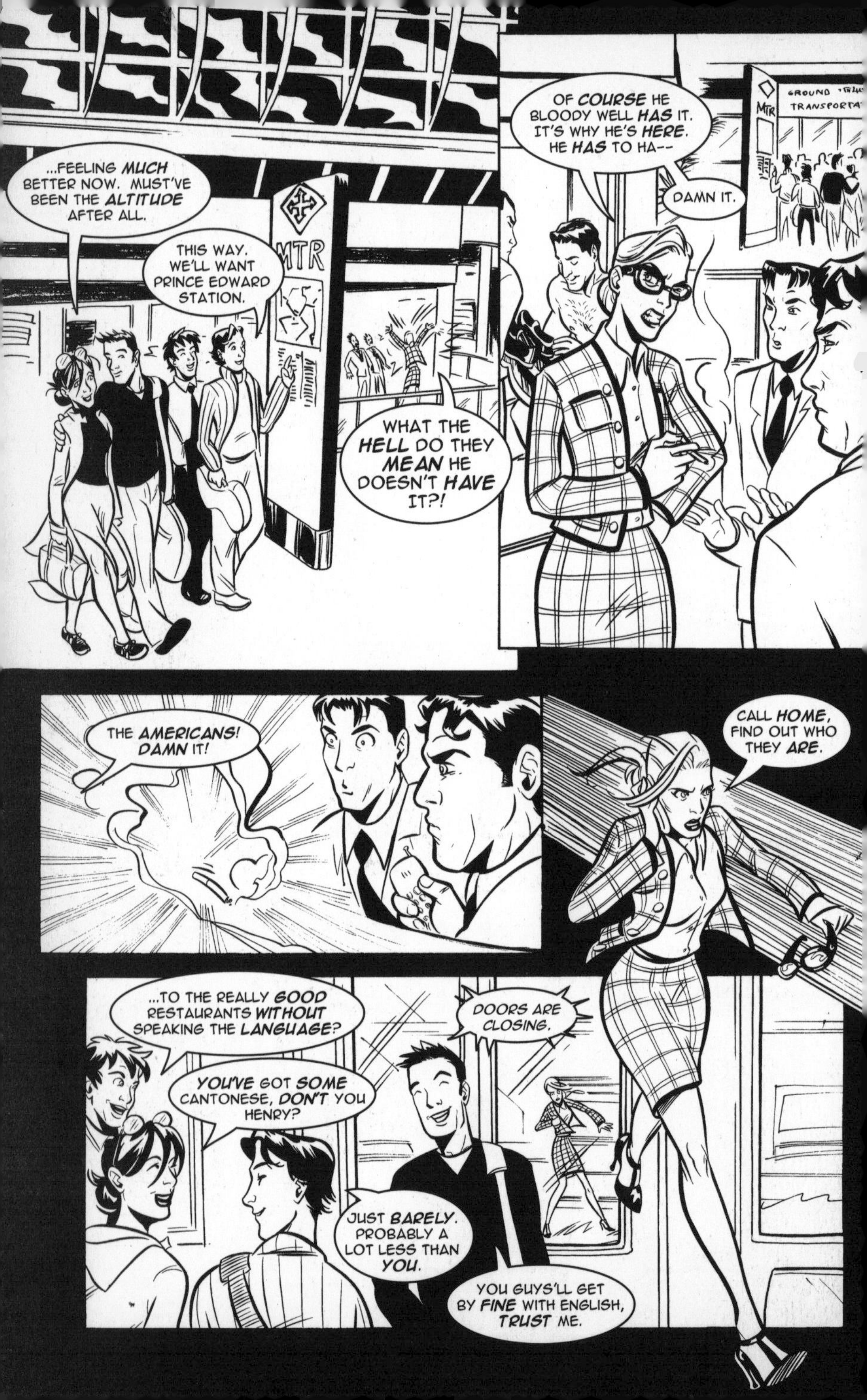

...FEELING MUCH BETTER NOW. MUST'VE BEEN THE ALTITUDE AFTER ALL.
THIS WAY. WE'LL WANT PRINCE EDWARD STATION.
MTR
WHAT THE HELL DO THEY MEAN HE DOESN'T HAVE IT?!
OF COURSE HE BLOODY WELL HAS IT. IT'S WHY HE'S HERE. HE HAS TO HA--
DAMN IT.
GROUND TRANSPORTA
THE AMERICANS! DAMN IT!
CALL HOME, FIND OUT WHO THEY ARE.
...TO THE REALLY GOOD RESTAURANTS WITHOUT SPEAKING THE LANGUAGE?
DOORS ARE CLOSING.
YOU'VE GOT SOME CANTONESE, DON'T YOU HENRY?
JUST BARELY. PROBABLY A LOT LESS THAN YOU.
YOU GUYS'LL GET BY FINE WITH ENGLISH, TRUST ME.

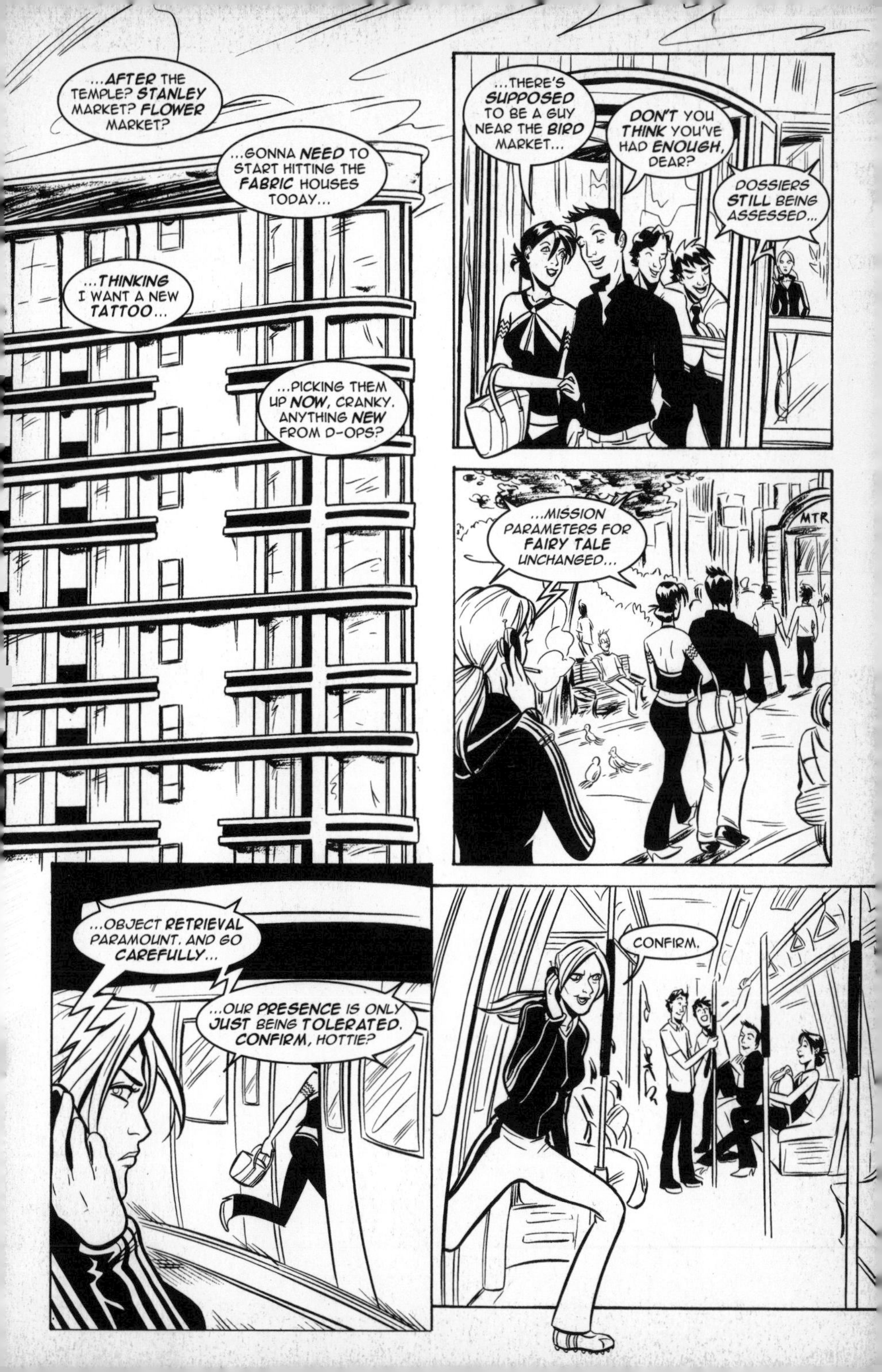
...AFTER THE TEMPLE? STANLEY MARKET? FLOWER MARKET?
...GONNA NEED TO START HITTING THE FABRIC HOUSES TODAY...
...THINKING I WANT A NEW TATTOO...
...PICKING THEM UP NOW, CRANKY. ANYTHING NEW FROM D-OPS?
...THERE'S SUPPOSED TO BE A GUY NEAR THE BIRD MARKET...
DON'T YOU THINK YOU'VE HAD ENOUGH, DEAR?
DOSSIERS STILL BEING ASSESSED...
MTR
...MISSION PARAMETERS FOR FAIRY TALE UNCHANGED...
...OBJECT RETRIEVAL PARAMOUNT, AND GO CAREFULLY...
...OUR PRESENCE IS ONLY JUST BEING TOLERATED. CONFIRM, HOTTIE?
CONFIRM.

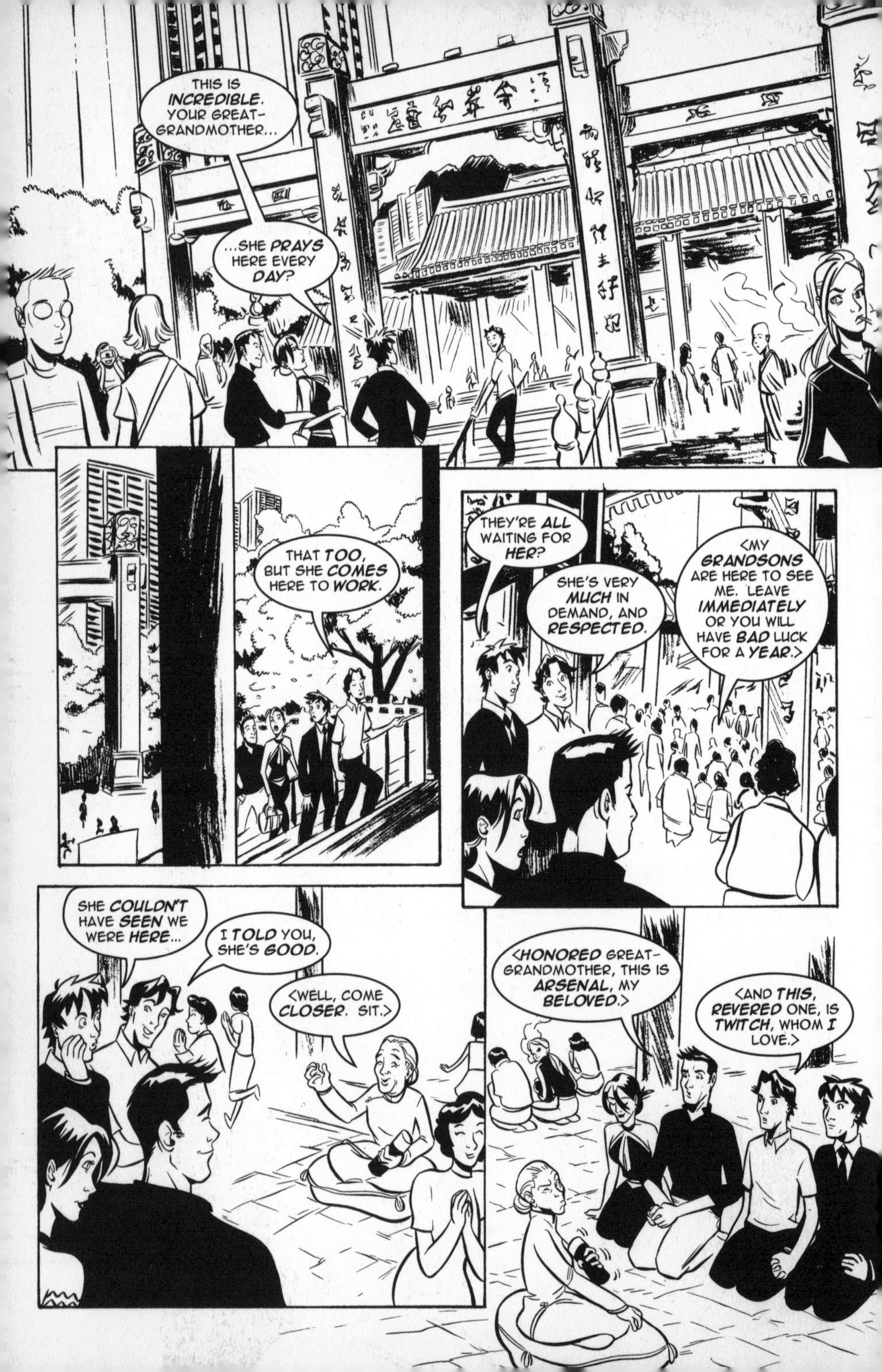

THIS IS INCREDIBLE. YOUR GREAT-GRANDMOTHER...
...SHE PRAYS HERE EVERY DAY?
THAT TOO, BUT SHE COMES HERE TO WORK.
THEY'RE ALL WAITING FOR HER?
SHE'S VERY MUCH IN DEMAND, AND RESPECTED.
<MY GRANDSONS ARE HERE TO SEE ME. LEAVE IMMEDIATELY OR YOU WILL HAVE BAD LUCK FOR A YEAR.>
SHE COULDN'T HAVE SEEN WE WERE HERE...
I TOLD YOU, SHE'S GOOD.
<WELL, COME CLOSER. SIT.>
<HONORED GREAT-GRANDMOTHER, THIS IS ARSENAL, MY BELOVED.>
<AND THIS, REVERED ONE, IS TWITCH, WHOM I LOVE.>

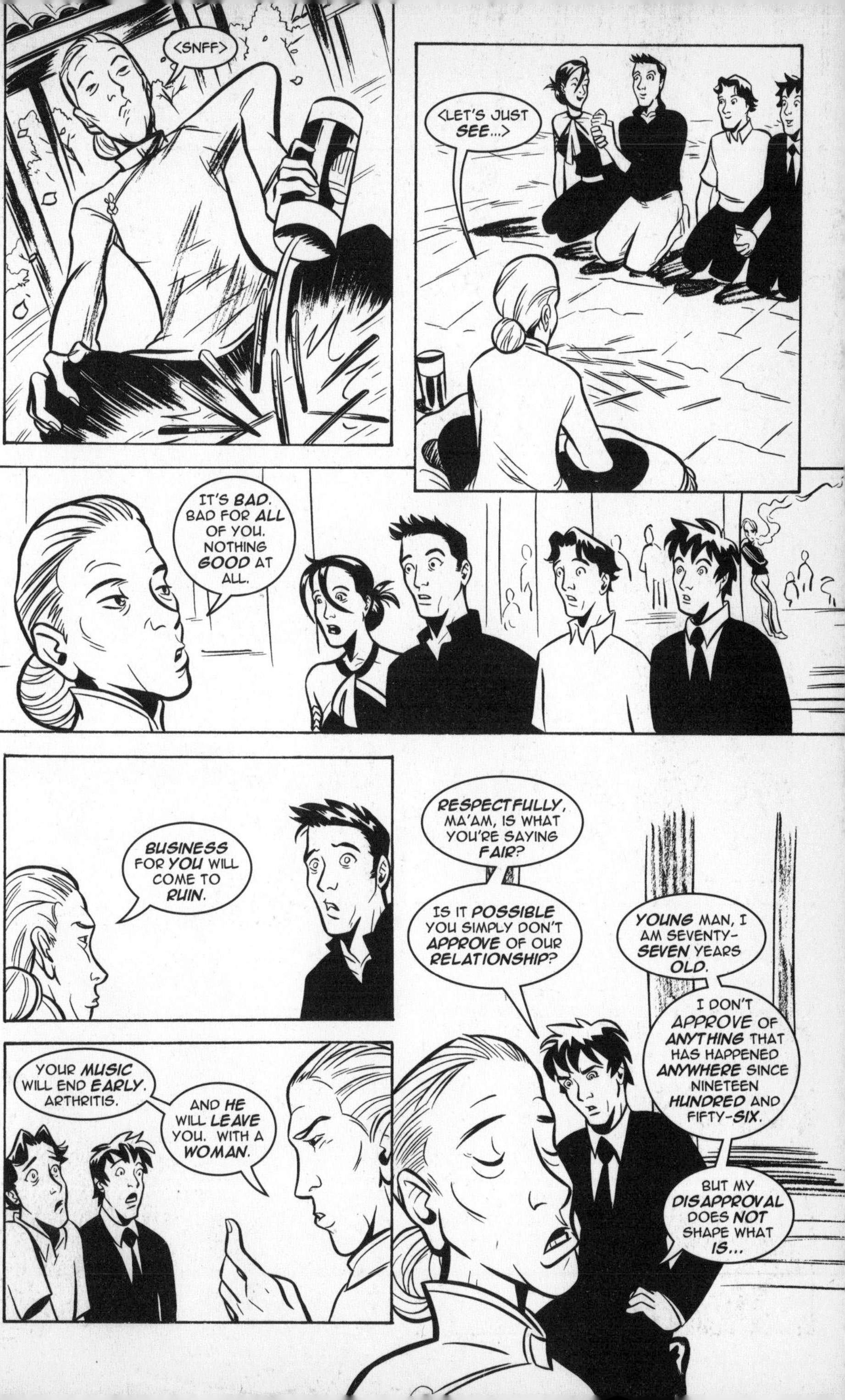
<SNFF>
<LET'S JUST SEE...>
IT'S BAD. BAD FOR ALL OF YOU. NOTHING GOOD AT ALL.
BUSINESS FOR YOU WILL COME TO RUIN.
RESPECTFULLY, MA'AM, IS WHAT YOU'RE SAYING FAIR?
IS IT POSSIBLE YOU SIMPLY DON'T APPROVE OF OUR RELATIONSHIP?
YOUR MUSIC WILL END EARLY. ARTHRITIS.
AND HE WILL LEAVE YOU. WITH A WOMAN.
YOUNG MAN, I AM SEVENTY-SEVEN YEARS OLD.
I DON'T APPROVE OF ANYTHING THAT HAS HAPPENED ANYWHERE SINCE NINETEEN HUNDRED AND FIFTY-SIX.
BUT MY DISAPPROVAL DOES NOT SHAPE WHAT IS...

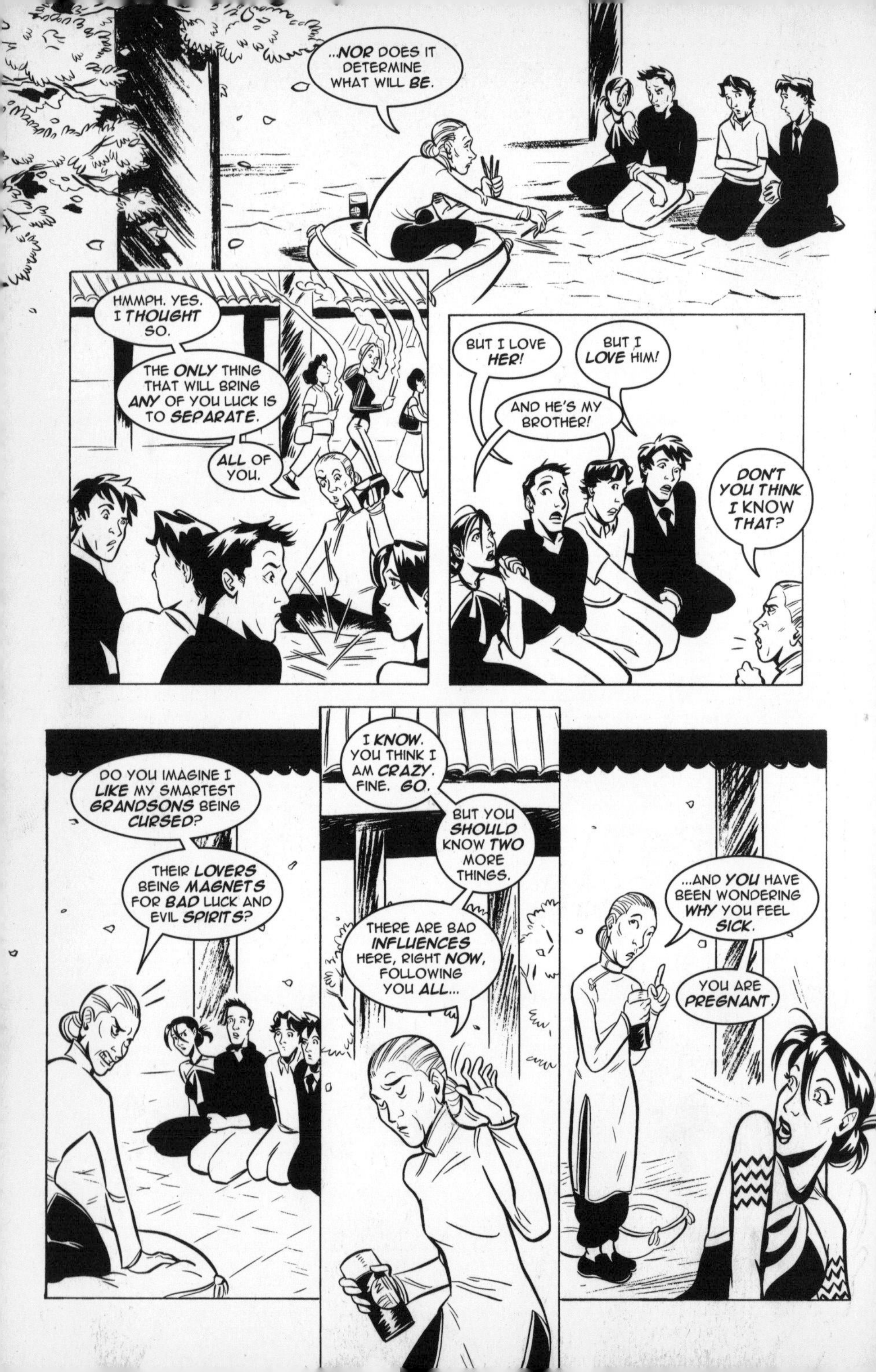
...NOR DOES IT DETERMINE WHAT WILL BE.
HMMPH. YES. I THOUGHT SO.
THE ONLY THING THAT WILL BRING ANY OF YOU LUCK IS TO SEPARATE.
ALL OF YOU.
BUT I LOVE HER!
BUT I LOVE HIM!
AND HE'S MY BROTHER!
DON'T YOU THINK I KNOW THAT?
DO YOU IMAGINE I LIKE MY SMARTEST GRANDSONS BEING CURSED?
THEIR LOVERS BEING MAGNETS FOR BAD LUCK AND EVIL SPIRITS?
I KNOW. YOU THINK I AM CRAZY. FINE. GO.
BUT YOU SHOULD KNOW TWO MORE THINGS.
THERE ARE BAD INFLUENCES HERE, RIGHT NOW, FOLLOWING YOU ALL...
...AND YOU HAVE BEEN WONDERING WHY YOU FEEL SICK.
YOU ARE PREGNANT.

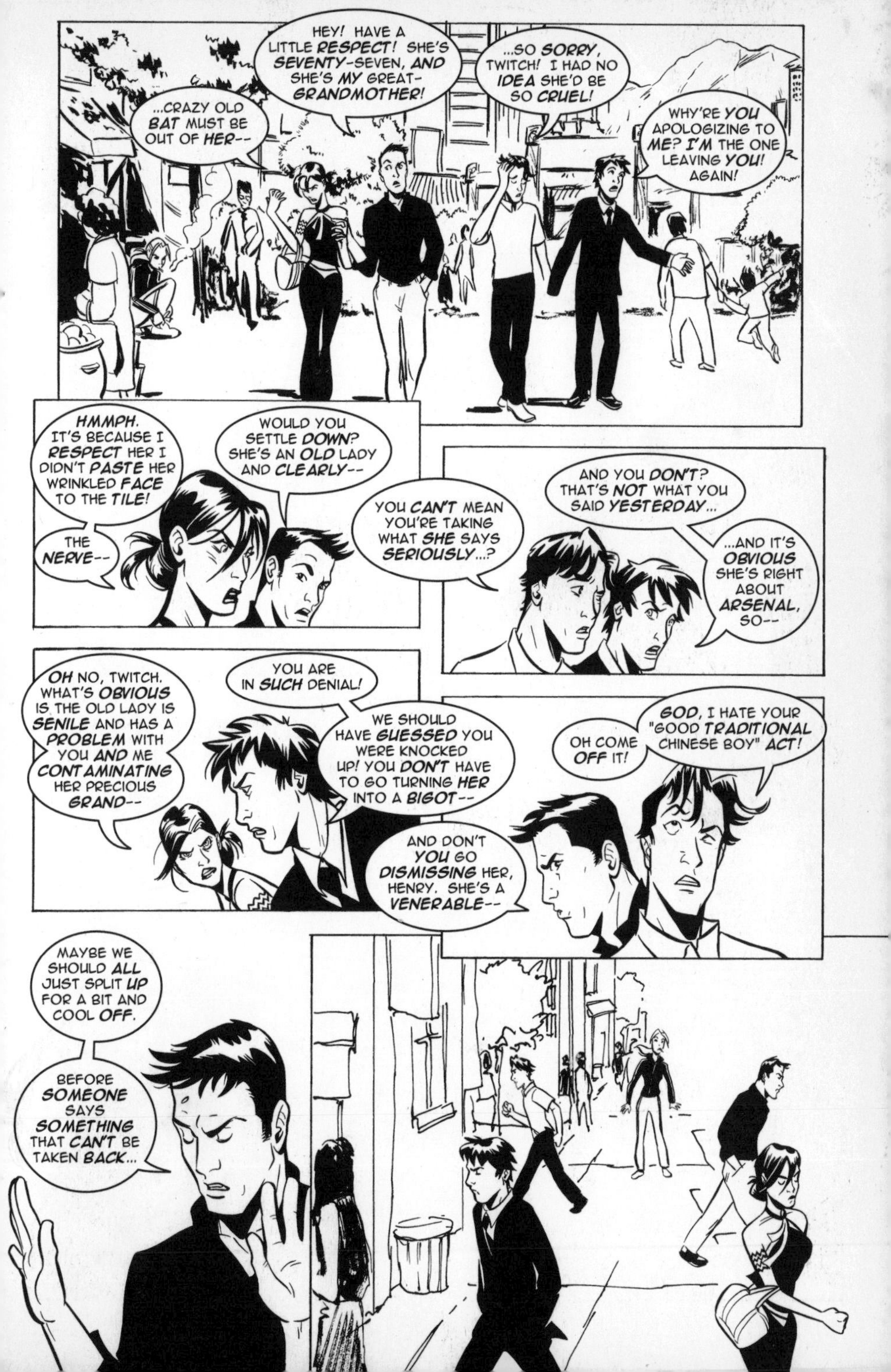
...CRAZY OLD BAT MUST BE OUT OF HER--
HEY! HAVE A LITTLE RESPECT! SHE'S SEVENTY-SEVEN, AND SHE'S MY GREAT-GRANDMOTHER!
...SO SORRY, TWITCH! I HAD NO IDEA SHE'D BE SO CRUEL!
WHY'RE YOU APOLOGIZING TO ME? I'M THE ONE LEAVING YOU! AGAIN!
HMMPH. IT'S BECAUSE I RESPECT HER I DIDN'T PASTE HER WRINKLED FACE TO THE TILE!
THE NERVE--
WOULD YOU SETTLE DOWN? SHE'S AN OLD LADY AND CLEARLY--
YOU CAN'T MEAN YOU'RE TAKING WHAT SHE SAYS SERIOUSLY...?
AND YOU DON'T? THAT'S NOT WHAT YOU SAID YESTERDAY...
...AND IT'S OBVIOUS SHE'S RIGHT ABOUT ARSENAL, SO--
OH NO, TWITCH. WHAT'S OBVIOUS IS THE OLD LADY IS SENILE AND HAS A PROBLEM WITH YOU AND ME CONTAMINATING HER PRECIOUS GRAND--
YOU ARE IN SUCH DENIAL!
WE SHOULD HAVE GUESSED YOU WERE KNOCKED UP! YOU DON'T HAVE TO GO TURNING HER INTO A BIGOT--
AND DON'T YOU GO DISMISSING HER, HENRY. SHE'S A VENERABLE--
OH COME OFF IT!
GOD, I HATE YOUR "GOOD TRADITIONAL CHINESE BOY" ACT!
MAYBE WE SHOULD ALL JUST SPLIT UP FOR A BIT AND COOL OFF.
BEFORE SOMEONE SAYS SOMETHING THAT CAN'T BE TAKEN BACK...

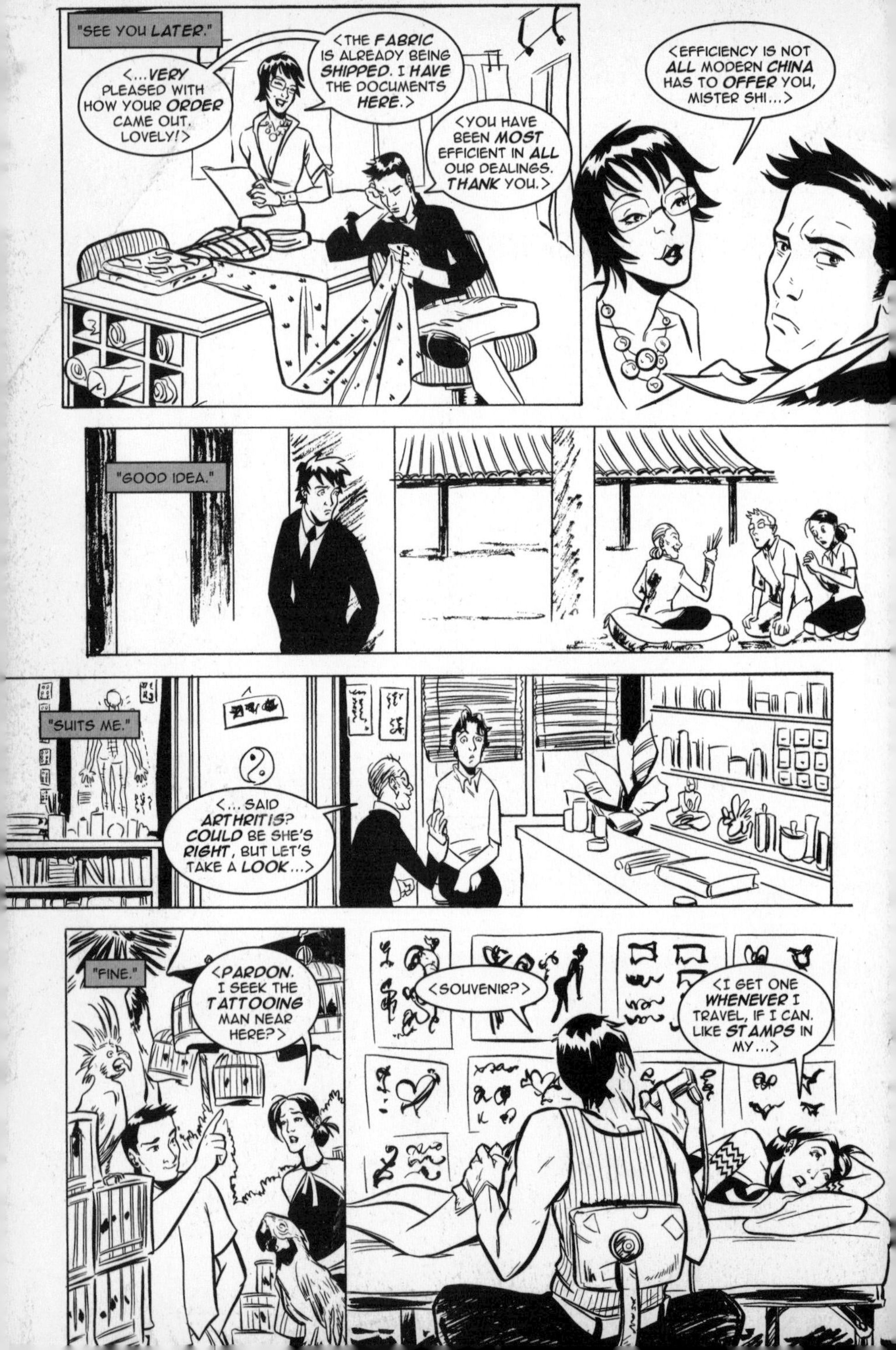
"SEE YOU LATER."
<...VERY PLEASED WITH HOW YOUR ORDER CAME OUT. LOVELY!>
<THE FABRIC IS ALREADY BEING SHIPPED. I HAVE THE DOCUMENTS HERE.>
<YOU HAVE BEEN MOST EFFICIENT IN ALL OUR DEALINGS. THANK YOU.>
<EFFICIENCY IS NOT ALL MODERN CHINA HAS TO OFFER YOU, MISTER SHI...>
"GOOD IDEA."
"SUITS ME."
<... SAID ARTHRITIS? COULD BE SHE'S RIGHT, BUT LET'S TAKE A LOOK...>
"FINE."
<PARDON. I SEEK THE TATTOOING MAN NEAR HERE?>
<SOUVENIR?>
<I GET ONE WHENEVER I TRAVEL, IF I CAN. LIKE STAMPS IN MY...>

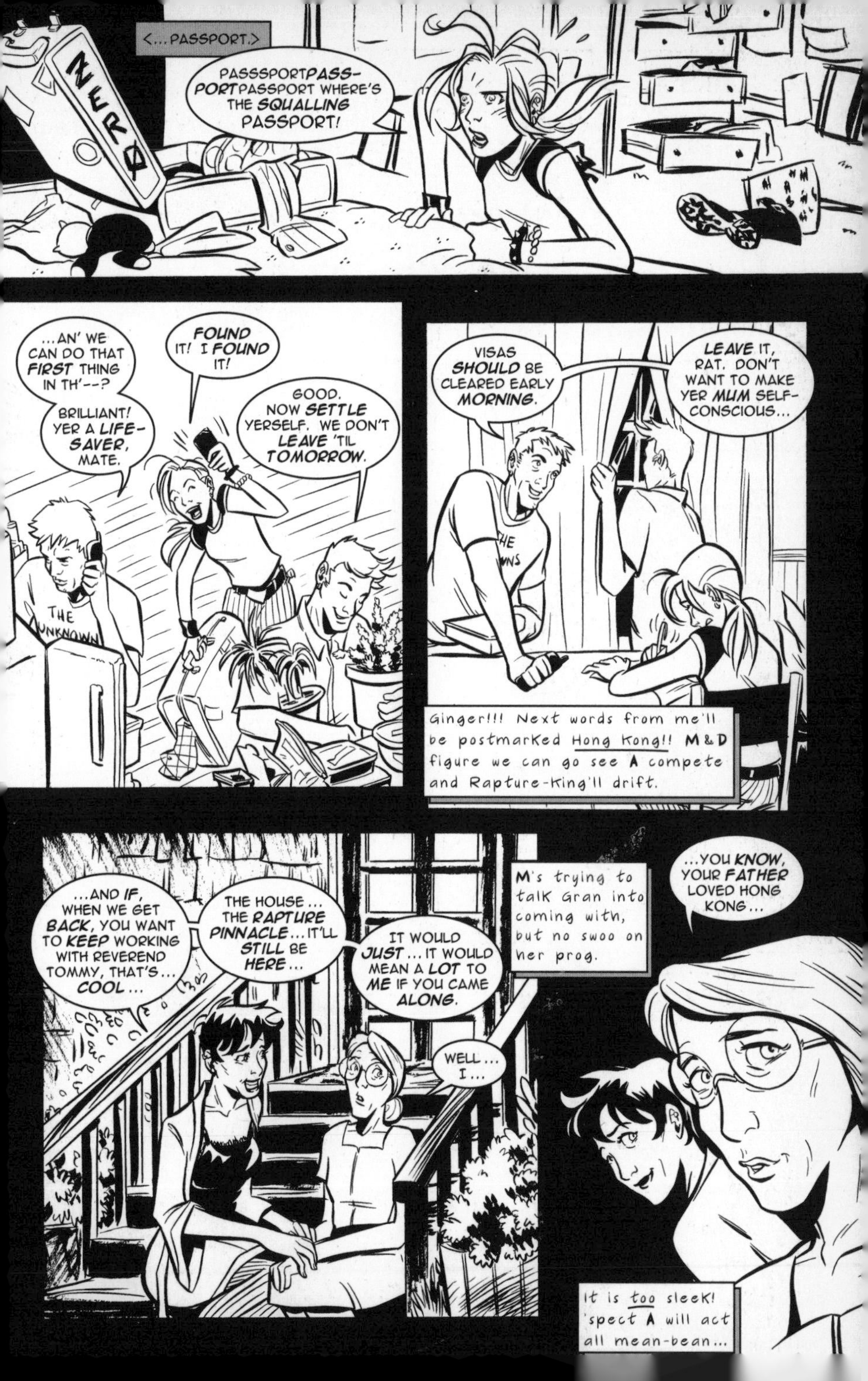

<...PASSPORT.>
PASSSPORTPASS-PORTPASSPORT WHERE'S THE SQUALLING PASSPORT!
...AN' WE CAN DO THAT FIRST THING IN TH'--?
BRILLIANT! YER A LIFE-SAVER, MATE.
FOUND IT! I FOUND IT!
GOOD. NOW SETTLE YERSELF. WE DON'T LEAVE 'TIL TOMORROW.
VISAS SHOULD BE CLEARED EARLY MORNING.
LEAVE IT, RAT. DON'T WANT TO MAKE YER MUM SELF-CONSCIOUS...
Ginger!!! Next words from me'll be postmarked Hong Kong!! M & D figure we can go see A compete and Rapture-King'll drift.
...AND IF, WHEN WE GET BACK, YOU WANT TO KEEP WORKING WITH REVEREND TOMMY, THAT'S... COOL...
THE HOUSE... THE RAPTURE PINNACLE... IT'LL STILL BE HERE...
IT WOULD JUST... IT WOULD MEAN A LOT TO ME IF YOU CAME ALONG.
WELL... I...
M's trying to talk Gran into coming with, but no swoo on her prog.
...YOU KNOW, YOUR FATHER LOVED HONG KONG...
It is too sleek! 'spect A will act all mean-bean...

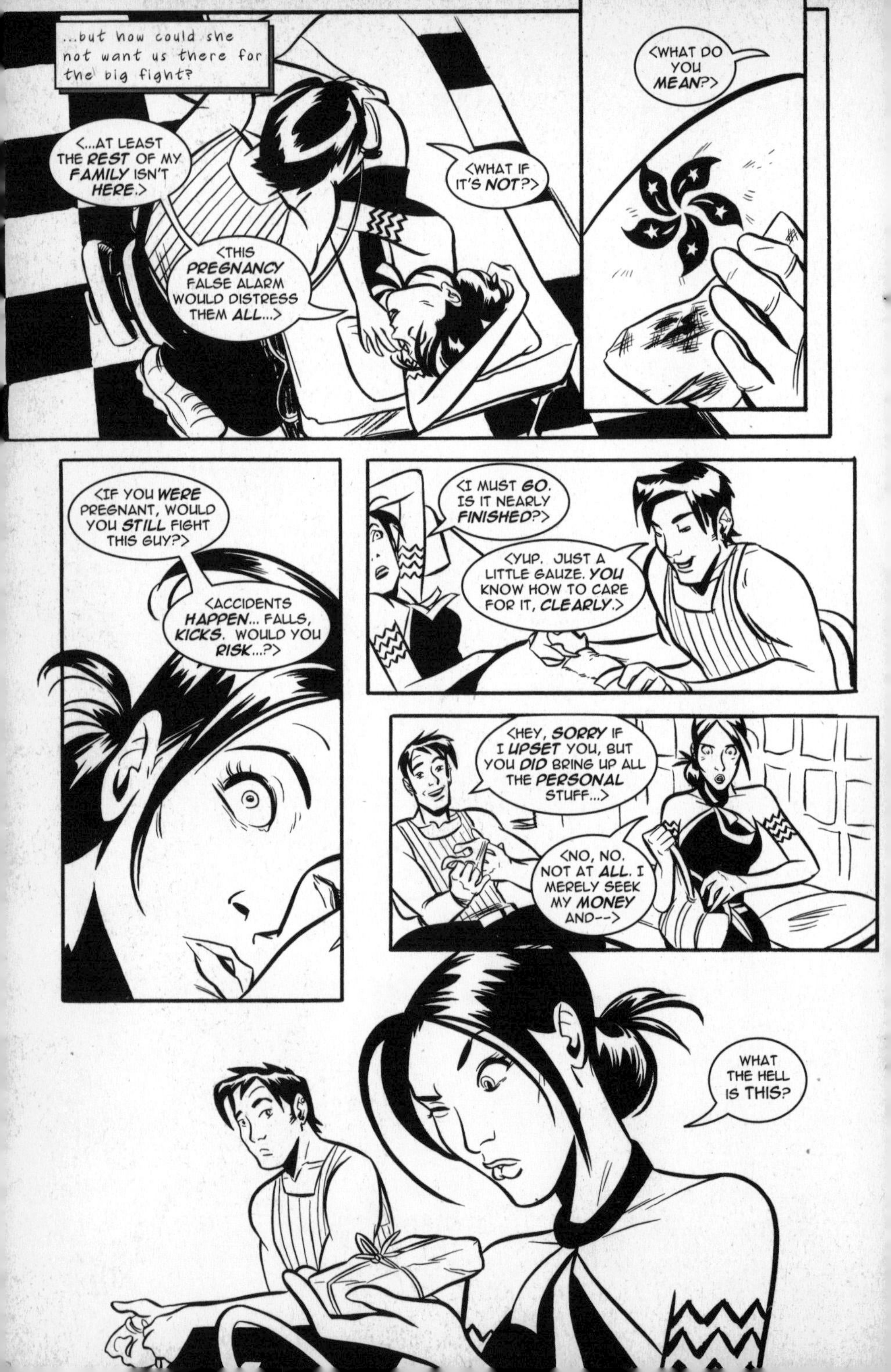

...but how could she not want us there for the big fight?
<...AT LEAST THE REST OF MY FAMILY ISN'T HERE.>
<THIS PREGNANCY FALSE ALARM WOULD DISTRESS THEM ALL...>
<WHAT IF IT'S NOT?>
<WHAT DO YOU MEAN?>
<IF YOU WERE PREGNANT, WOULD YOU STILL FIGHT THIS GUY?>
<ACCIDENTS HAPPEN... FALLS, KICKS. WOULD YOU RISK...?>
<I MUST GO. IS IT NEARLY FINISHED?>
<YUP. JUST A LITTLE GAUZE. YOU KNOW HOW TO CARE FOR IT, CLEARLY.>
<HEY, SORRY IF I UPSET YOU, BUT YOU DID BRING UP ALL THE PERSONAL STUFF...>
<NO, NO. NOT AT ALL. I MERELY SEEK MY MONEY AND-->
WHAT THE HELL IS THIS?

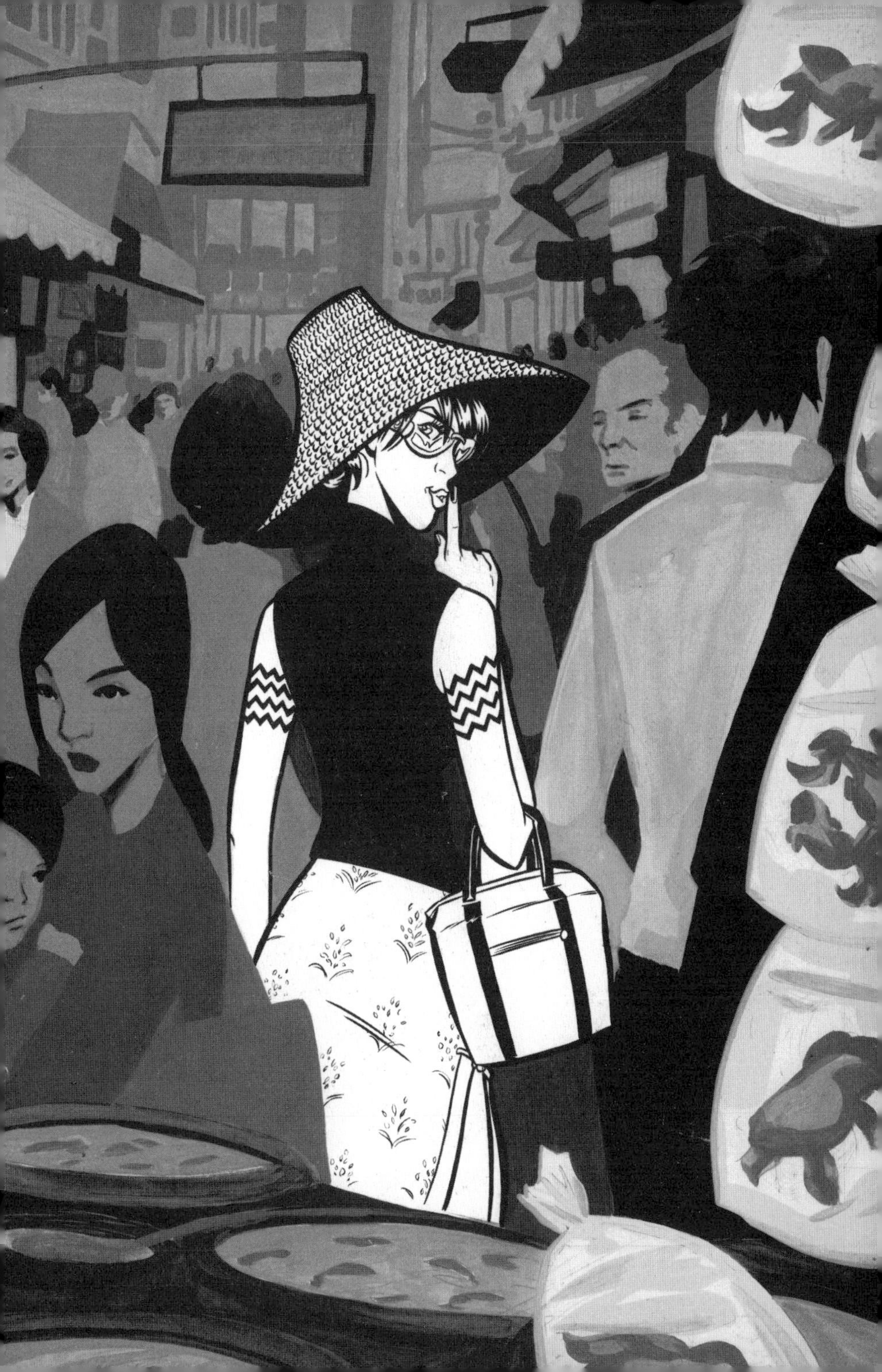

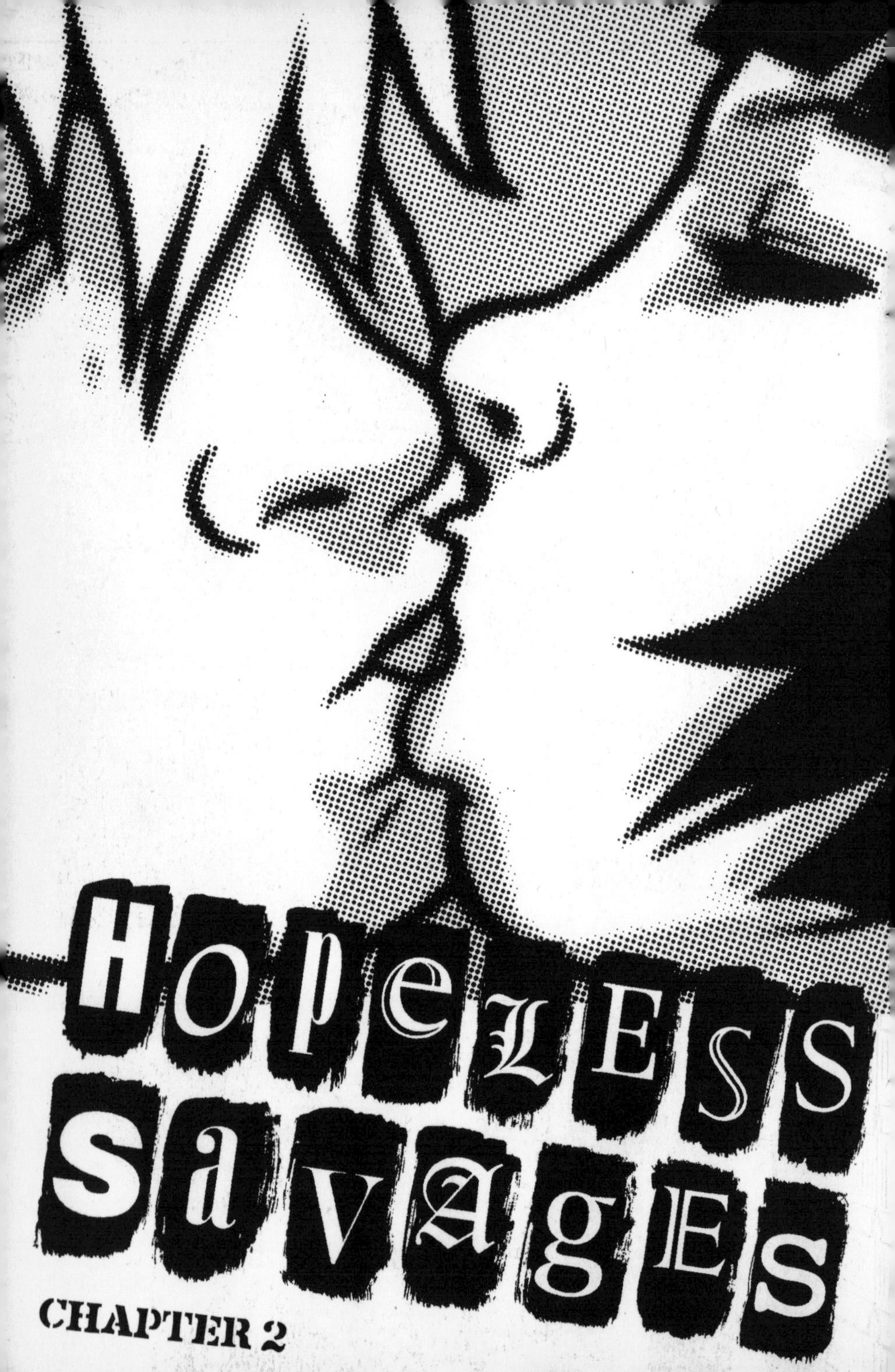

Hopeless Savages

CHAPTER 2

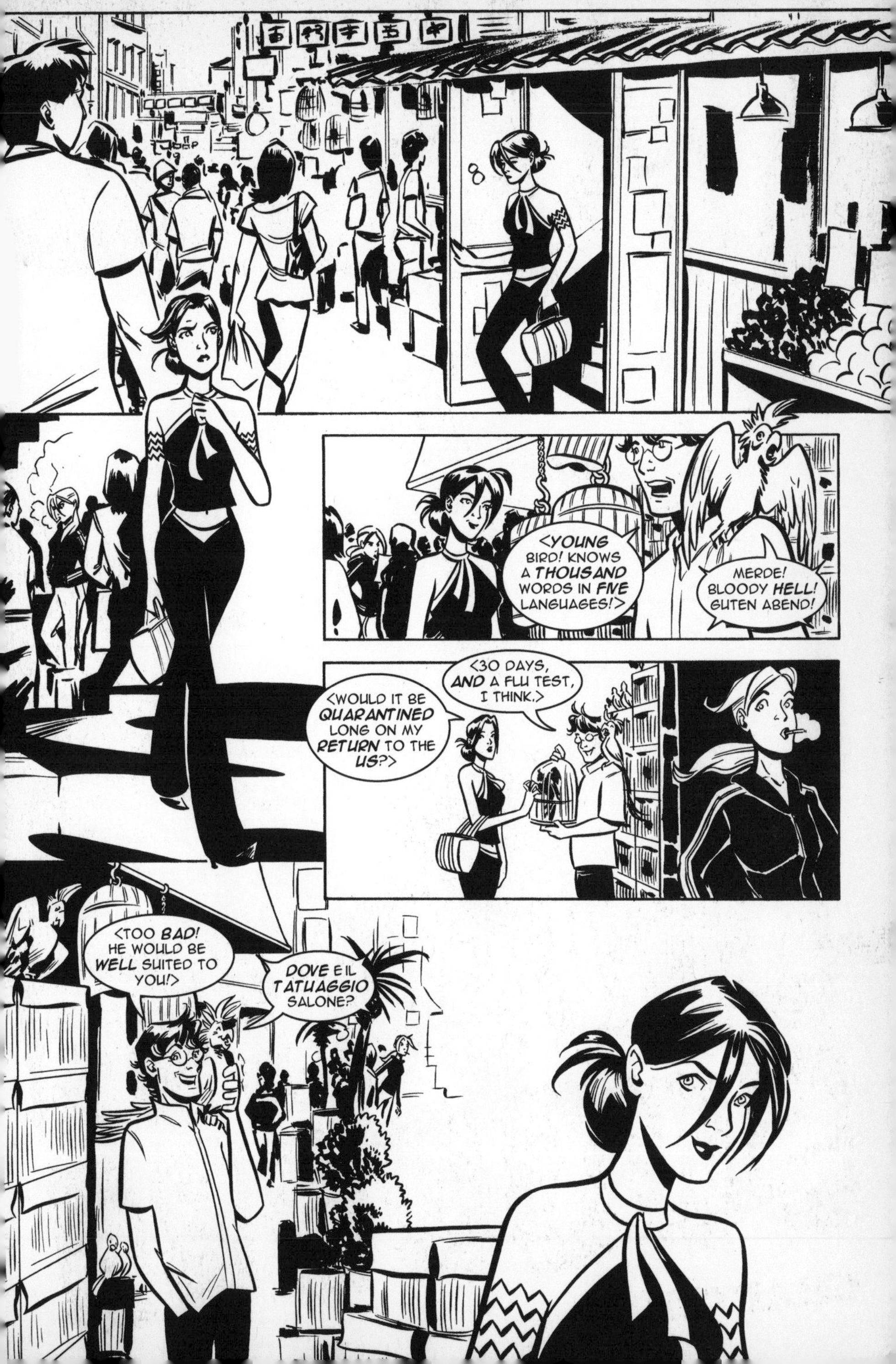
<YOUNG BIRD! KNOWS A THOUSAND WORDS IN FIVE LANGUAGES!>
MERDE! BLOODY HELL! GUTEN ABEND!
<WOULD IT BE QUARANTINED LONG ON MY RETURN TO THE US?>
<30 DAYS, AND A FLU TEST, I THINK.>
<TOO BAD! HE WOULD BE WELL SUITED TO YOU!>
DOVE E IL TATUAGGIO SALONE?

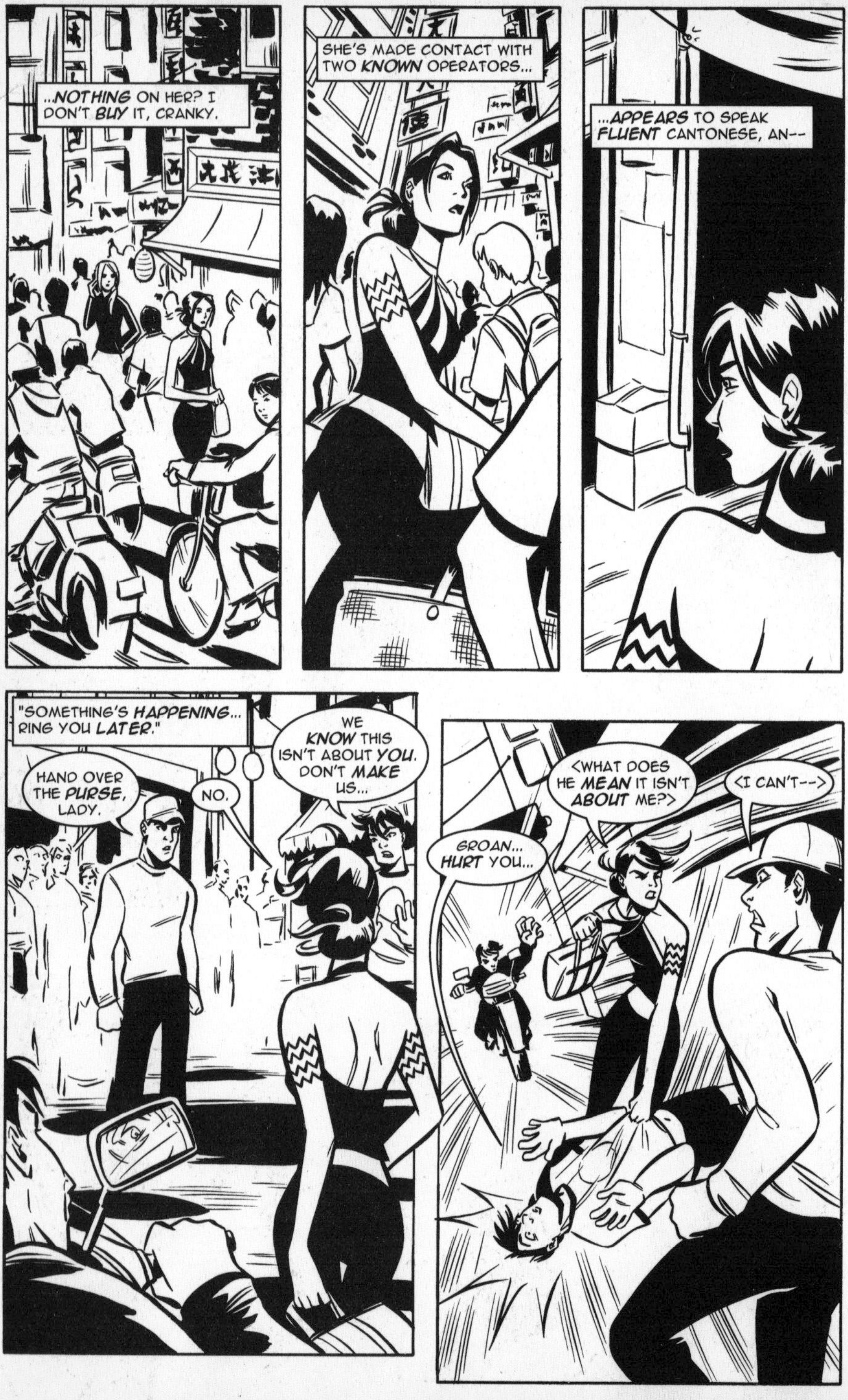
...NOTHING ON HER? I DON'T BUY IT, CRANKY.
SHE'S MADE CONTACT WITH TWO KNOWN OPERATORS...
...APPEARS TO SPEAK FLUENT CANTONESE, AN--
"SOMETHING'S HAPPENING... RING YOU LATER."
HAND OVER THE PURSE, LADY.
NO.
WE KNOW THIS ISN'T ABOUT YOU. DON'T MAKE US...
GROAN... HURT YOU...
<WHAT DOES HE MEAN IT ISN'T ABOUT ME?>
<I CAN'T-->

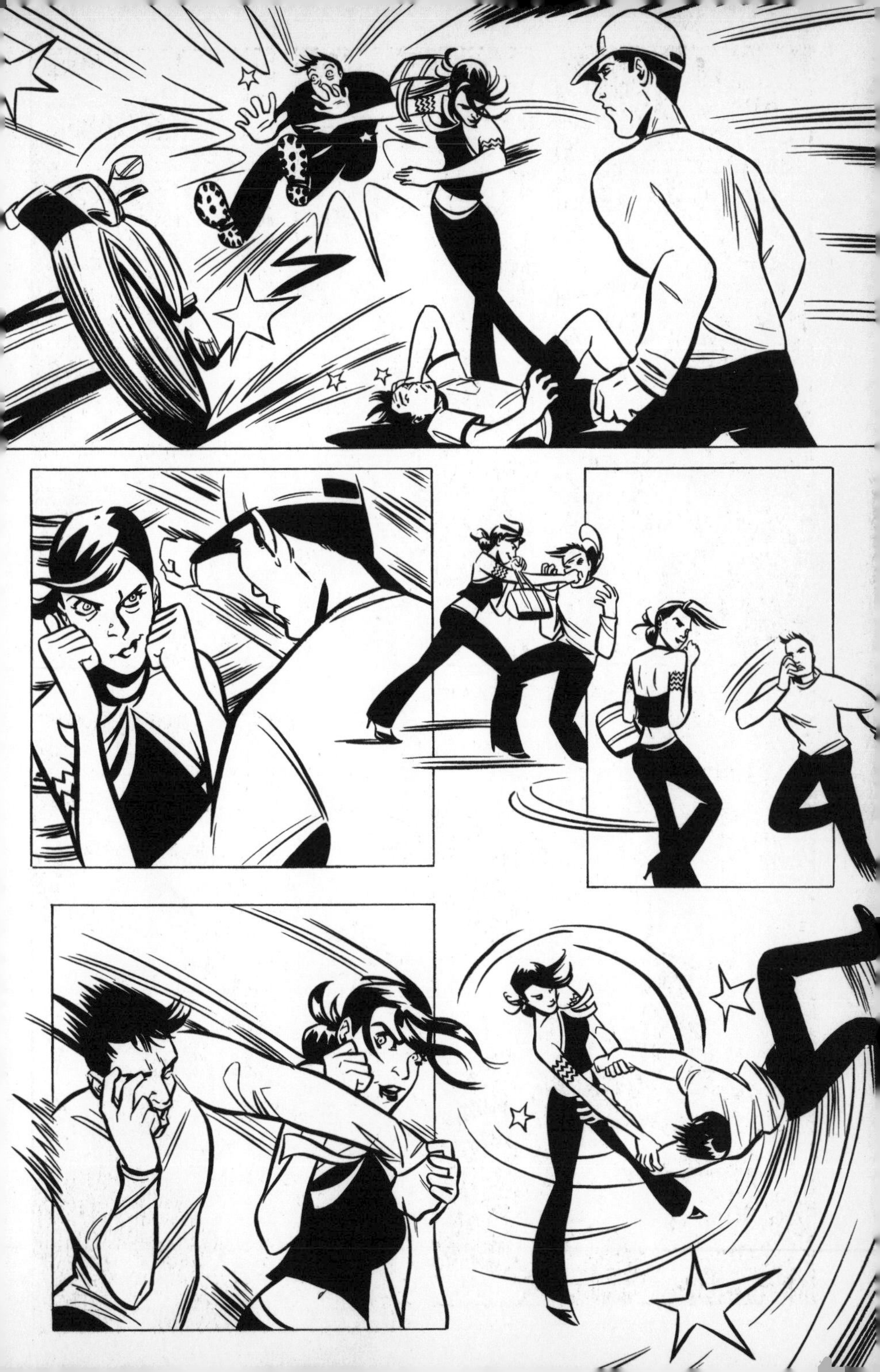

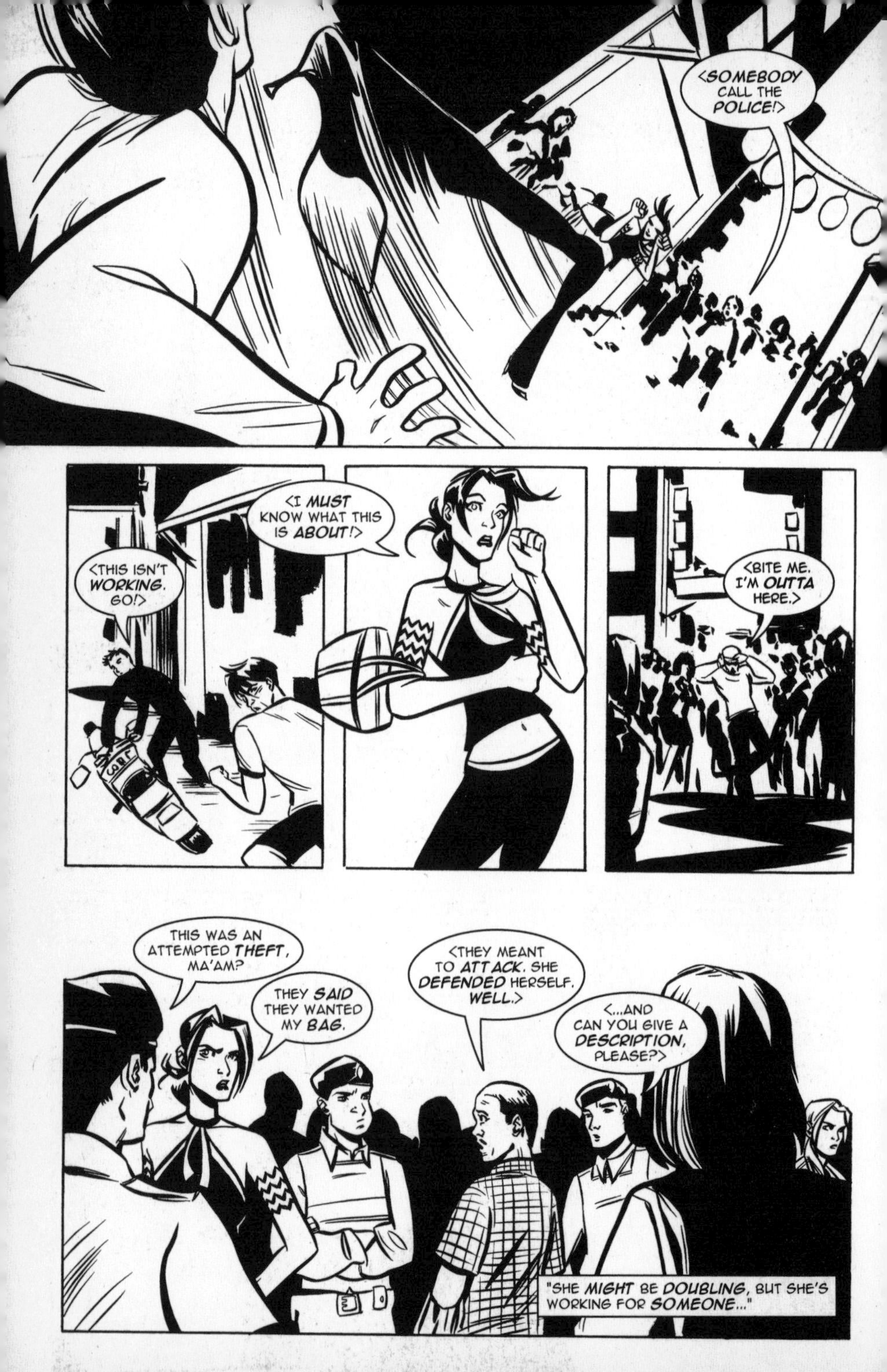
<SOMEBODY CALL THE POLICE!>
<THIS ISN'T WORKING. GO!>
<I MUST KNOW WHAT THIS IS ABOUT!>
<BITE ME. I'M OUTTA HERE.>
THIS WAS AN ATTEMPTED THEFT, MA'AM?
THEY SAID THEY WANTED MY BAG.
<THEY MEANT TO ATTACK. SHE DEFENDED HERSELF, WELL.>
<...AND CAN YOU GIVE A DESCRIPTION, PLEASE?>
"SHE MIGHT BE DOUBLING, BUT SHE'S WORKING FOR SOMEONE..."

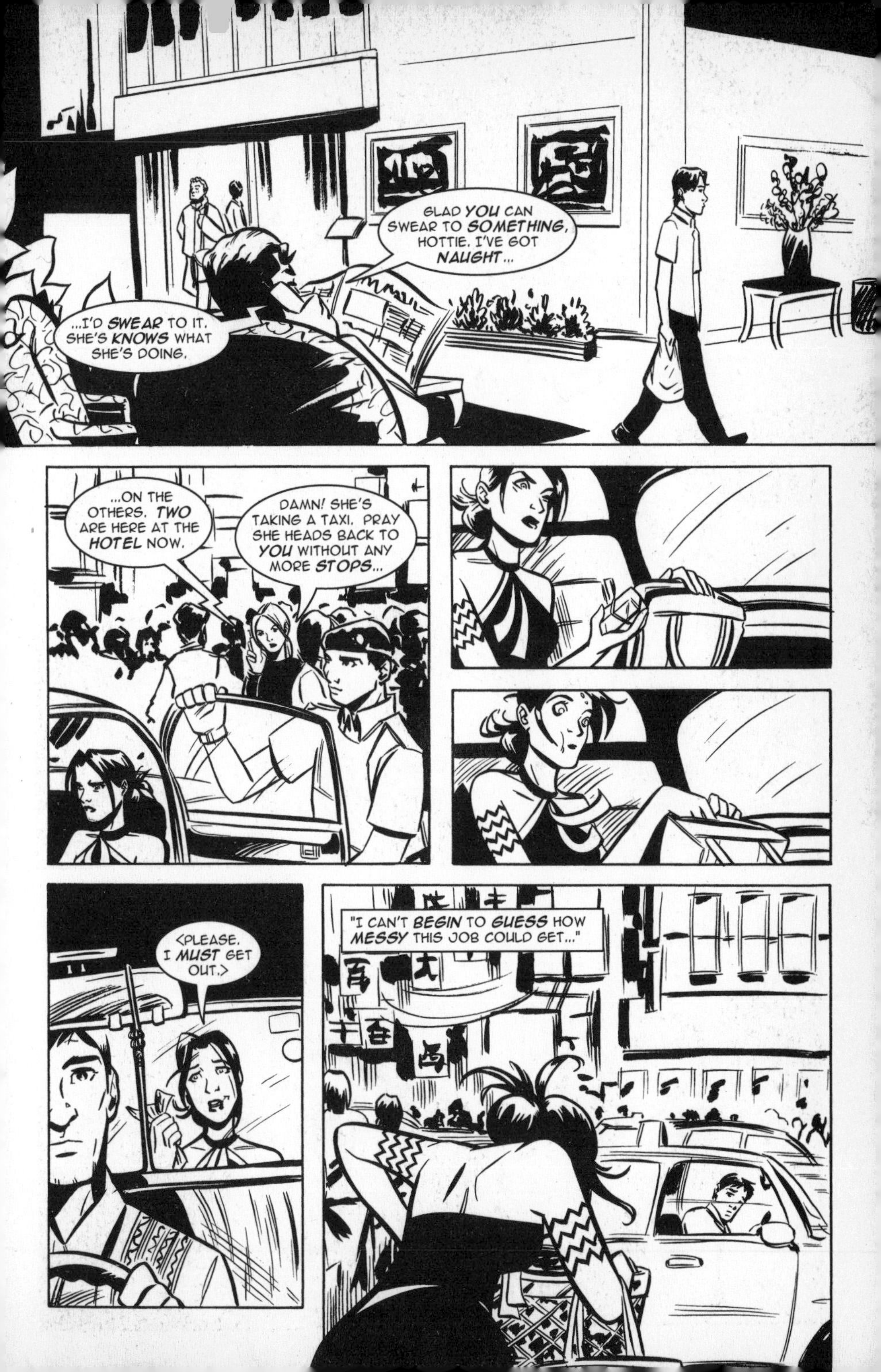
...I'D SWEAR TO IT. SHE'S KNOWS WHAT SHE'S DOING.
GLAD YOU CAN SWEAR TO SOMETHING, HOTTIE. I'VE GOT NAUGHT...
...ON THE OTHERS. TWO ARE HERE AT THE HOTEL NOW.
DAMN! SHE'S TAKING A TAXI. PRAY SHE HEADS BACK TO YOU WITHOUT ANY MORE STOPS...
<PLEASE. I MUST GET OUT.>
"I CAN'T BEGIN TO GUESS HOW MESSY THIS JOB COULD GET..."

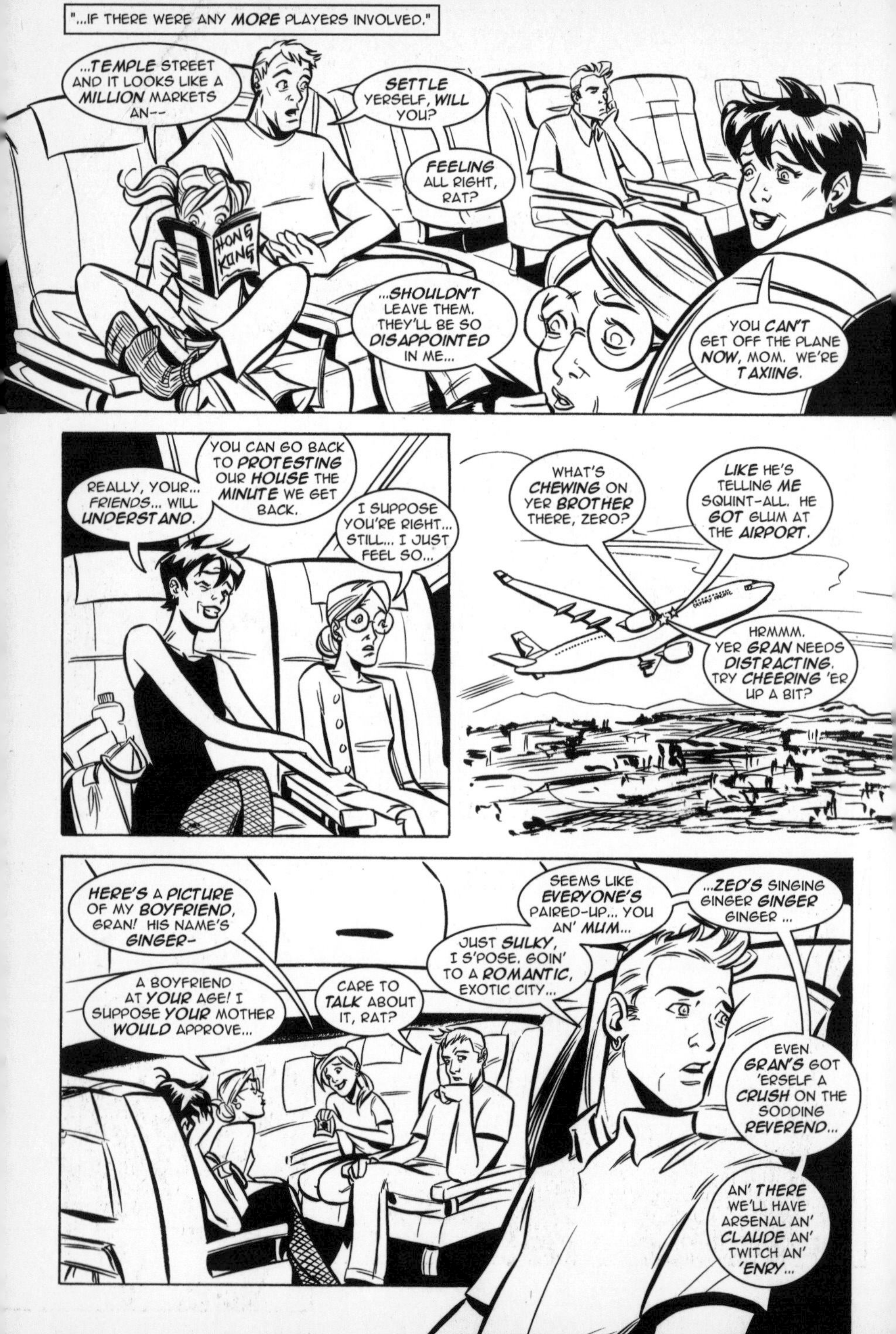
"...IF THERE WERE ANY MORE PLAYERS INVOLVED."
...TEMPLE STREET AND IT LOOKS LIKE A MILLION MARKETS AN--
SETTLE YERSELF, WILL YOU?
FEELING ALL RIGHT, RAT?
HONG KONG
...SHOULDN'T LEAVE THEM. THEY'LL BE SO DISAPPOINTED IN ME...
YOU CAN'T GET OFF THE PLANE NOW, MOM. WE'RE TAXIING.
REALLY, YOUR... FRIENDS... WILL UNDERSTAND.
YOU CAN GO BACK TO PROTESTING OUR HOUSE THE MINUTE WE GET BACK.
I SUPPOSE YOU'RE RIGHT... STILL... I JUST FEEL SO...
WHAT'S CHEWING ON YER BROTHER THERE, ZERO?
LIKE HE'S TELLING ME SQUINT-ALL. HE GOT GLUM AT THE AIRPORT.
HRMMM. YER GRAN NEEDS DISTRACTING. TRY CHEERING 'ER UP A BIT?
HERE'S A PICTURE OF MY BOYFRIEND, GRAN! HIS NAME'S GINGER-
A BOYFRIEND AT YOUR AGE! I SUPPOSE YOUR MOTHER WOULD APPROVE...
CARE TO TALK ABOUT IT, RAT?
JUST SULKY, I S'POSE. GOIN' TO A ROMANTIC, EXOTIC CITY...
SEEMS LIKE EVERYONE'S PAIRED-UP... YOU AN' MUM...
...ZED'S SINGING GINGER GINGER GINGER ...
EVEN GRAN'S GOT 'ERSELF A CRUSH ON THE SODDING REVEREND...
AN' THERE WE'LL HAVE ARSENAL AN' CLAUDE AN' TWITCH AN' 'ENRY...

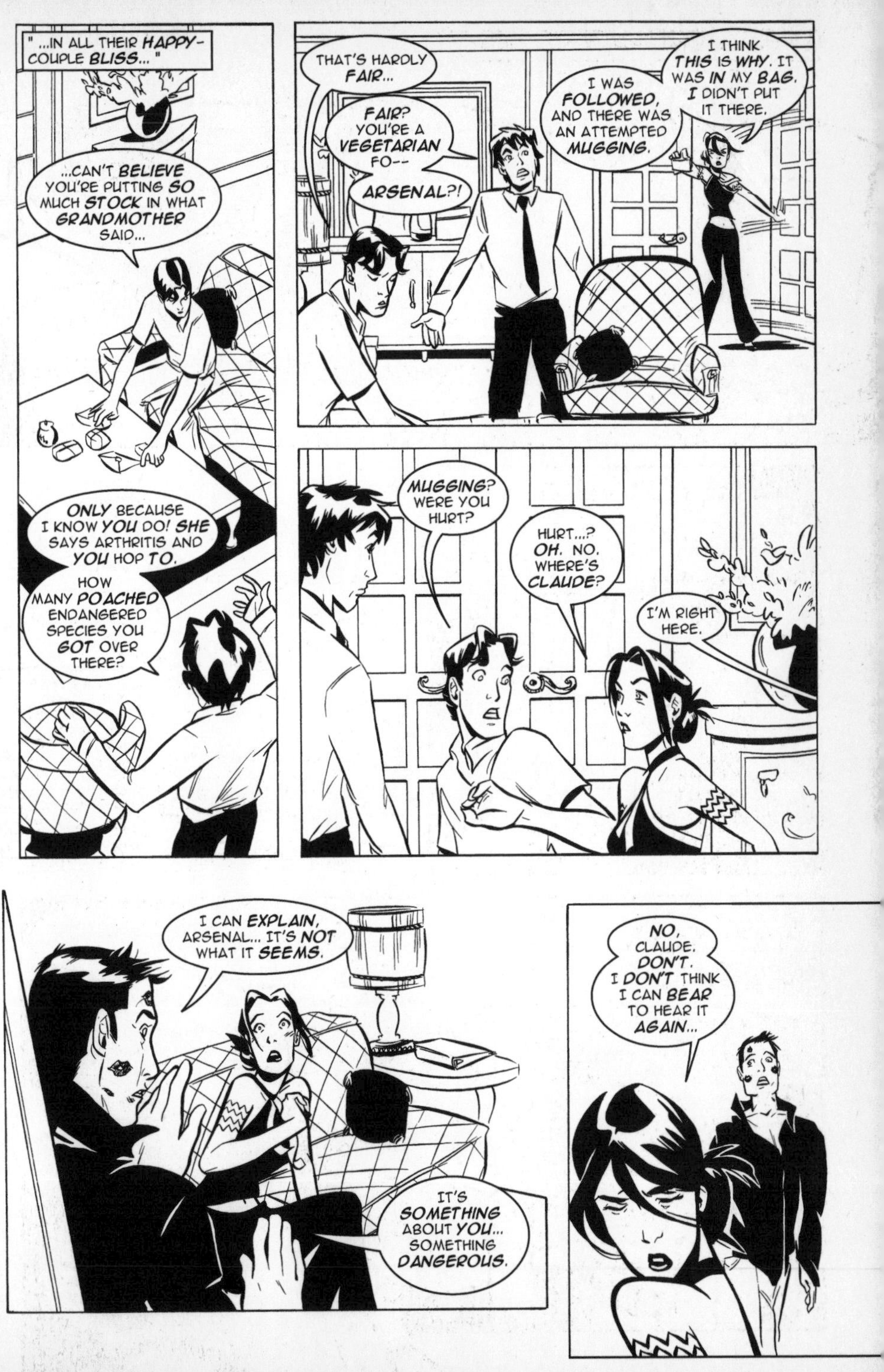

"...IN ALL THEIR HAPPY-COUPLE BLISS..."
...CAN'T BELIEVE YOU'RE PUTTING SO MUCH STOCK IN WHAT GRANDMOTHER SAID...
ONLY BECAUSE I KNOW YOU DO! SHE SAYS ARTHRITIS AND YOU HOP TO.
HOW MANY POACHED ENDANGERED SPECIES YOU GOT OVER THERE?
THAT'S HARDLY FAIR...
FAIR? YOU'RE A VEGETARIAN FO--
ARSENAL?!
I WAS FOLLOWED, AND THERE WAS AN ATTEMPTED MUGGING.
I THINK THIS IS WHY. IT WAS IN MY BAG. I DIDN'T PUT IT THERE.
MUGGING? WERE YOU HURT?
HURT...? OH. NO. WHERE'S CLAUDE?
I'M RIGHT HERE.
I CAN EXPLAIN, ARSENAL... IT'S NOT WHAT IT SEEMS.
IT'S SOMETHING ABOUT YOU... SOMETHING DANGEROUS.
NO, CLAUDE. DON'T. I DON'T THINK I CAN BEAR TO HEAR IT AGAIN...

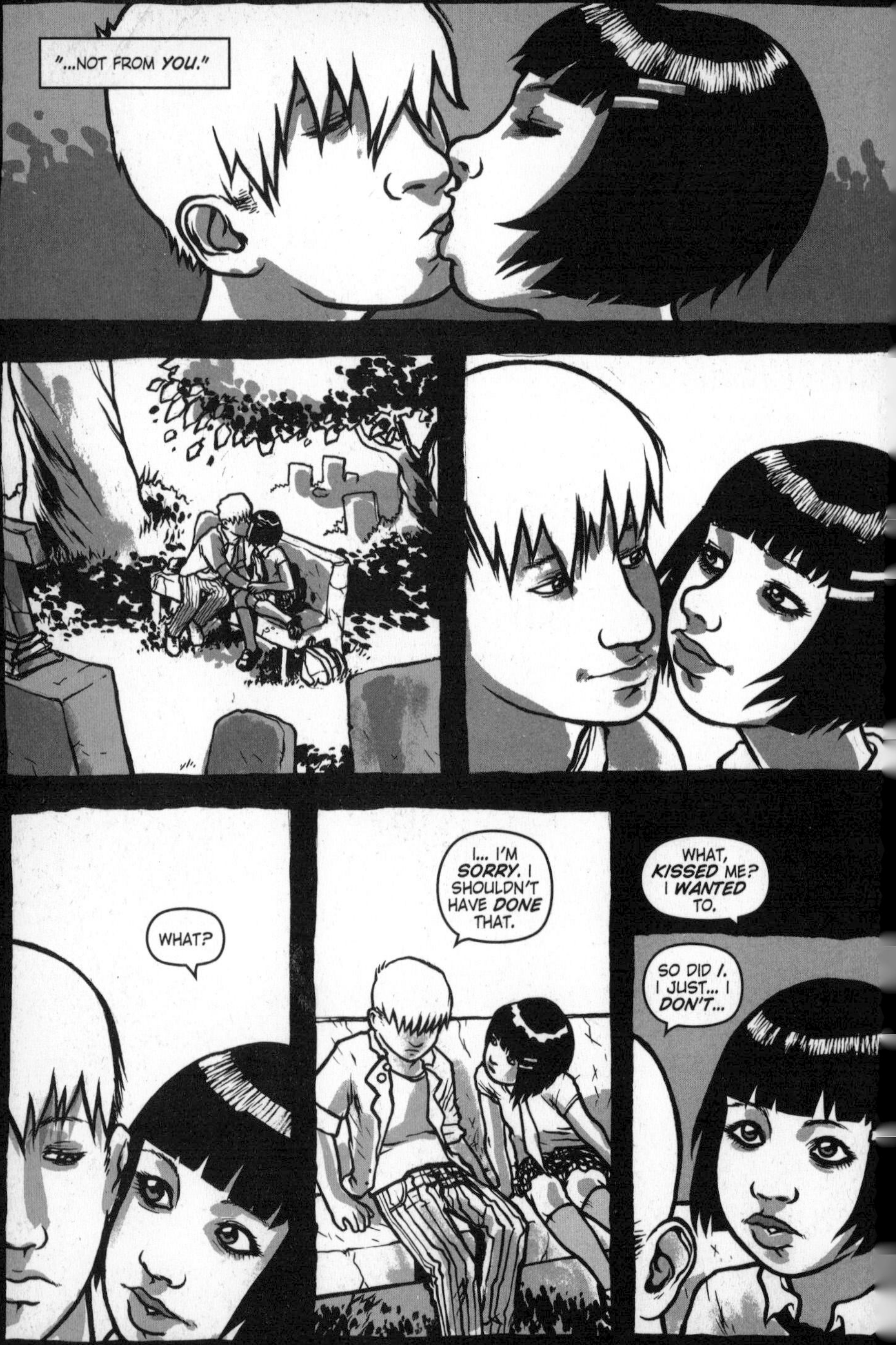
"...NOT FROM *YOU*."
WHAT?
I... I'M *SORRY*. I SHOULDN'T HAVE *DONE* THAT.
WHAT, *KISSED* ME? I *WANTED* TO.
SO DID *I*. I JUST... I *DON'T*...

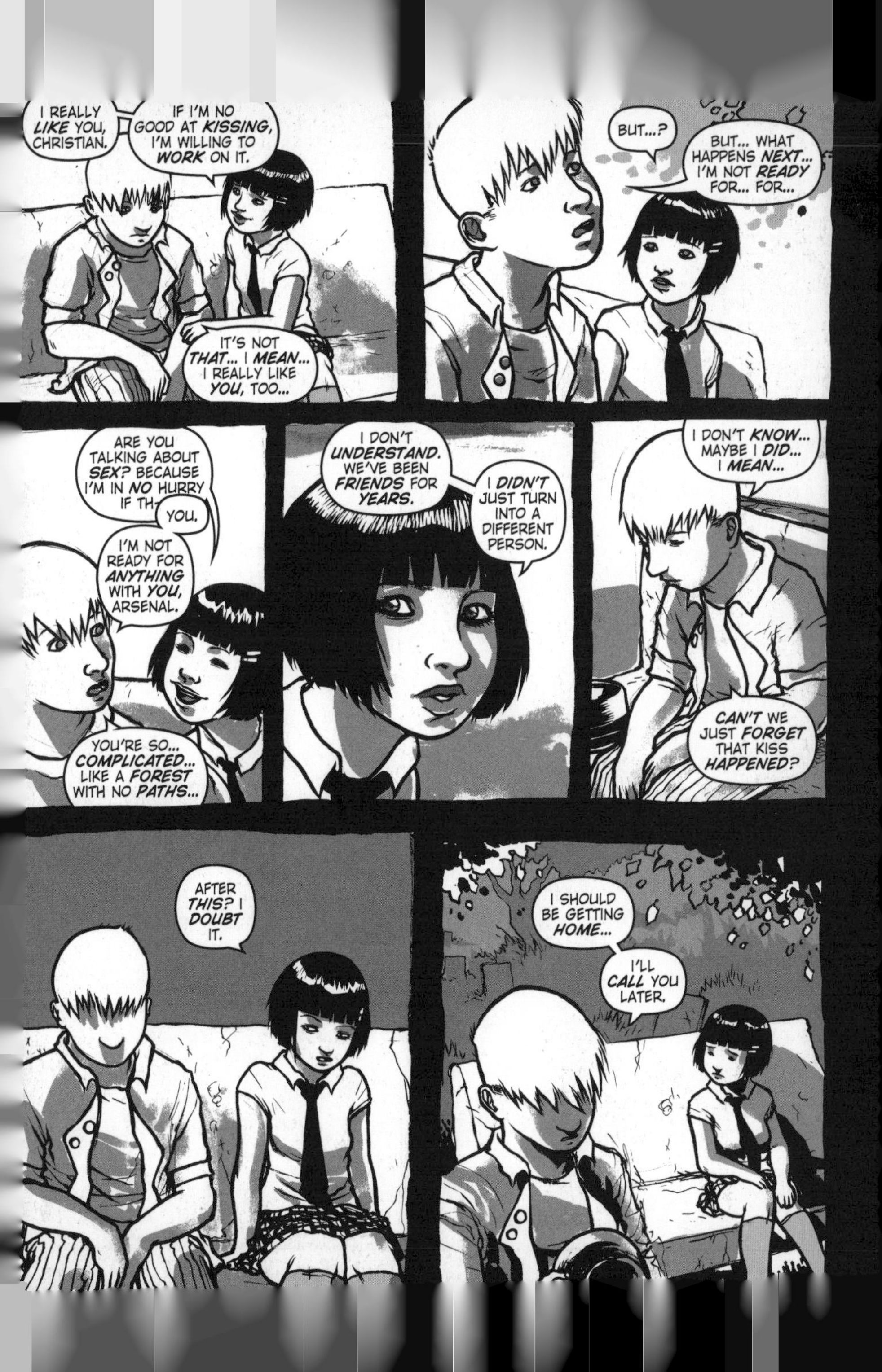
I REALLY LIKE YOU, CHRISTIAN.
IF I'M NO GOOD AT KISSING, I'M WILLING TO WORK ON IT.
IT'S NOT THAT... I MEAN... I REALLY LIKE YOU, TOO...
BUT...?
BUT... WHAT HAPPENS NEXT... I'M NOT READY FOR... FOR...
ARE YOU TALKING ABOUT SEX? BECAUSE I'M IN NO HURRY IF TH-
YOU.
I'M NOT READY FOR ANYTHING WITH YOU, ARSENAL.
YOU'RE SO... COMPLICATED... LIKE A FOREST WITH NO PATHS...
I DON'T UNDERSTAND. WE'VE BEEN FRIENDS FOR YEARS.
I DIDN'T JUST TURN INTO A DIFFERENT PERSON.
I DON'T KNOW... MAYBE I DID... I MEAN...
CAN'T WE JUST FORGET THAT KISS HAPPENED?
AFTER THIS? I DOUBT IT.
I SHOULD BE GETTING HOME...
I'LL CALL YOU LATER.

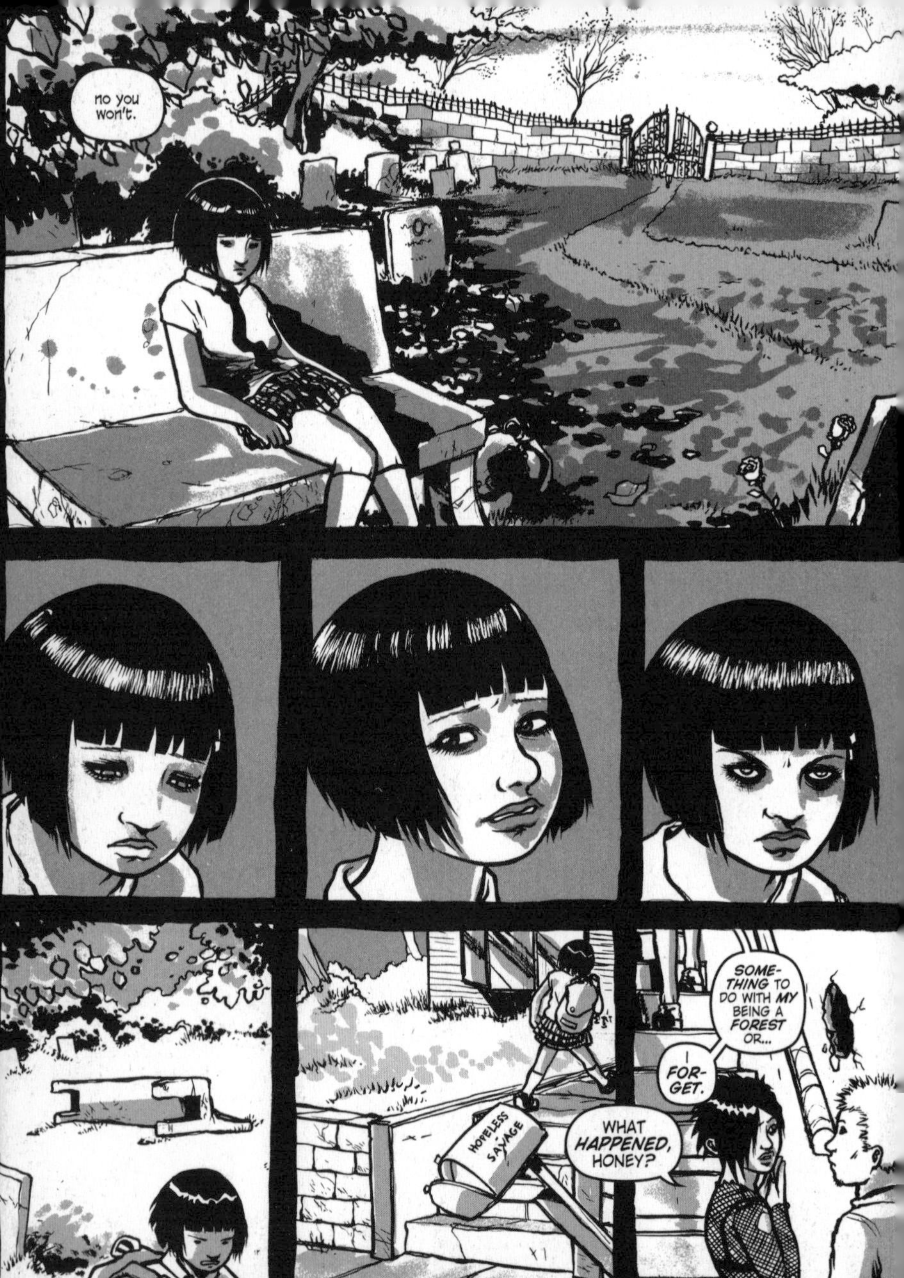
no you won't.
SOME-THING TO DO WITH MY BEING A FOREST OR...
I FOR-GET.
WHAT HAPPENED, HONEY?
HOPELESS SAVAGE

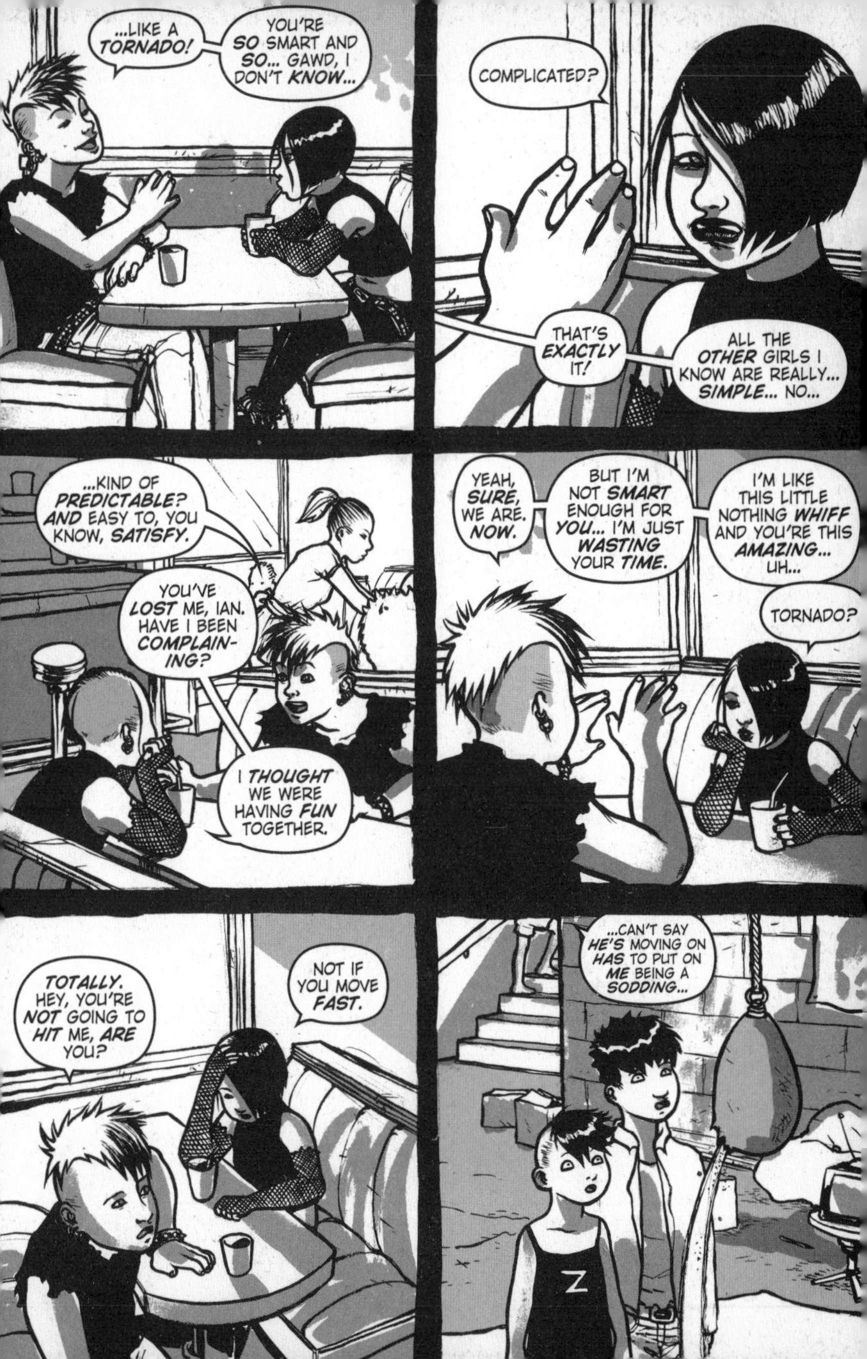
...LIKE A TORNADO!
YOU'RE SO SMART AND SO... GAWD, I DON'T KNOW...
COMPLICATED?
THAT'S EXACTLY IT!
ALL THE OTHER GIRLS I KNOW ARE REALLY... SIMPLE... NO...
...KIND OF PREDICTABLE? AND EASY TO, YOU KNOW, SATISFY.
YOU'VE LOST ME, IAN. HAVE I BEEN COMPLAIN-ING?
I THOUGHT WE WERE HAVING FUN TOGETHER.
YEAH, SURE, WE ARE. NOW.
BUT I'M NOT SMART ENOUGH FOR YOU... I'M JUST WASTING YOUR TIME.
I'M LIKE THIS LITTLE NOTHING WHIFF AND YOU'RE THIS AMAZING... UH...
TORNADO?
TOTALLY. HEY, YOU'RE NOT GOING TO HIT ME, ARE YOU?
NOT IF YOU MOVE FAST.
...CAN'T SAY HE'S MOVING ON HAS TO PUT ON ME BEING A SODDING...
Z

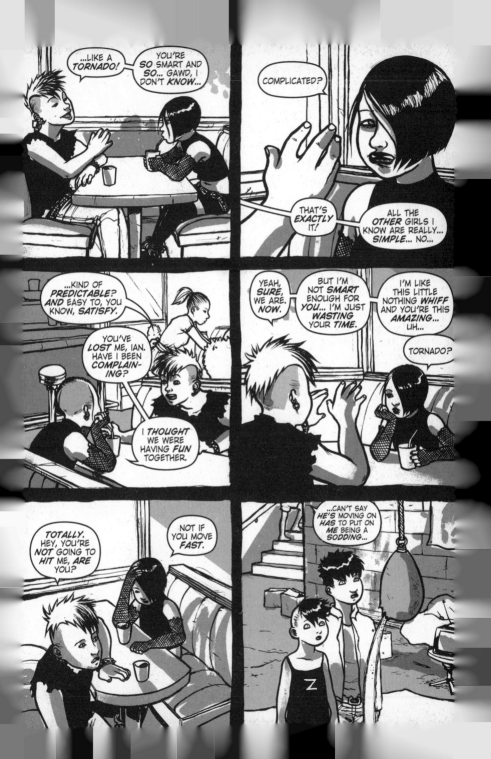

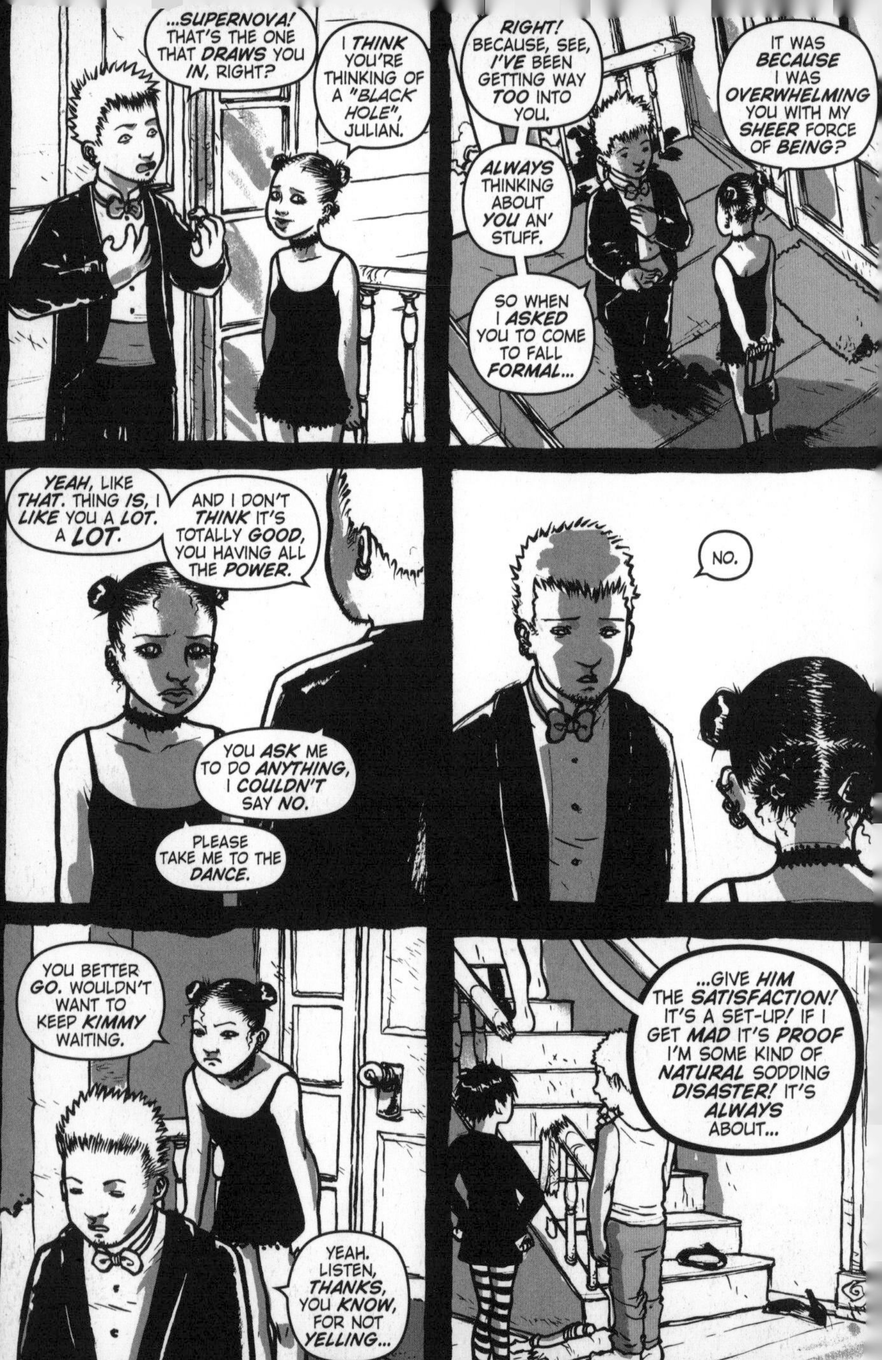

...SUPERNOVA! THAT'S THE ONE THAT DRAWS YOU IN, RIGHT?
I THINK YOU'RE THINKING OF A "BLACK HOLE", JULIAN.
RIGHT! BECAUSE, SEE, I'VE BEEN GETTING WAY TOO INTO YOU.
ALWAYS THINKING ABOUT YOU AN' STUFF.
SO WHEN I ASKED YOU TO COME TO FALL FORMAL...
IT WAS BECAUSE I WAS OVERWHELMING YOU WITH MY SHEER FORCE OF BEING?
YEAH, LIKE THAT. THING IS, I LIKE YOU A LOT. A LOT.
AND I DON'T THINK IT'S TOTALLY GOOD, YOU HAVING ALL THE POWER.
YOU ASK ME TO DO ANYTHING, I COULDN'T SAY NO.
PLEASE TAKE ME TO THE DANCE.
NO.
YOU BETTER GO. WOULDN'T WANT TO KEEP KIMMY WAITING.
YEAH. LISTEN, THANKS, YOU KNOW, FOR NOT YELLING...
...GIVE HIM THE SATISFACTION! IT'S A SET-UP! IF I GET MAD IT'S PROOF I'M SOME KIND OF NATURAL SODDING DISASTER! IT'S ALWAYS ABOUT...

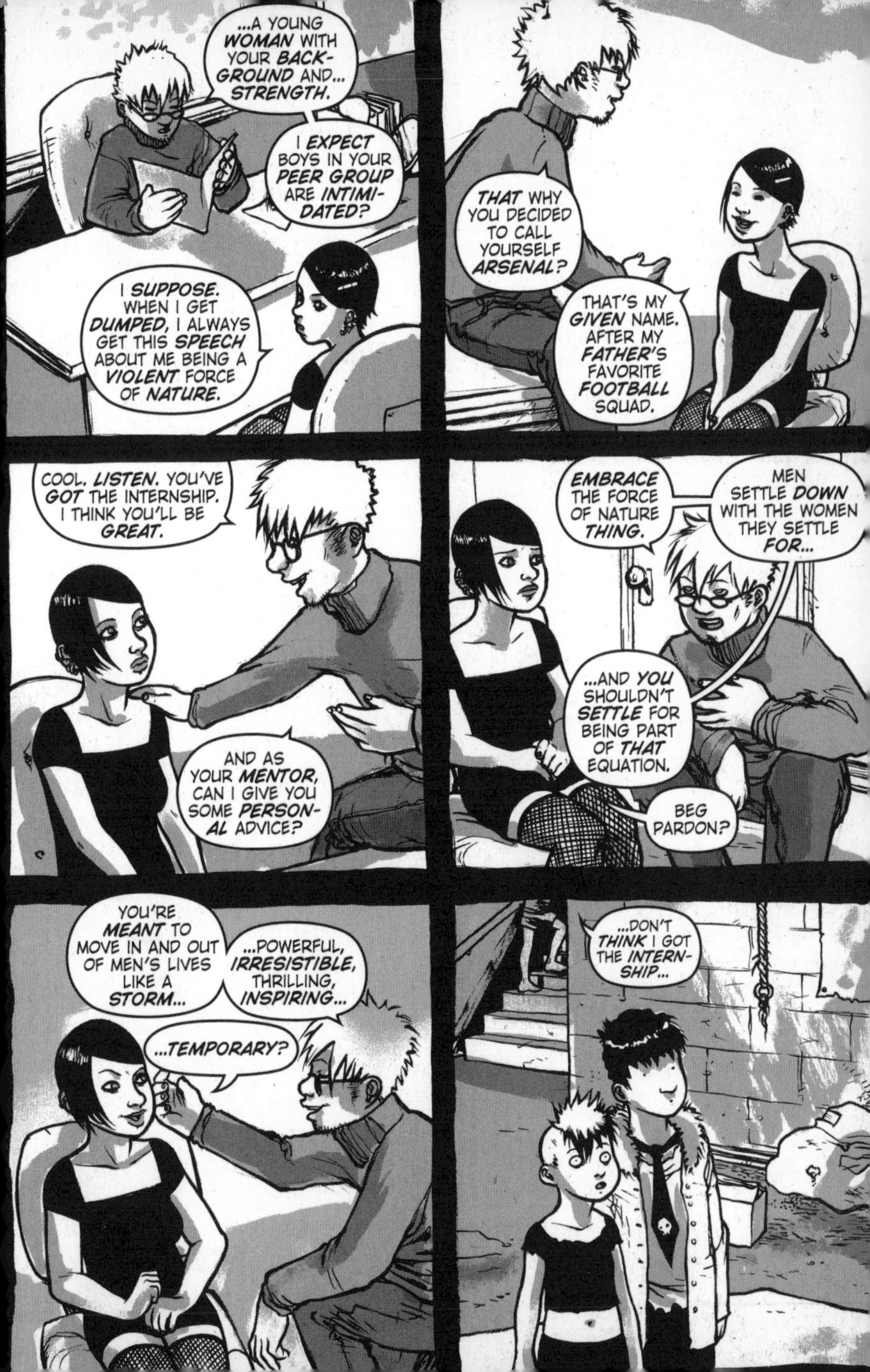
...A YOUNG WOMAN WITH YOUR BACKGROUND AND... STRENGTH.
I EXPECT BOYS IN YOUR PEER GROUP ARE INTIMIDATED?
I SUPPOSE. WHEN I GET DUMPED, I ALWAYS GET THIS SPEECH ABOUT ME BEING A VIOLENT FORCE OF NATURE.
THAT WHY YOU DECIDED TO CALL YOURSELF ARSENAL?
THAT'S MY GIVEN NAME. AFTER MY FATHER'S FAVORITE FOOTBALL SQUAD.
COOL. LISTEN. YOU'VE GOT THE INTERNSHIP. I THINK YOU'LL BE GREAT.
AND AS YOUR MENTOR, CAN I GIVE YOU SOME PERSONAL ADVICE?
EMBRACE THE FORCE OF NATURE THING.
MEN SETTLE DOWN WITH THE WOMEN THEY SETTLE FOR...
...AND YOU SHOULDN'T SETTLE FOR BEING PART OF THAT EQUATION.
BEG PARDON?
YOU'RE MEANT TO MOVE IN AND OUT OF MEN'S LIVES LIKE A STORM...
...POWERFUL, IRRESISTIBLE, THRILLING, INSPIRING...
...TEMPORARY?
...DON'T THINK I GOT THE INTERNSHIP...

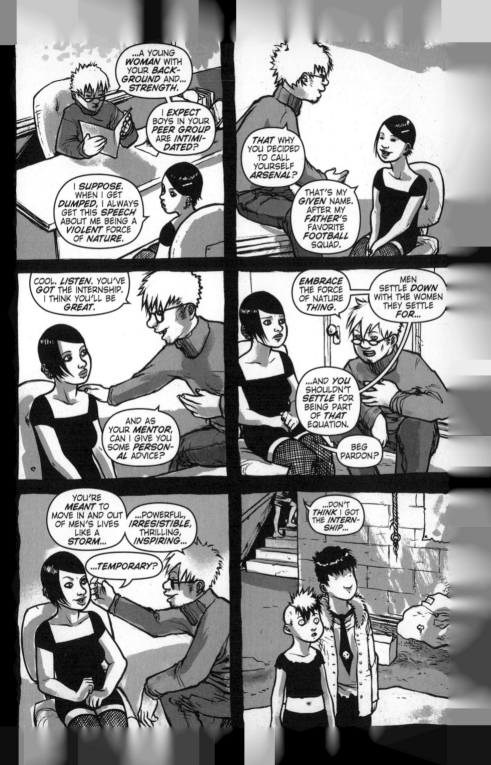

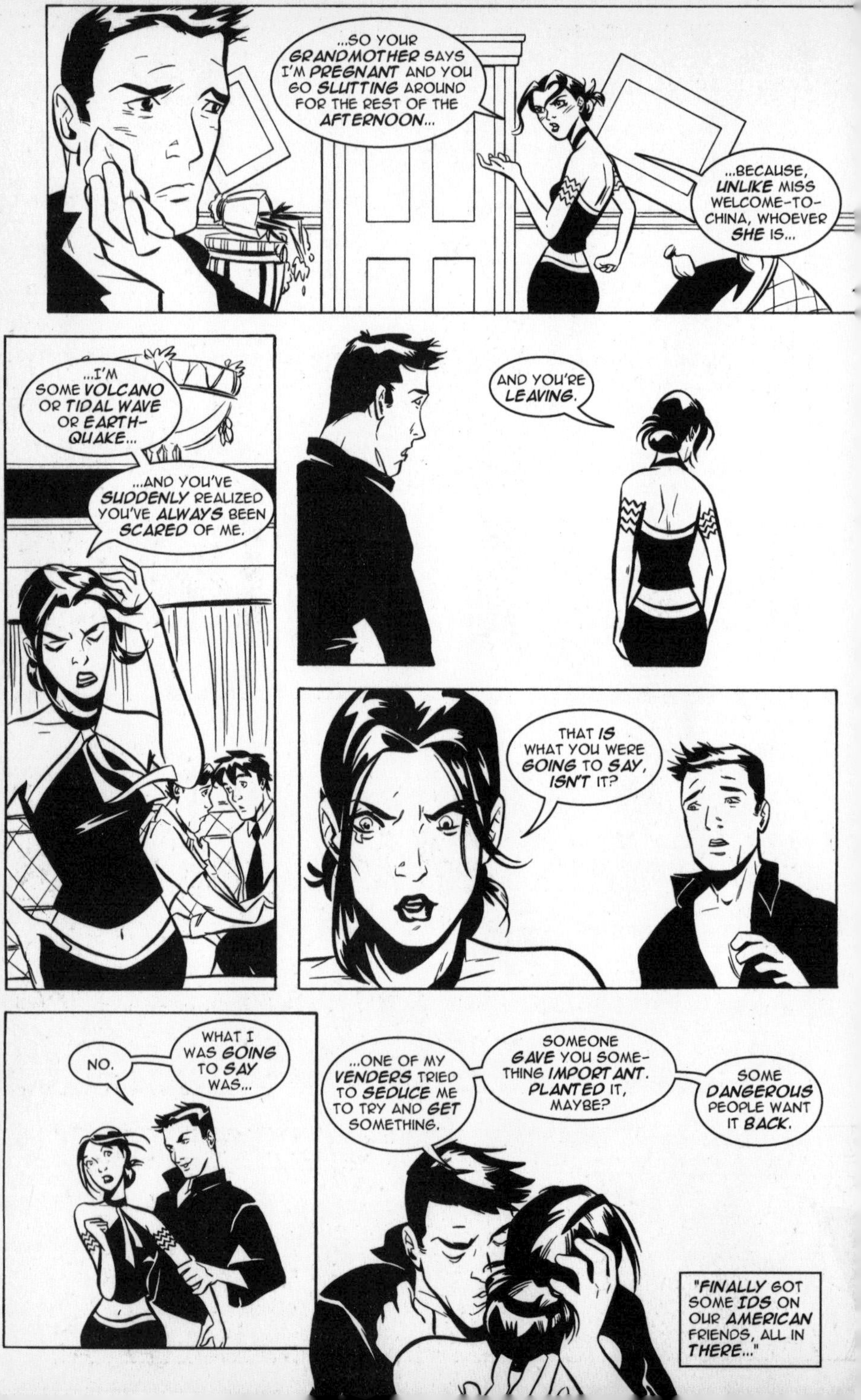
...SO YOUR GRANDMOTHER SAYS I'M PREGNANT AND YOU GO SLUTTING AROUND FOR THE REST OF THE AFTERNOON...
...BECAUSE, UNLIKE MISS WELCOME-TO-CHINA, WHOEVER SHE IS...
...I'M SOME VOLCANO OR TIDAL WAVE OR EARTH-QUAKE...
...AND YOU'VE SUDDENLY REALIZED YOU'VE ALWAYS BEEN SCARED OF ME.
AND YOU'RE LEAVING.
THAT IS WHAT YOU WERE GOING TO SAY, ISN'T IT?
NO.
WHAT I WAS GOING TO SAY WAS...
...ONE OF MY VENDERS TRIED TO SEDUCE ME TO TRY AND GET SOMETHING.
SOMEONE GAVE YOU SOME-THING IMPORTANT. PLANTED IT, MAYBE?
SOME DANGEROUS PEOPLE WANT IT BACK.
"FINALLY GOT SOME IDS ON OUR AMERICAN FRIENDS, ALL IN THERE..."

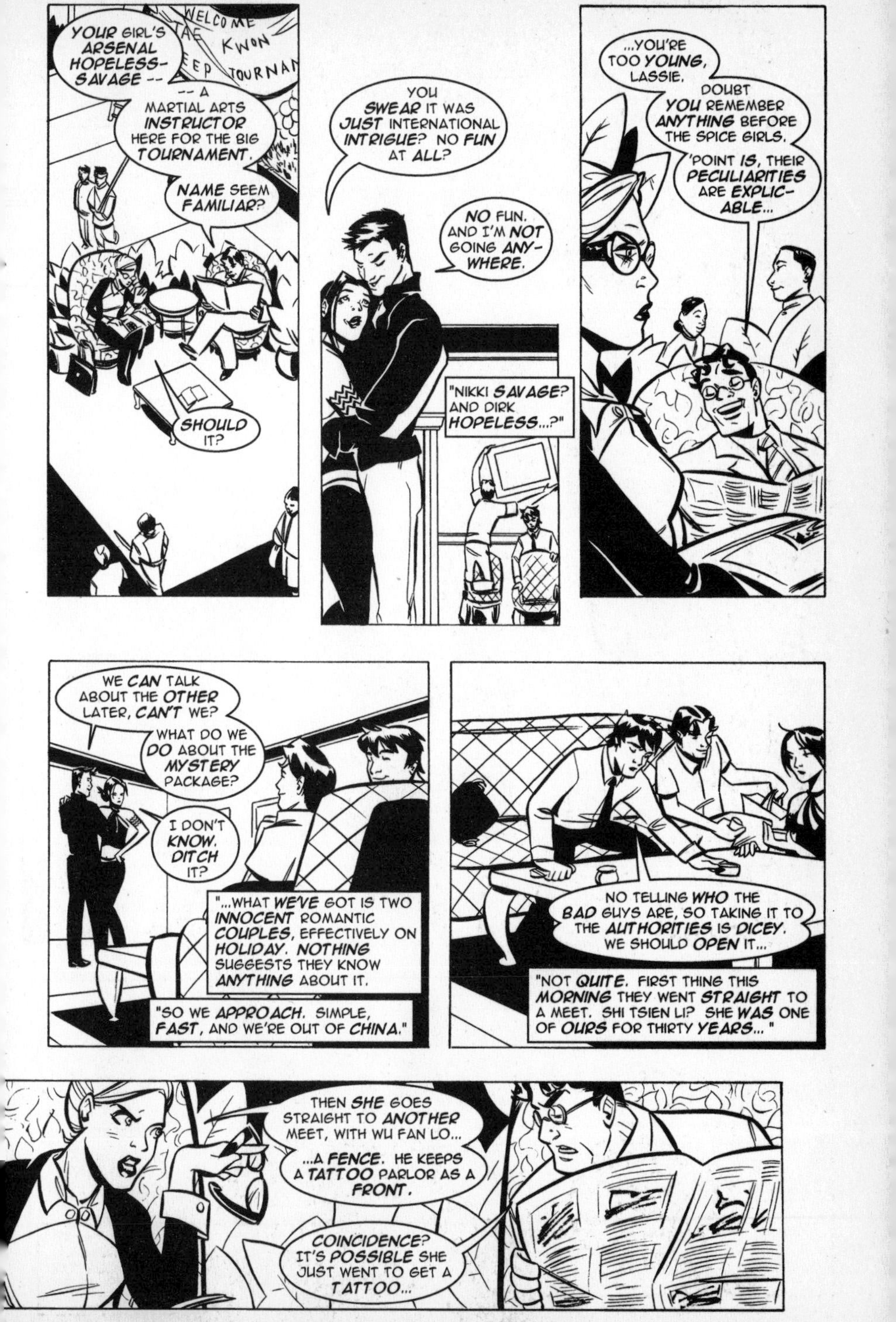
WELCOME TAE KWON ... TOURNAM
YOUR GIRL'S ARSENAL HOPELESS-SAVAGE --
-- A MARTIAL ARTS INSTRUCTOR HERE FOR THE BIG TOURNAMENT.
NAME SEEM FAMILIAR?
SHOULD IT?
YOU SWEAR IT WAS JUST INTERNATIONAL INTRIGUE? NO FUN AT ALL?
NO FUN. AND I'M NOT GOING ANYWHERE.
"NIKKI SAVAGE? AND DIRK HOPELESS...?"
...YOU'RE TOO YOUNG, LASSIE.
DOUBT YOU REMEMBER ANYTHING BEFORE THE SPICE GIRLS.
'POINT IS, THEIR PECULIARITIES ARE EXPLICABLE...
WE CAN TALK ABOUT THE OTHER LATER, CAN'T WE?
WHAT DO WE DO ABOUT THE MYSTERY PACKAGE?
I DON'T KNOW. DITCH IT?
"...WHAT WE'VE GOT IS TWO INNOCENT ROMANTIC COUPLES, EFFECTIVELY ON HOLIDAY. NOTHING SUGGESTS THEY KNOW ANYTHING ABOUT IT.
"SO WE APPROACH. SIMPLE, FAST, AND WE'RE OUT OF CHINA."
NO TELLING WHO THE BAD GUYS ARE, SO TAKING IT TO THE AUTHORITIES IS DICEY. WE SHOULD OPEN IT...
"NOT QUITE. FIRST THING THIS MORNING THEY WENT STRAIGHT TO A MEET. SHI TSIEN LI? SHE WAS ONE OF OURS FOR THIRTY YEARS..."
THEN SHE GOES STRAIGHT TO ANOTHER MEET, WITH WU FAN LO...
...A FENCE. HE KEEPS A TATTOO PARLOR AS A FRONT.
COINCIDENCE? IT'S POSSIBLE SHE JUST WENT TO GET A TATTOO...

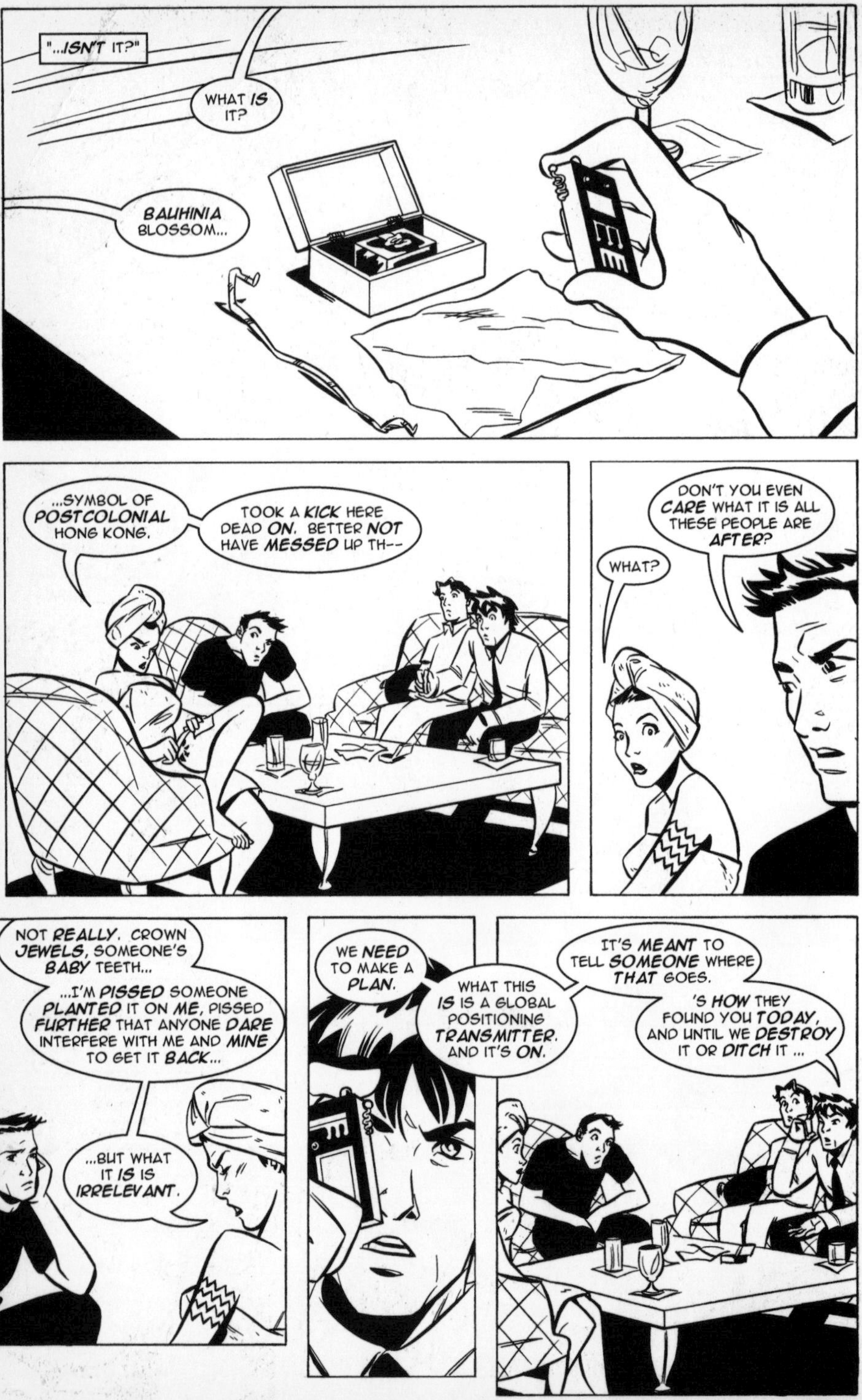
"...ISN'T IT?"
WHAT IS IT?
BAUHINIA BLOSSOM...
...SYMBOL OF POSTCOLONIAL HONG KONG.
TOOK A KICK HERE DEAD ON. BETTER NOT HAVE MESSED UP TH--
DON'T YOU EVEN CARE WHAT IT IS ALL THESE PEOPLE ARE AFTER?
WHAT?
NOT REALLY. CROWN JEWELS, SOMEONE'S BABY TEETH...
...I'M PISSED SOMEONE PLANTED IT ON ME, PISSED FURTHER THAT ANYONE DARE INTERFERE WITH ME AND MINE TO GET IT BACK...
...BUT WHAT IT IS IS IRRELEVANT.
WE NEED TO MAKE A PLAN.
WHAT THIS IS IS A GLOBAL POSITIONING TRANSMITTER. AND IT'S ON.
IT'S MEANT TO TELL SOMEONE WHERE THAT GOES.
'S HOW THEY FOUND YOU TODAY, AND UNTIL WE DESTROY IT OR DITCH IT ...

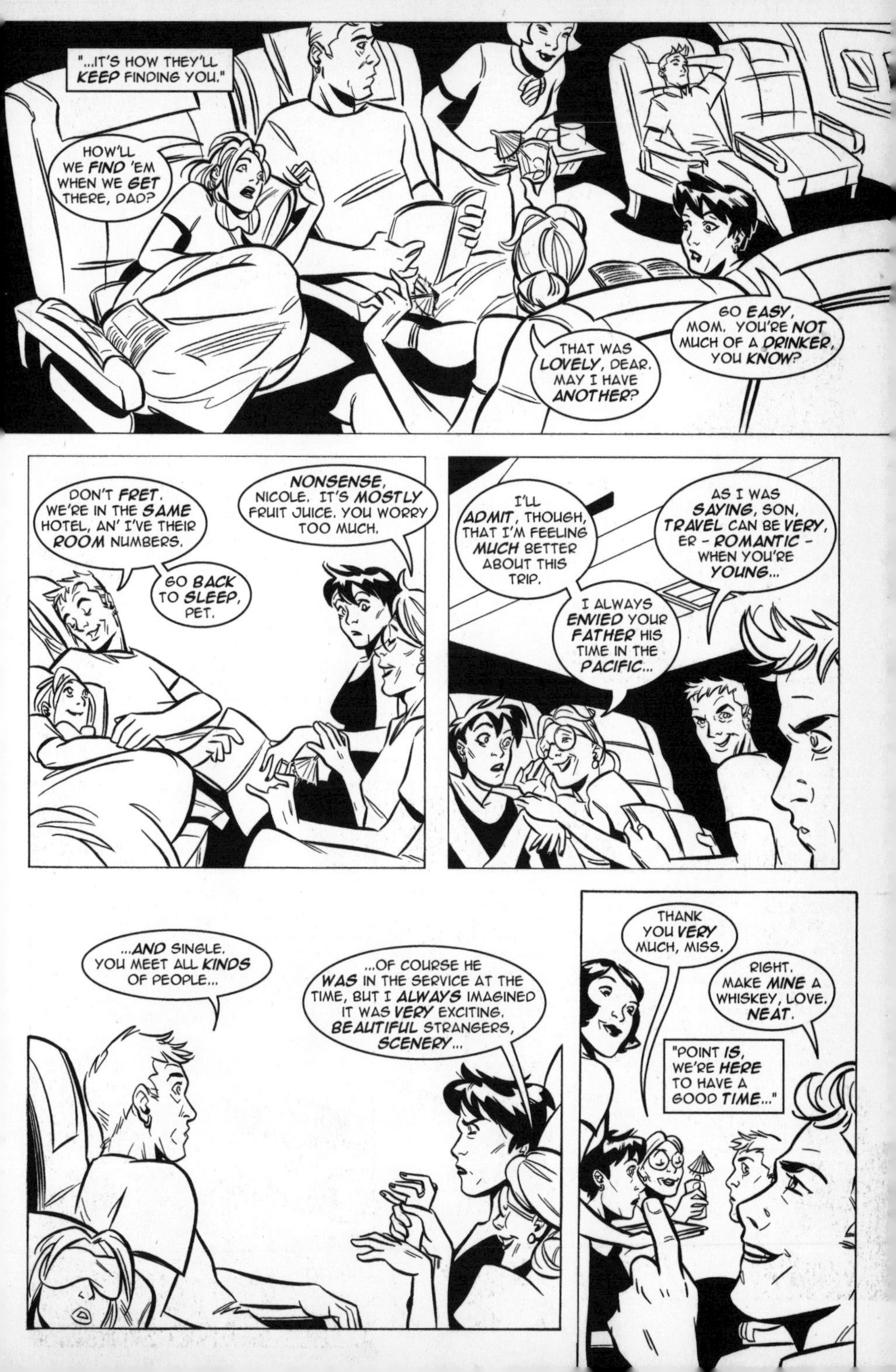
"...IT'S HOW THEY'LL KEEP FINDING YOU."
HOW'LL WE FIND 'EM WHEN WE GET THERE, DAD?
THAT WAS LOVELY, DEAR. MAY I HAVE ANOTHER?
GO EASY, MOM. YOU'RE NOT MUCH OF A DRINKER, YOU KNOW?
DON'T FRET. WE'RE IN THE SAME HOTEL, AN' I'VE THEIR ROOM NUMBERS.
GO BACK TO SLEEP, PET.
NONSENSE, NICOLE. IT'S MOSTLY FRUIT JUICE. YOU WORRY TOO MUCH.
I'LL ADMIT, THOUGH, THAT I'M FEELING MUCH BETTER ABOUT THIS TRIP.
I ALWAYS ENVIED YOUR FATHER HIS TIME IN THE PACIFIC...
AS I WAS SAYING, SON, TRAVEL CAN BE VERY, ER - ROMANTIC - WHEN YOU'RE YOUNG...
...AND SINGLE. YOU MEET ALL KINDS OF PEOPLE...
...OF COURSE HE WAS IN THE SERVICE AT THE TIME, BUT I ALWAYS IMAGINED IT WAS VERY EXCITING. BEAUTIFUL STRANGERS, SCENERY...
THANK YOU VERY MUCH, MISS.
RIGHT. MAKE MINE A WHISKEY, LOVE. NEAT.
"POINT IS, WE'RE HERE TO HAVE A GOOD TIME..."

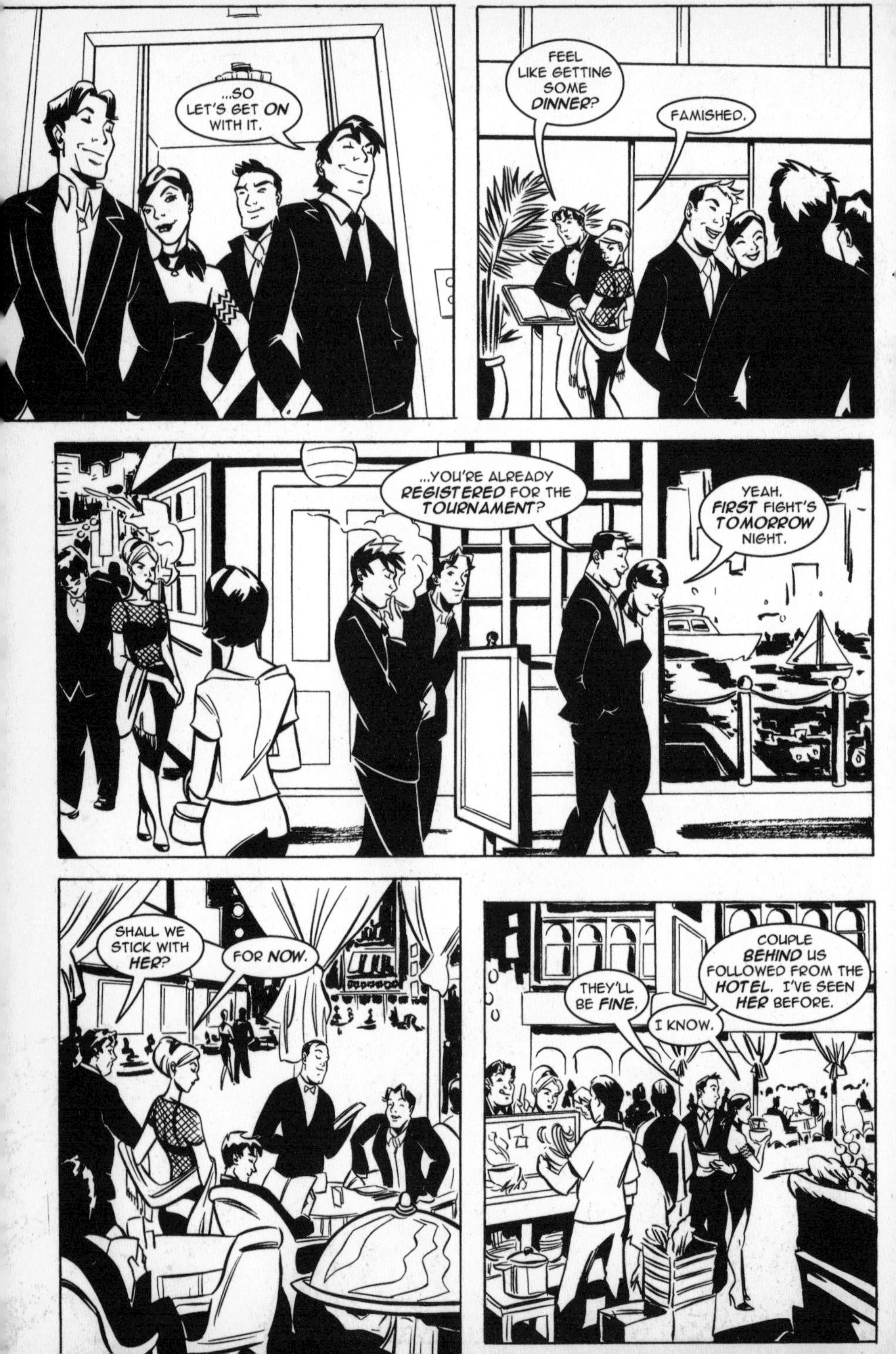
...SO LET'S GET ON WITH IT.
FEEL LIKE GETTING SOME DINNER?
FAMISHED.
...YOU'RE ALREADY REGISTERED FOR THE TOURNAMENT?
YEAH. FIRST FIGHT'S TOMORROW NIGHT.
SHALL WE STICK WITH HER?
FOR NOW.
COUPLE BEHIND US FOLLOWED FROM THE HOTEL. I'VE SEEN HER BEFORE.
THEY'LL BE FINE.
I KNOW.

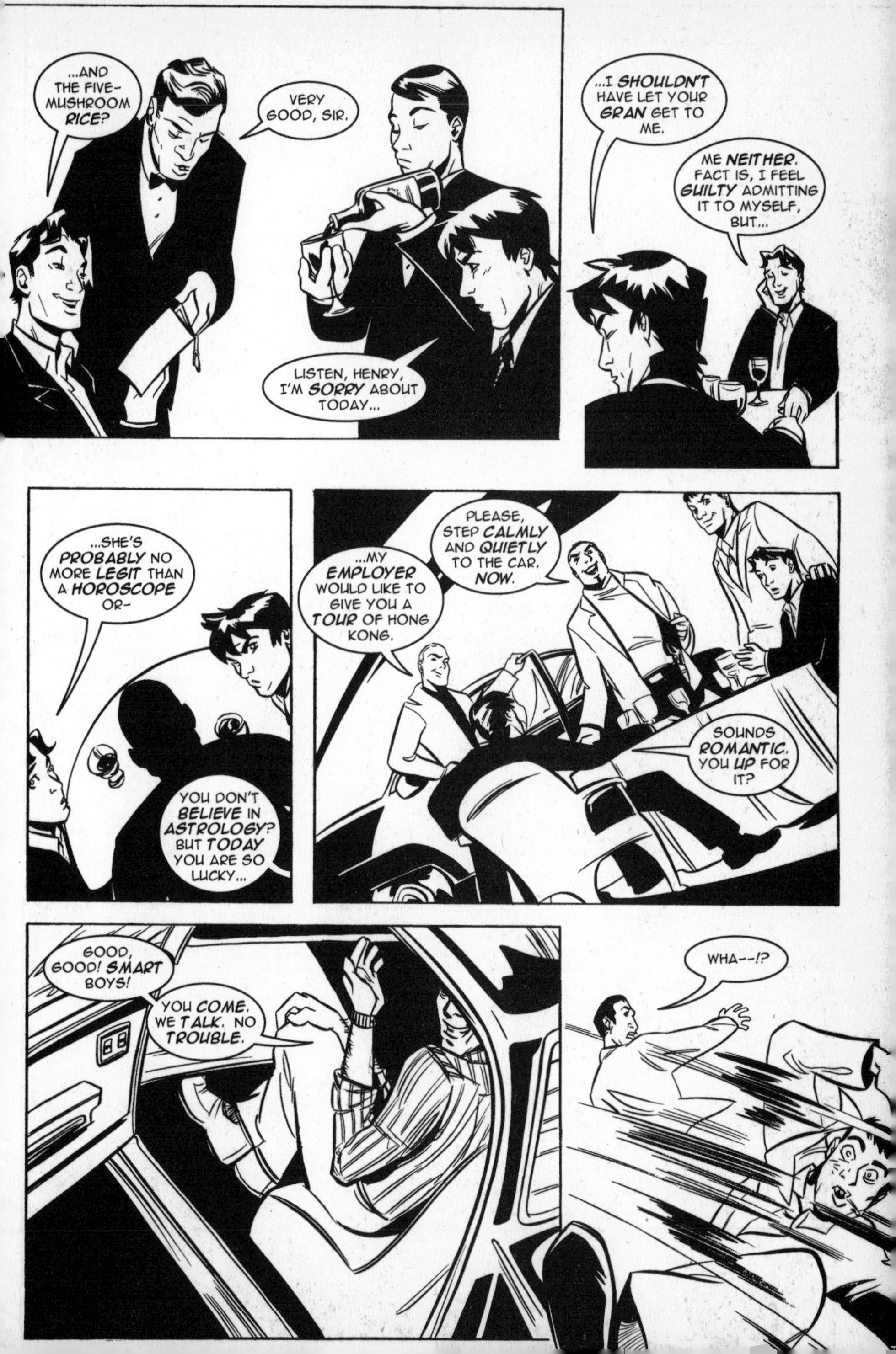
...AND THE FIVE-MUSHROOM RICE?
VERY GOOD, SIR.
LISTEN, HENRY, I'M SORRY ABOUT TODAY...
...I SHOULDN'T HAVE LET YOUR GRAN GET TO ME.
ME NEITHER. FACT IS, I FEEL GUILTY ADMITTING IT TO MYSELF, BUT...
...SHE'S PROBABLY NO MORE LEGIT THAN A HOROSCOPE OR-
YOU DON'T BELIEVE IN ASTROLOGY? BUT TODAY YOU ARE SO LUCKY...
...MY EMPLOYER WOULD LIKE TO GIVE YOU A TOUR OF HONG KONG.
PLEASE, STEP CALMLY AND QUIETLY TO THE CAR. NOW.
SOUNDS ROMANTIC. YOU UP FOR IT?
GOOD, GOOD! SMART BOYS!
YOU COME. WE TALK. NO TROUBLE.
WHA--!?

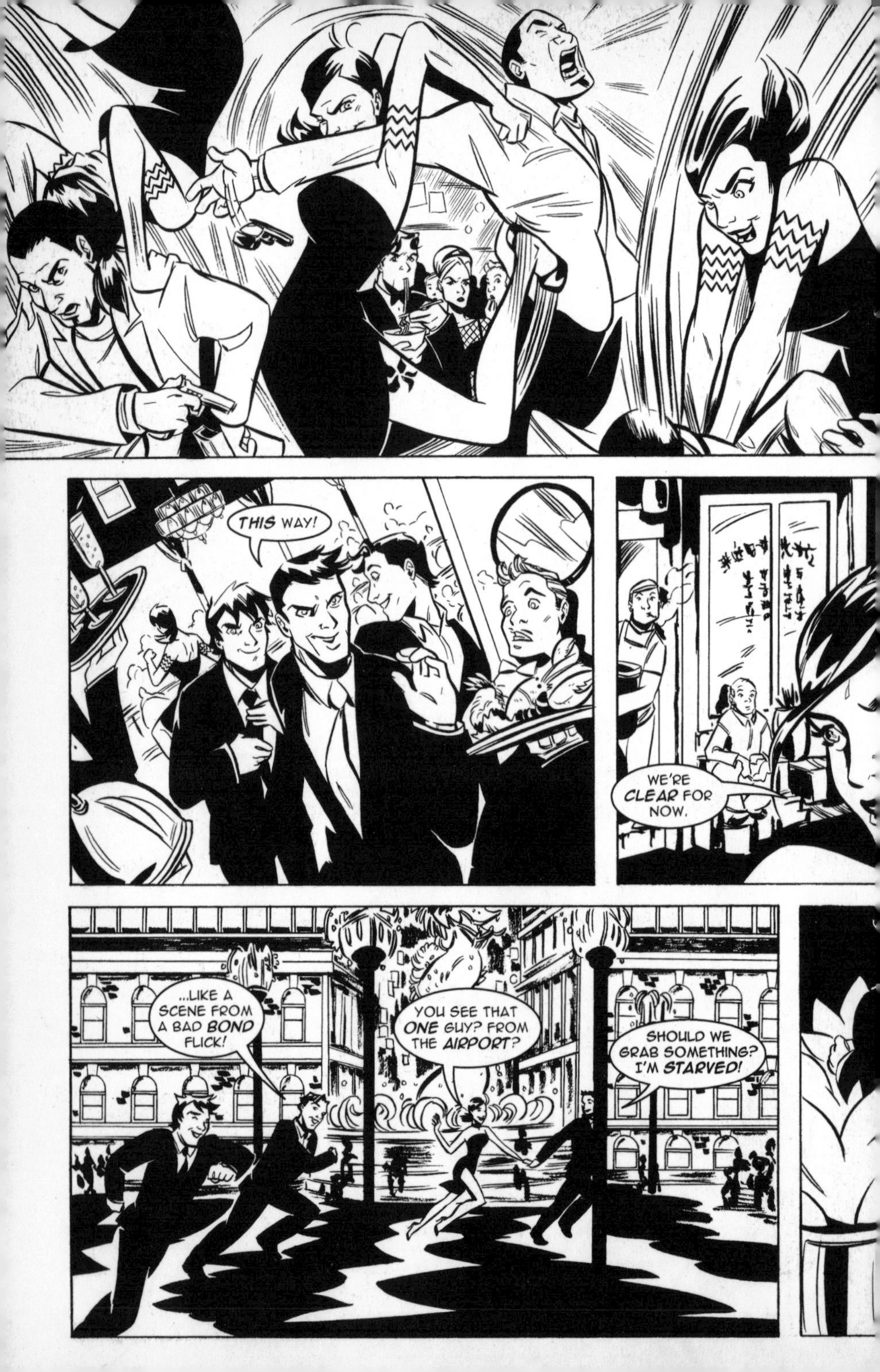
THIS WAY!
WE'RE CLEAR FOR NOW.
...LIKE A SCENE FROM A BAD BOND FLICK!
YOU SEE THAT ONE GUY? FROM THE AIRPORT?
SHOULD WE GRAB SOMETHING? I'M STARVED!

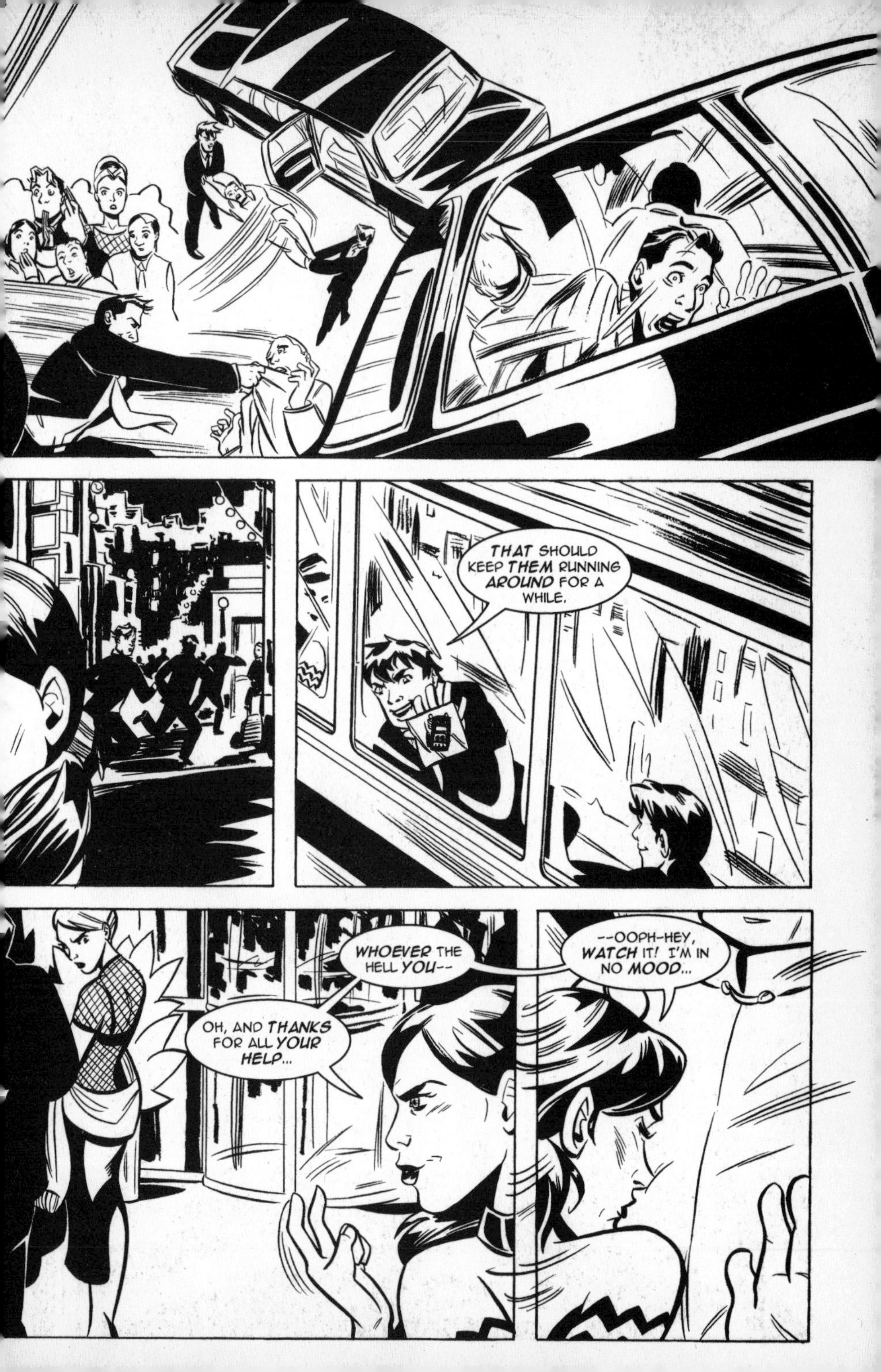
THAT SHOULD KEEP THEM RUNNING AROUND FOR A WHILE.
WHOEVER THE HELL YOU--
OH, AND THANKS FOR ALL YOUR HELP...
--OOPH-HEY, WATCH IT! I'M IN NO MOOD...

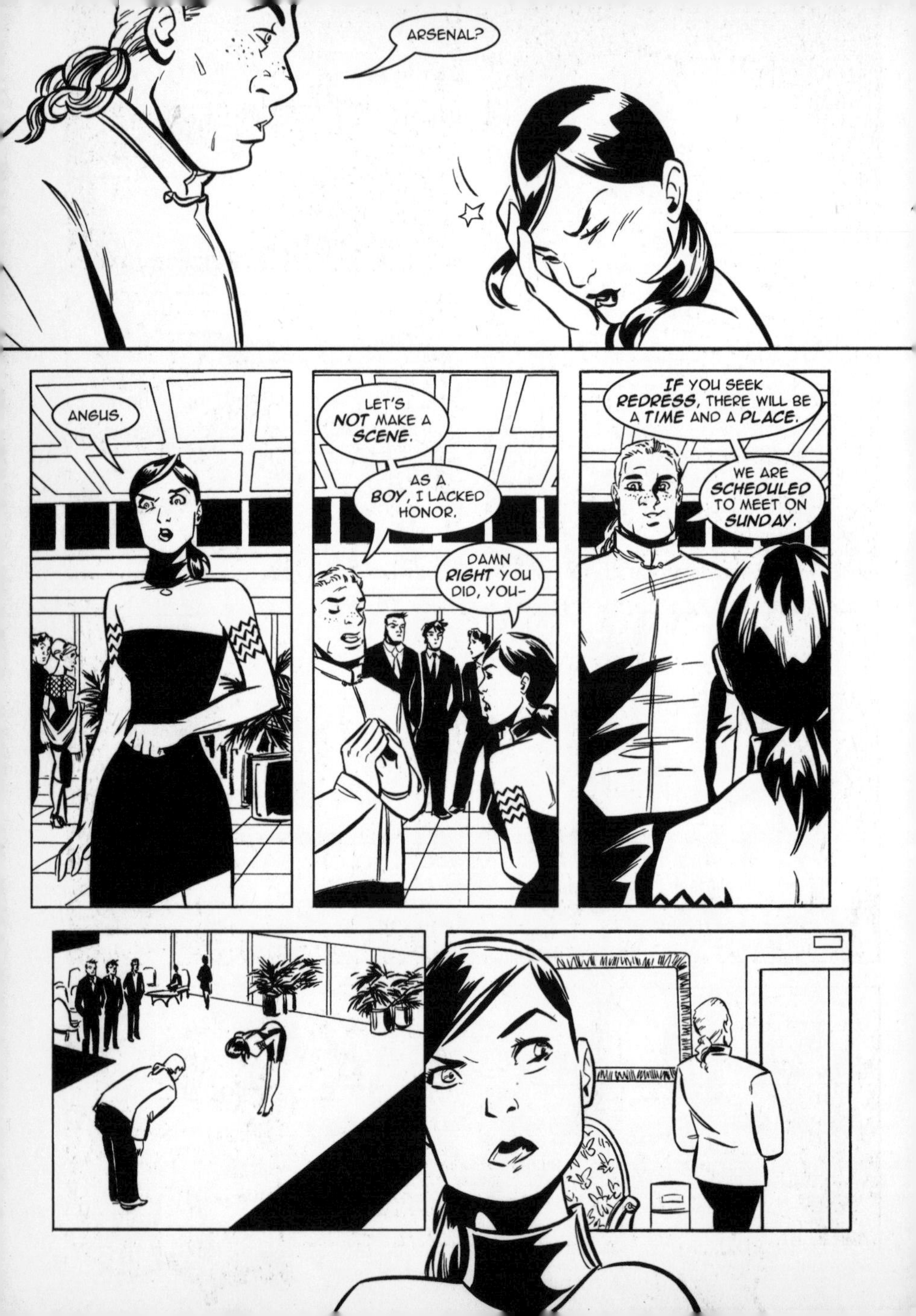
ARSENAL?
ANGUS.
LET'S NOT MAKE A SCENE.
AS A BOY, I LACKED HONOR.
DAMN RIGHT YOU DID, YOU-
IF YOU SEEK REDRESS, THERE WILL BE A TIME AND A PLACE.
WE ARE SCHEDULED TO MEET ON SUNDAY.

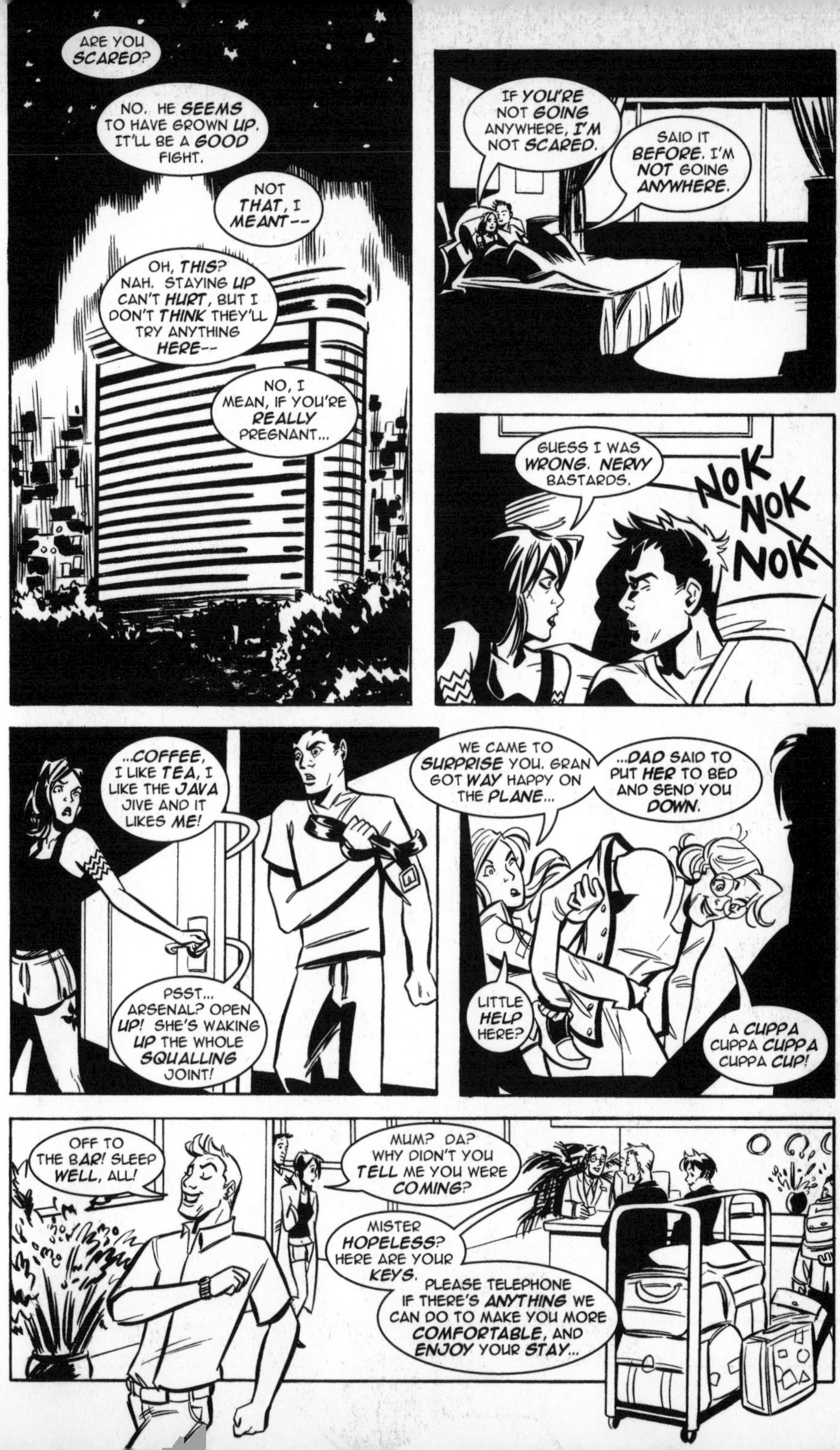
ARE YOU SCARED?
NO. HE SEEMS TO HAVE GROWN UP. IT'LL BE A GOOD FIGHT.
NOT THAT, I MEANT--
OH, THIS? NAH. STAYING UP CAN'T HURT, BUT I DON'T THINK THEY'LL TRY ANYTHING HERE--
NO, I MEAN, IF YOU'RE REALLY PREGNANT...
IF YOU'RE NOT GOING ANYWHERE, I'M NOT SCARED.
SAID IT BEFORE. I'M NOT GOING ANYWHERE.
GUESS I WAS WRONG. NERVY BASTARDS.
NOK NOK NOK
...COFFEE, I LIKE TEA, I LIKE THE JAVA JIVE AND IT LIKES ME!
PSST... ARSENAL? OPEN UP! SHE'S WAKING UP THE WHOLE SQUALLING JOINT!
WE CAME TO SURPRISE YOU. GRAN GOT WAY HAPPY ON THE PLANE...
...DAD SAID TO PUT HER TO BED AND SEND YOU DOWN.
LITTLE HELP HERE?
A CUPPA CUPPA CUPPA CUPPA CUP!
OFF TO THE BAR! SLEEP WELL, ALL!
MUM? DA? WHY DIDN'T YOU TELL ME YOU WERE COMING?
MISTER HOPELESS? HERE ARE YOUR KEYS.
PLEASE TELEPHONE IF THERE'S ANYTHING WE CAN DO TO MAKE YOU MORE COMFORTABLE, AND ENJOY YOUR STAY...

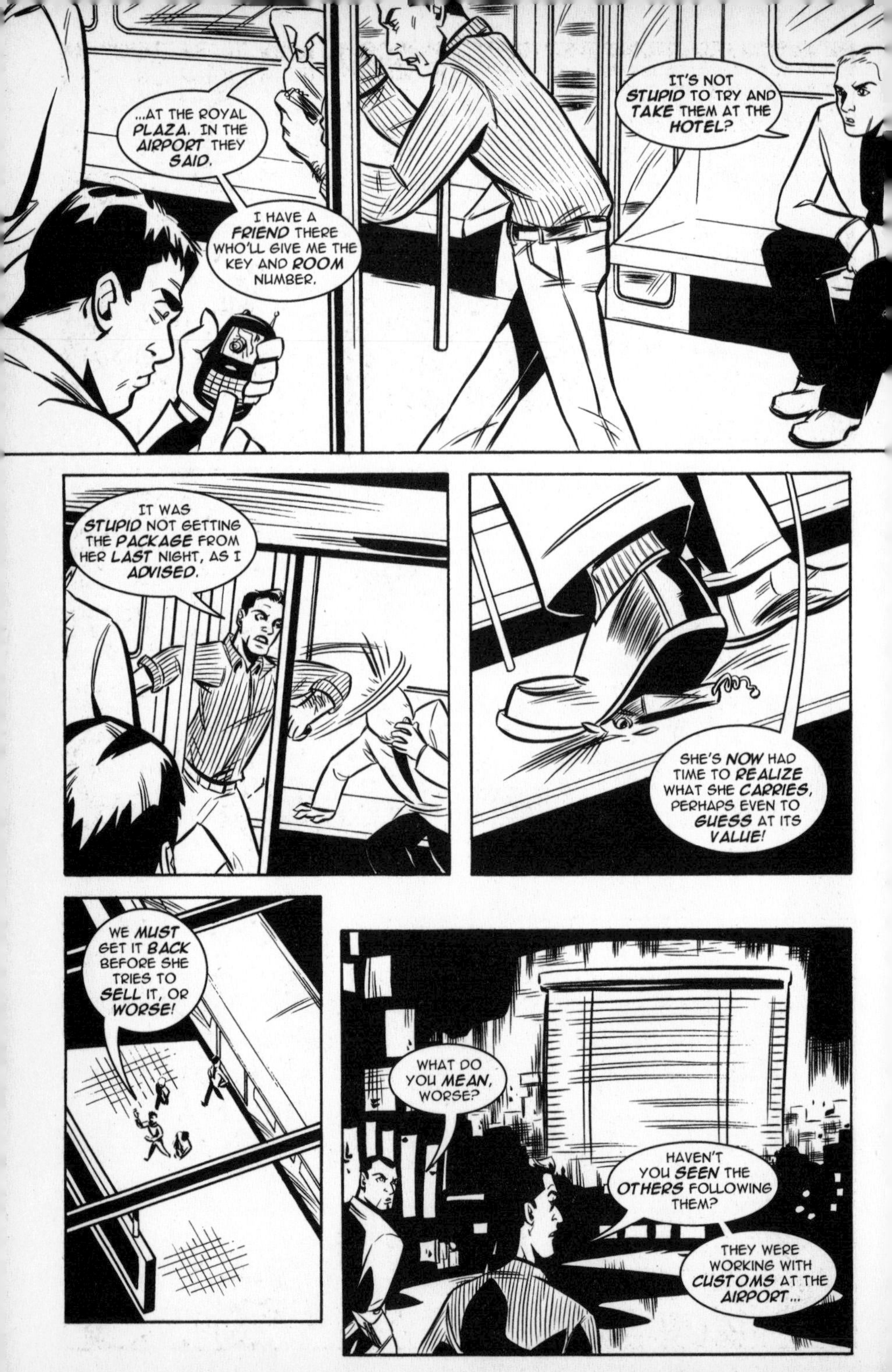
...AT THE ROYAL PLAZA. IN THE AIRPORT THEY SAID.
I HAVE A FRIEND THERE WHO'LL GIVE ME THE KEY AND ROOM NUMBER.
IT'S NOT STUPID TO TRY AND TAKE THEM AT THE HOTEL?
IT WAS STUPID NOT GETTING THE PACKAGE FROM HER LAST NIGHT, AS I ADVISED.
SHE'S NOW HAD TIME TO REALIZE WHAT SHE CARRIES, PERHAPS EVEN TO GUESS AT ITS VALUE!
WE MUST GET IT BACK BEFORE SHE TRIES TO SELL IT, OR WORSE!
WHAT DO YOU MEAN, WORSE?
HAVEN'T YOU SEEN THE OTHERS FOLLOWING THEM?
THEY WERE WORKING WITH CUSTOMS AT THE AIRPORT...

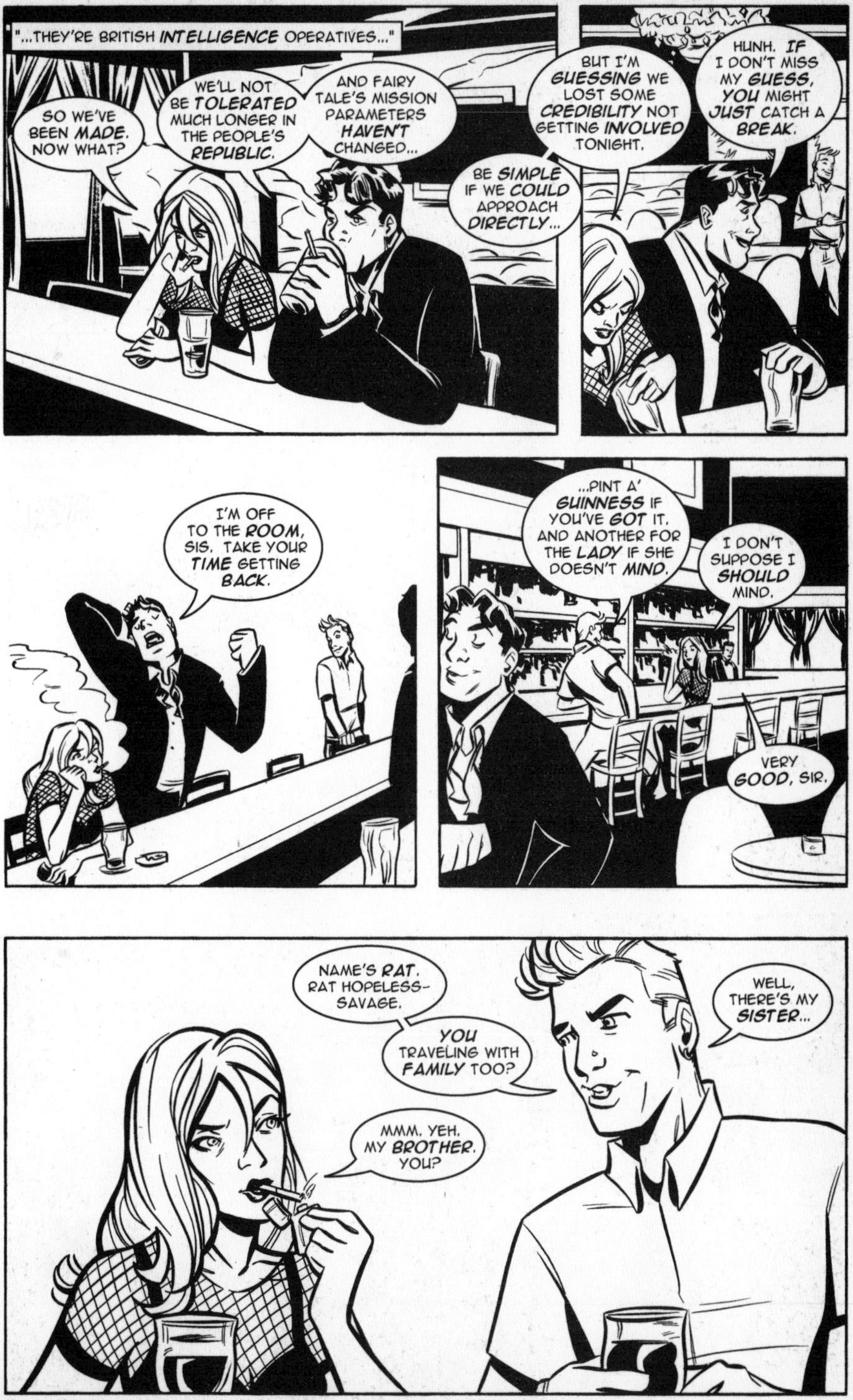
"...THEY'RE BRITISH INTELLIGENCE OPERATIVES..."
SO WE'VE BEEN MADE. NOW WHAT?
WE'LL NOT BE TOLERATED MUCH LONGER IN THE PEOPLE'S REPUBLIC.
AND FAIRY TALE'S MISSION PARAMETERS HAVEN'T CHANGED...
BE SIMPLE IF WE COULD APPROACH DIRECTLY...
BUT I'M GUESSING WE LOST SOME CREDIBILITY NOT GETTING INVOLVED TONIGHT.
HUNH. IF I DON'T MISS MY GUESS, YOU MIGHT JUST CATCH A BREAK.
I'M OFF TO THE ROOM, SIS. TAKE YOUR TIME GETTING BACK.
...PINT A' GUINNESS IF YOU'VE GOT IT. AND ANOTHER FOR THE LADY IF SHE DOESN'T MIND.
I DON'T SUPPOSE I SHOULD MIND.
VERY GOOD, SIR.
NAME'S RAT. RAT HOPELESS-SAVAGE.
YOU TRAVELING WITH FAMILY TOO?
MMM. YEH. MY BROTHER. YOU?
WELL, THERE'S MY SISTER...

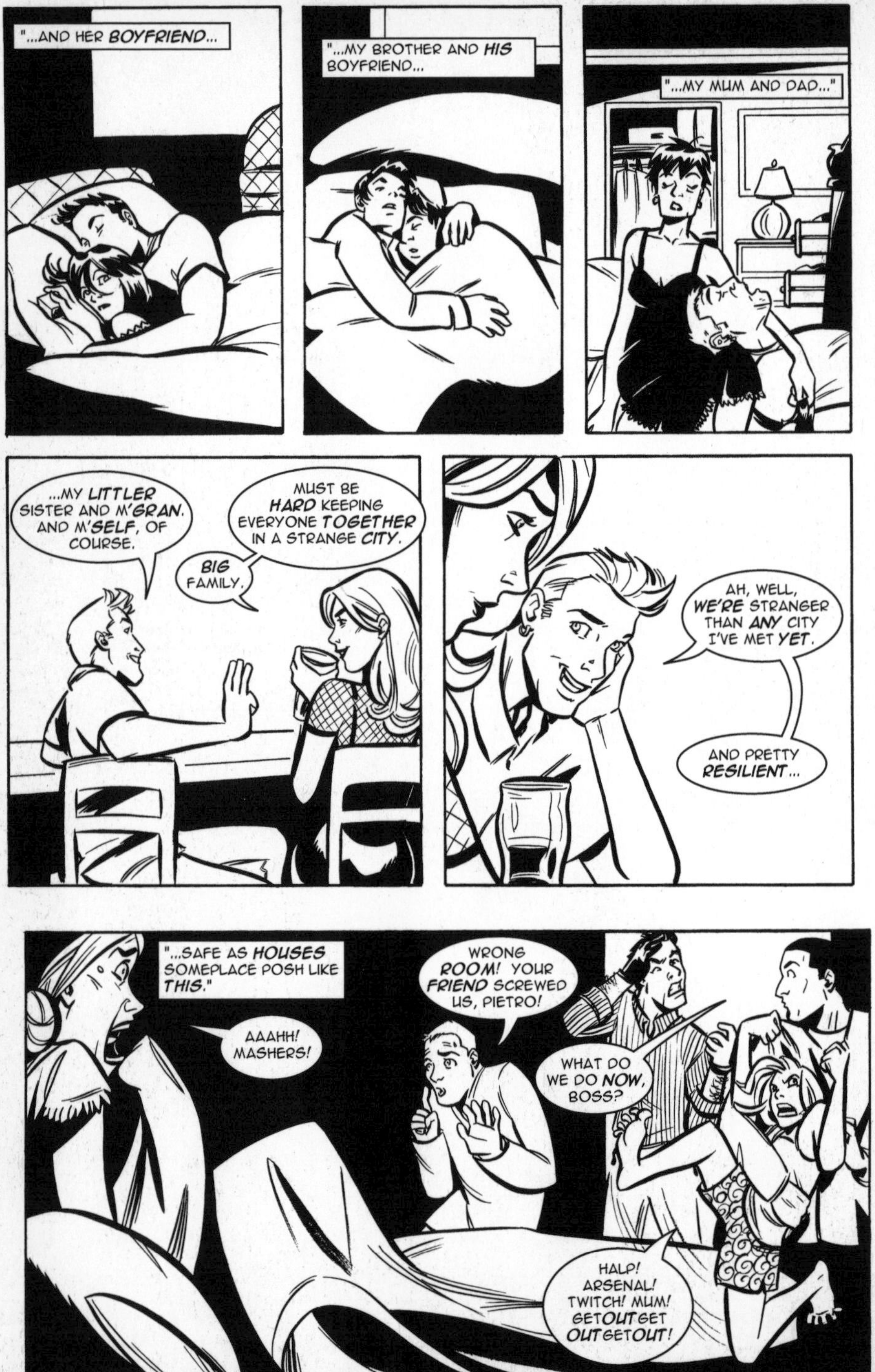
"...AND HER BOYFRIEND...
"...MY BROTHER AND HIS BOYFRIEND...
"...MY MUM AND DAD..."
...MY LITTLER SISTER AND M'GRAN. AND M'SELF, OF COURSE.
BIG FAMILY.
MUST BE HARD KEEPING EVERYONE TOGETHER IN A STRANGE CITY.
AH, WELL, WE'RE STRANGER THAN ANY CITY I'VE MET YET.
AND PRETTY RESILIENT...
"...SAFE AS HOUSES SOMEPLACE POSH LIKE THIS."
AAAHH! MASHERS!
WRONG ROOM! YOUR FRIEND SCREWED US, PIETRO!
WHAT DO WE DO NOW, BOSS?
HALP! ARSENAL! TWITCH! MUM! GETOUTGET OUTGETOUT!

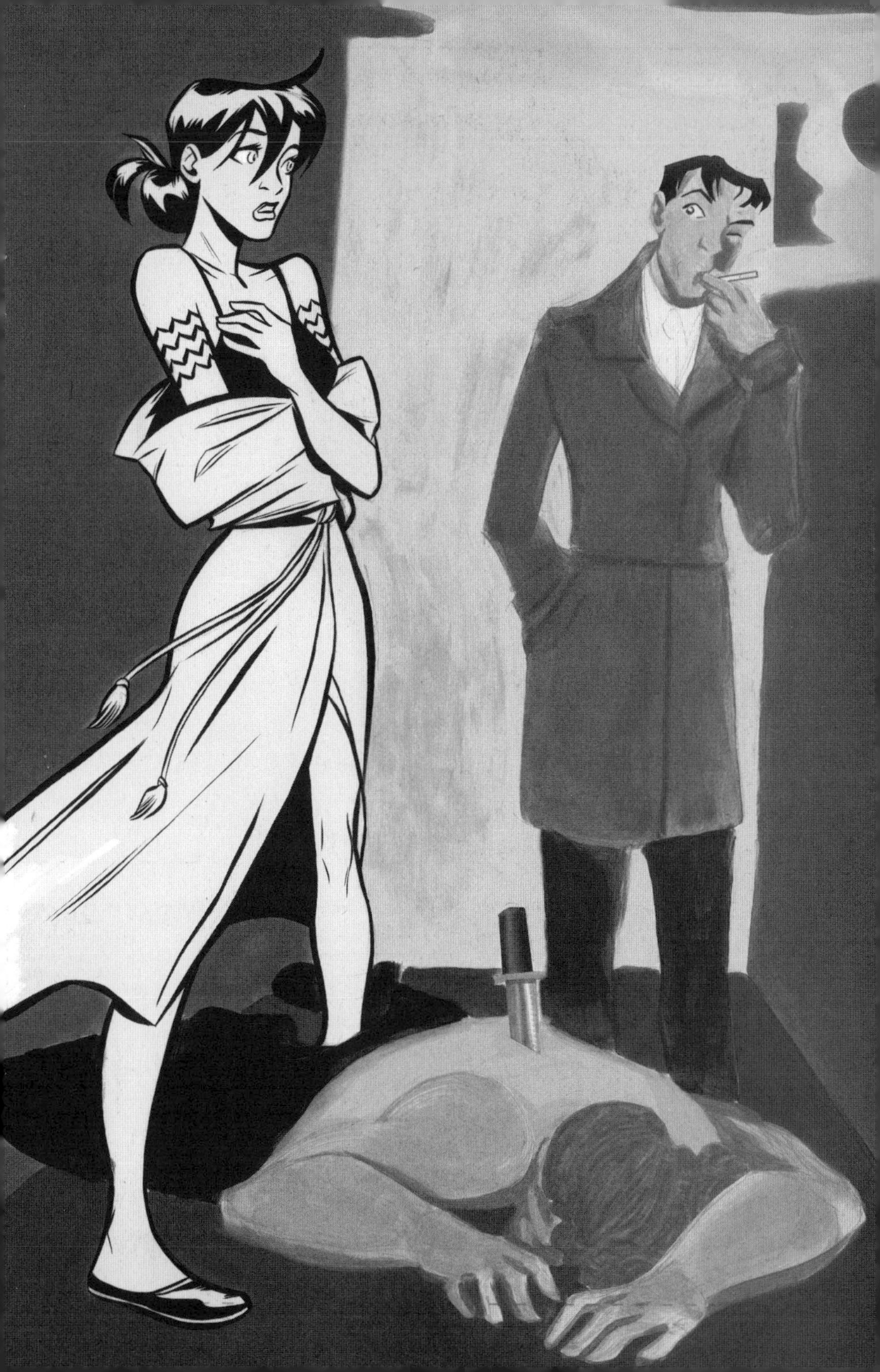

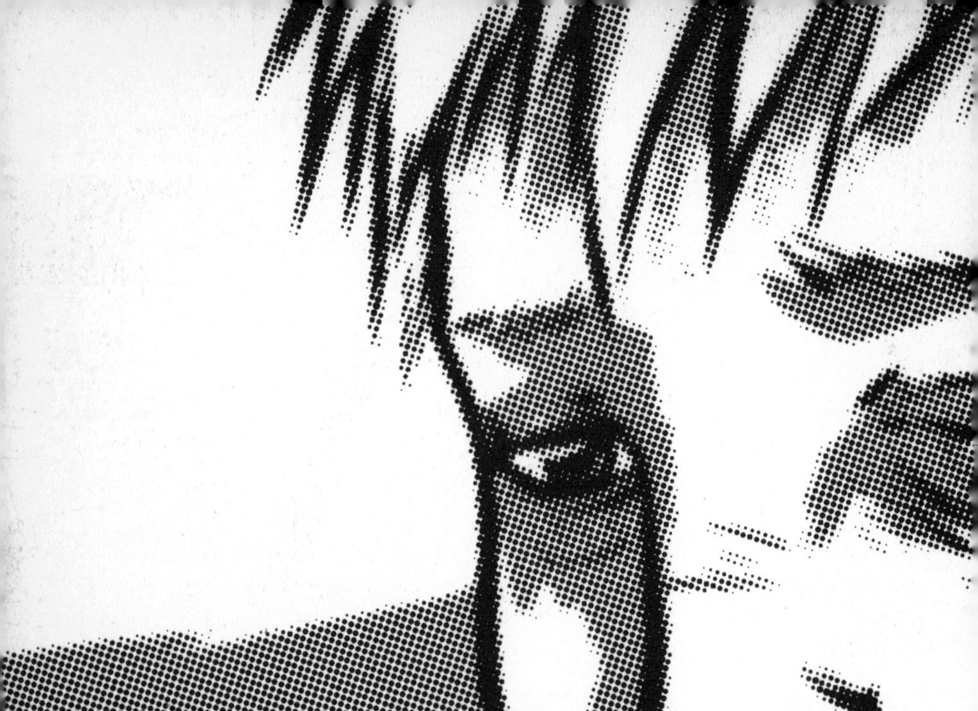

Hopeless Savages

CHAPTER 3

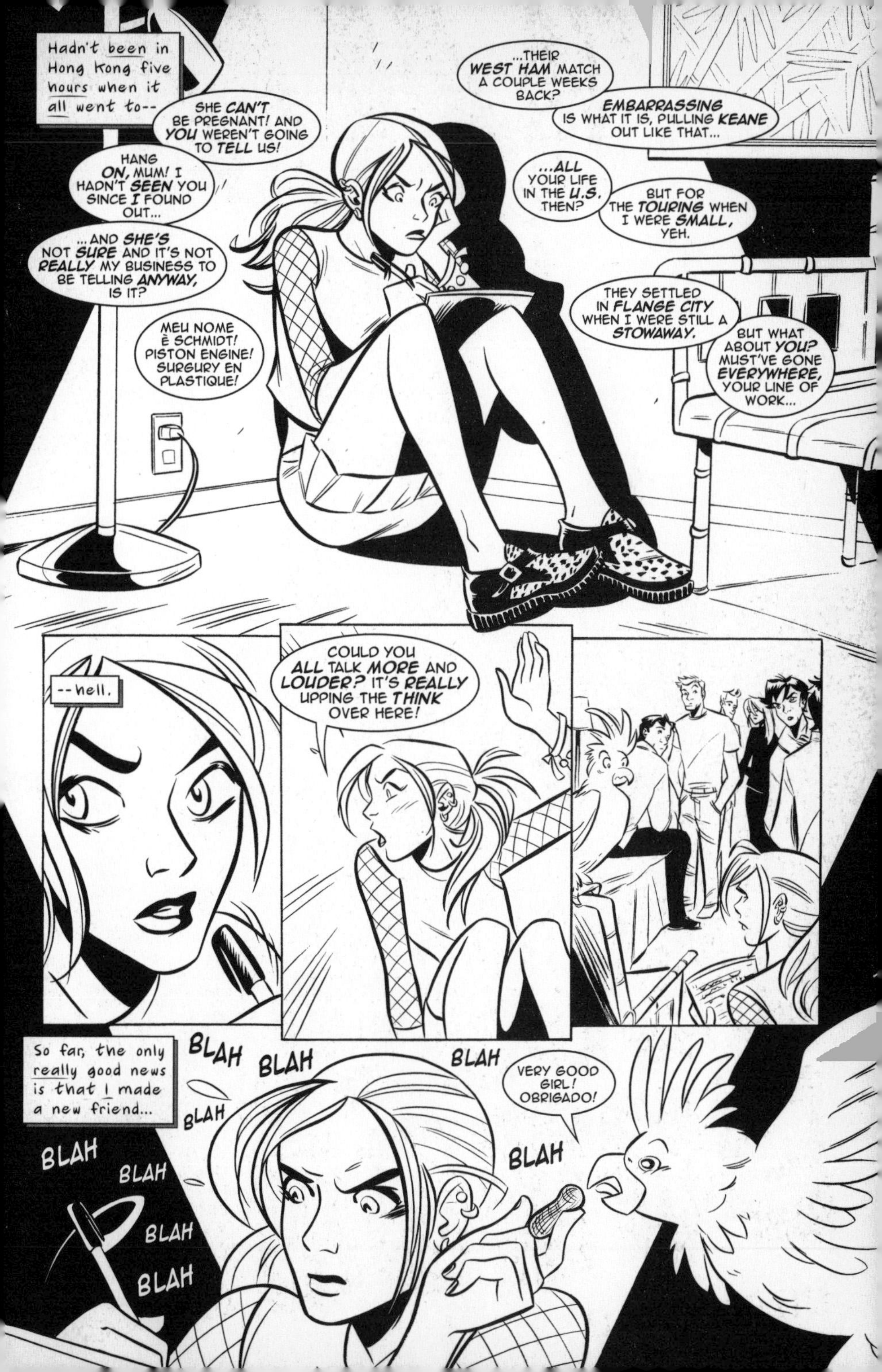

Hadn't been in Hong Kong five hours when it all went to--
SHE CAN'T BE PREGNANT! AND YOU WEREN'T GOING TO TELL US!
HANG ON, MUM! I HADN'T SEEN YOU SINCE I FOUND OUT...
...AND SHE'S NOT SURE AND IT'S NOT REALLY MY BUSINESS TO BE TELLING ANYWAY, IS IT?
MEU NOME È SCHMIDT! PISTON ENGINE! SURGURY EN PLASTIQUE!
...THEIR WEST HAM MATCH A COUPLE WEEKS BACK?
EMBARRASSING IS WHAT IT IS, PULLING KEANE OUT LIKE THAT...
...ALL YOUR LIFE IN THE U.S. THEN?
BUT FOR THE TOURING WHEN I WERE SMALL, YEH.
THEY SETTLED IN FLANGE CITY WHEN I WERE STILL A STOWAWAY.
BUT WHAT ABOUT YOU? MUST'VE GONE EVERYWHERE, YOUR LINE OF WORK...
--hell.
COULD YOU ALL TALK MORE AND LOUDER? IT'S REALLY UPPING THE THINK OVER HERE!
So far, the only really good news is that I made a new friend...
BLAH
BLAH
BLAH
BLAH
VERY GOOD GIRL! OBRIGADO!
BLAH
BLAH
BLAH
BLAH
BLAH

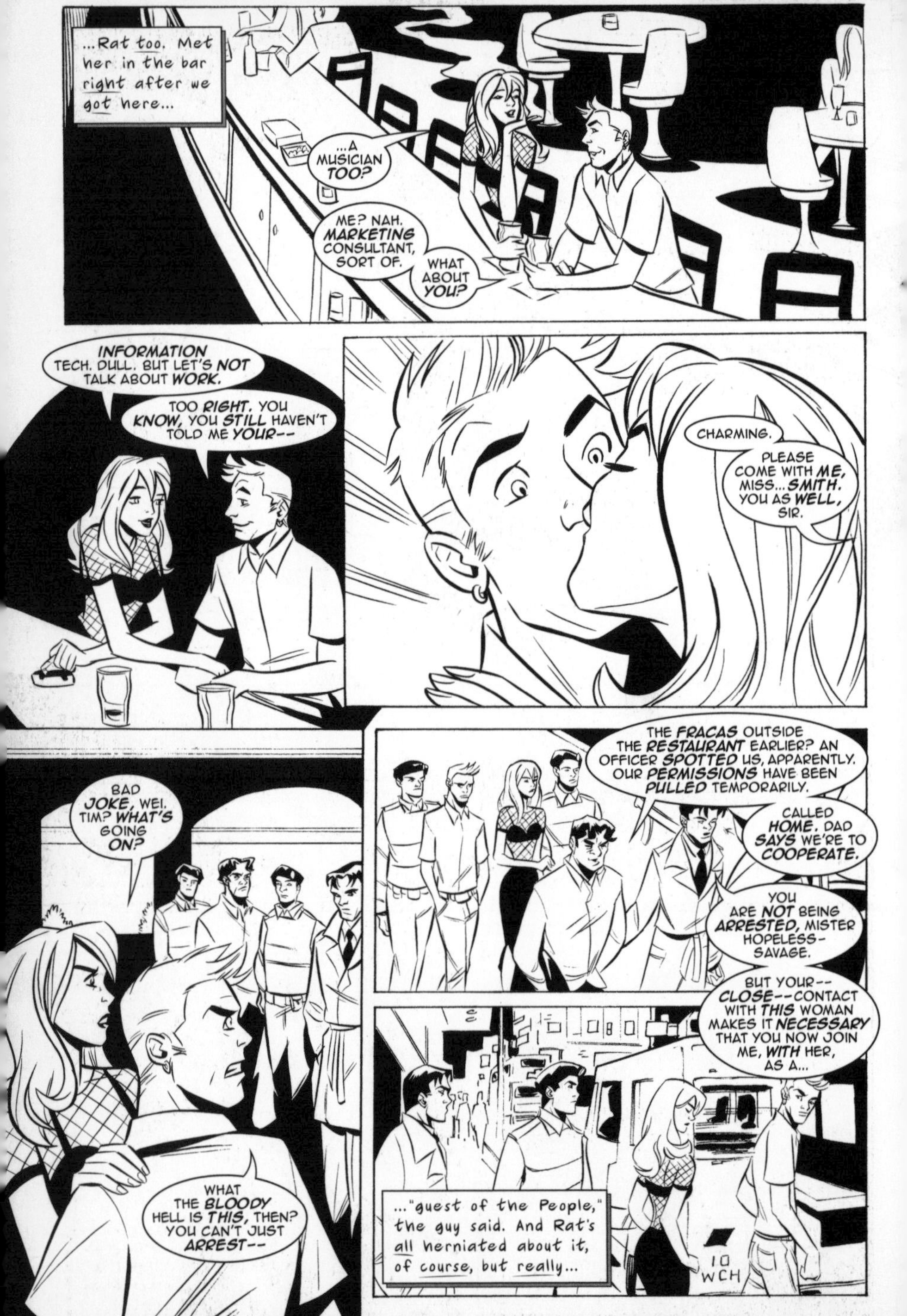
...Rat too. Met her in the bar right after we got here...
...A MUSICIAN TOO?
ME? NAH. MARKETING CONSULTANT, SORT OF.
WHAT ABOUT YOU?
INFORMATION TECH. DULL. BUT LET'S NOT TALK ABOUT WORK.
TOO RIGHT. YOU KNOW, YOU STILL HAVEN'T TOLD ME YOUR--
CHARMING.
PLEASE COME WITH ME, MISS... SMITH. YOU AS WELL, SIR.
BAD JOKE, WEI. TIM? WHAT'S GOING ON?
WHAT THE BLOODY HELL IS THIS, THEN? YOU CAN'T JUST ARREST--
THE FRACAS OUTSIDE THE RESTAURANT EARLIER? AN OFFICER SPOTTED US, APPARENTLY. OUR PERMISSIONS HAVE BEEN PULLED TEMPORARILY.
CALLED HOME. DAD SAYS WE'RE TO COOPERATE.
YOU ARE NOT BEING ARRESTED, MISTER HOPELESS-SAVAGE.
BUT YOUR--CLOSE--CONTACT WITH THIS WOMAN MAKES IT NECESSARY THAT YOU NOW JOIN ME, WITH HER, AS A...
..."guest of the People," the guy said. And Rat's all herniated about it, of course, but really...
10
WCH

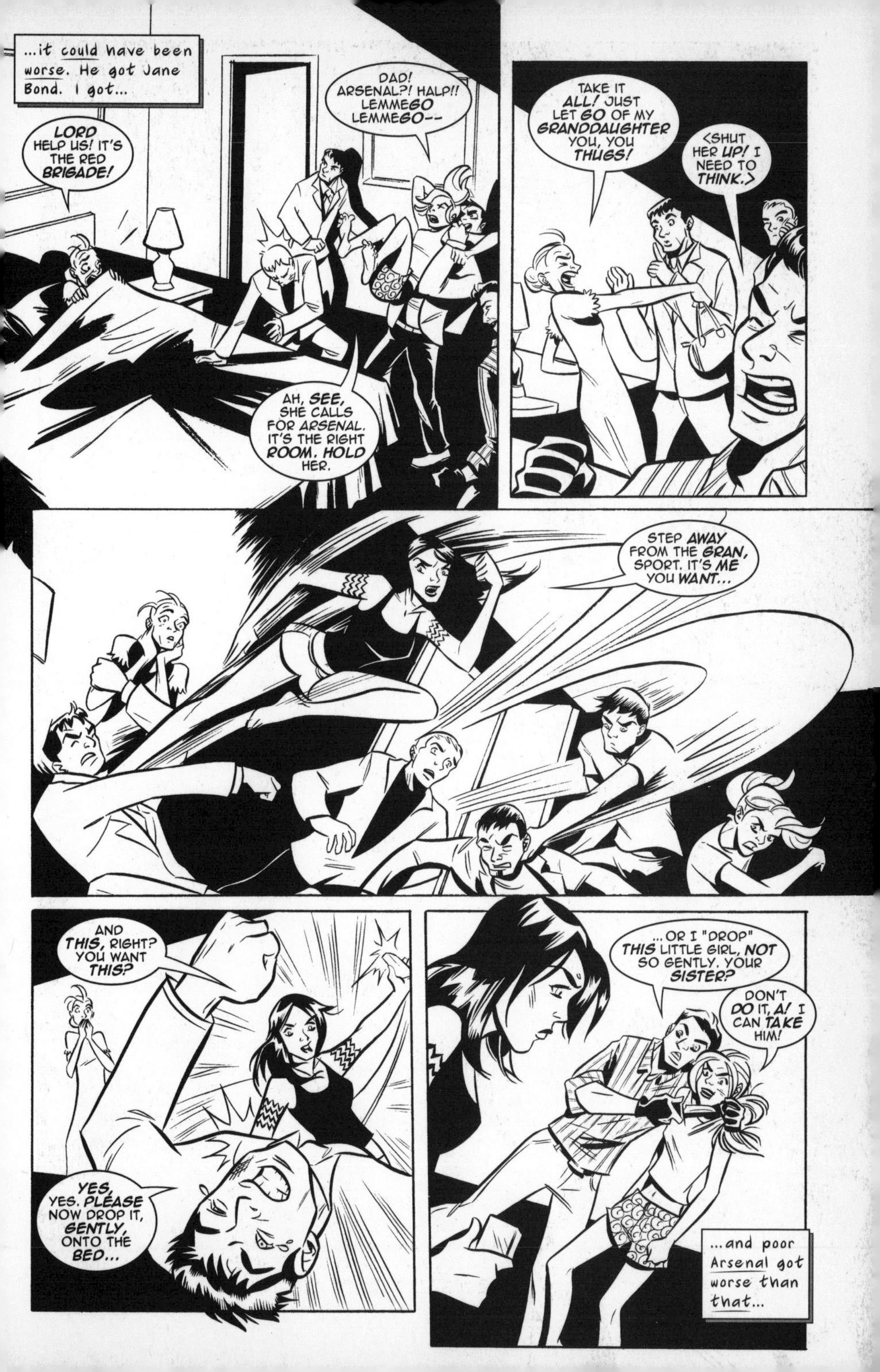
...it could have been worse. He got Jane Bond. I got...
LORD HELP US! IT'S THE RED BRIGADE!
DAD! ARSENAL?! HALP!! LEMMEGO LEMMEGO--
AH, SEE, SHE CALLS FOR ARSENAL. IT'S THE RIGHT ROOM. HOLD HER.
TAKE IT ALL! JUST LET GO OF MY GRANDDAUGHTER YOU, YOU THUGS!
<SHUT HER UP! I NEED TO THINK.>
STEP AWAY FROM THE GRAN, SPORT. IT'S ME YOU WANT...
AND THIS, RIGHT? YOU WANT THIS?
YES, YES. PLEASE NOW DROP IT, GENTLY, ONTO THE BED...
...OR I "DROP" THIS LITTLE GIRL, NOT SO GENTLY. YOUR SISTER?
DON'T DO IT, A! I CAN TAKE HIM!
...and poor Arsenal got worse than that...

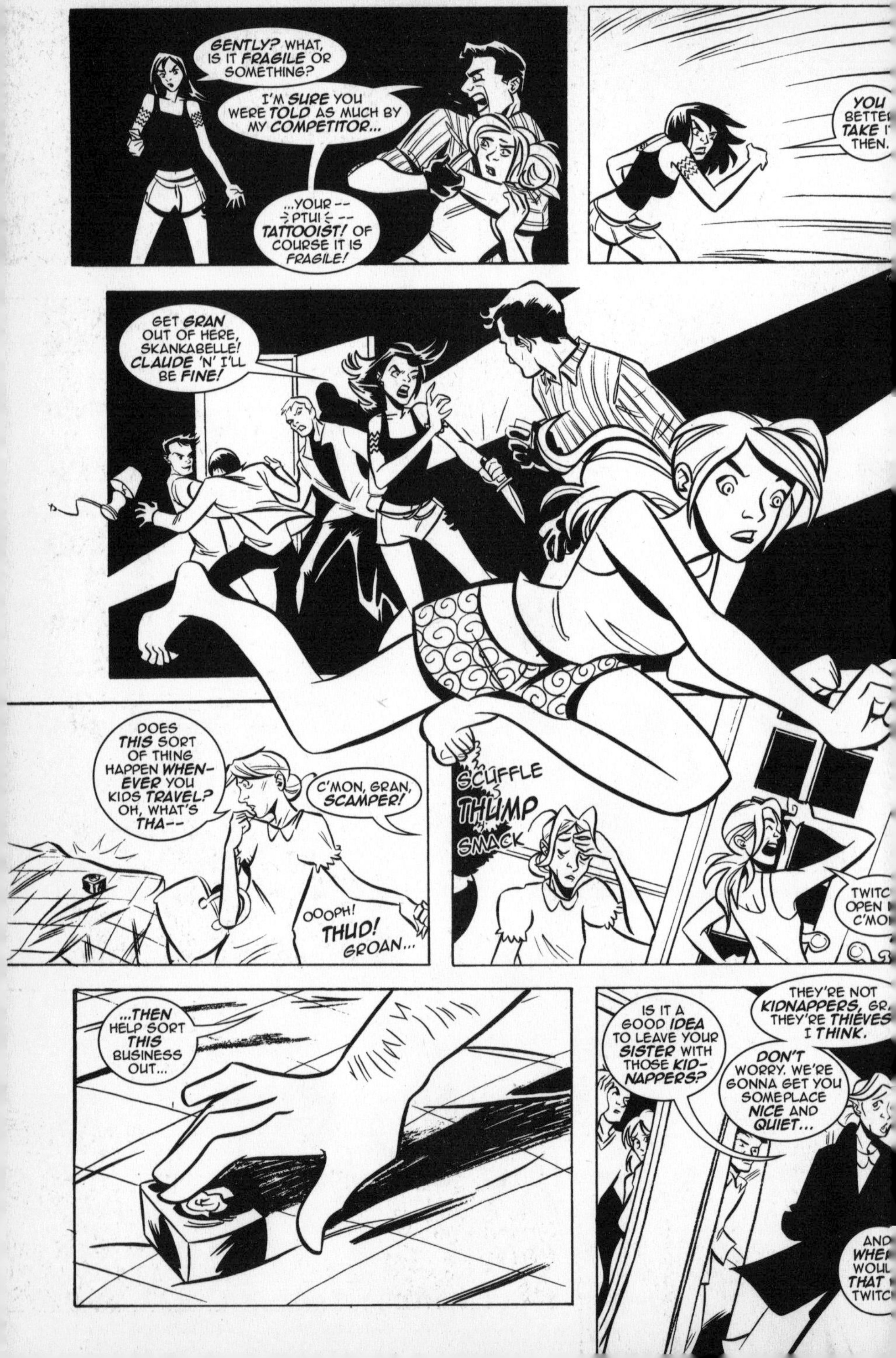
GENTLY? WHAT, IS IT FRAGILE OR SOMETHING?
I'M SURE YOU WERE TOLD AS MUCH BY MY COMPETITOR...
...YOUR -- PTUI -- TATTOOIST! OF COURSE IT IS FRAGILE!
YOU BETTER TAKE IT THEN.
GET GRAN OUT OF HERE, SKANKABELLE! CLAUDE 'N' I'LL BE FINE!
DOES THIS SORT OF THING HAPPEN WHENEVER YOU KIDS TRAVEL? OH, WHAT'S THA--
C'MON, GRAN, SCAMPER!
OOOPH! THUD! GROAN...
SCUFFLE
THUMP
SMACK
...THEN HELP SORT THIS BUSINESS OUT...
IS IT A GOOD IDEA TO LEAVE YOUR SISTER WITH THOSE KIDNAPPERS?
DON'T WORRY. WE'RE GONNA GET YOU SOMEPLACE NICE AND QUIET...

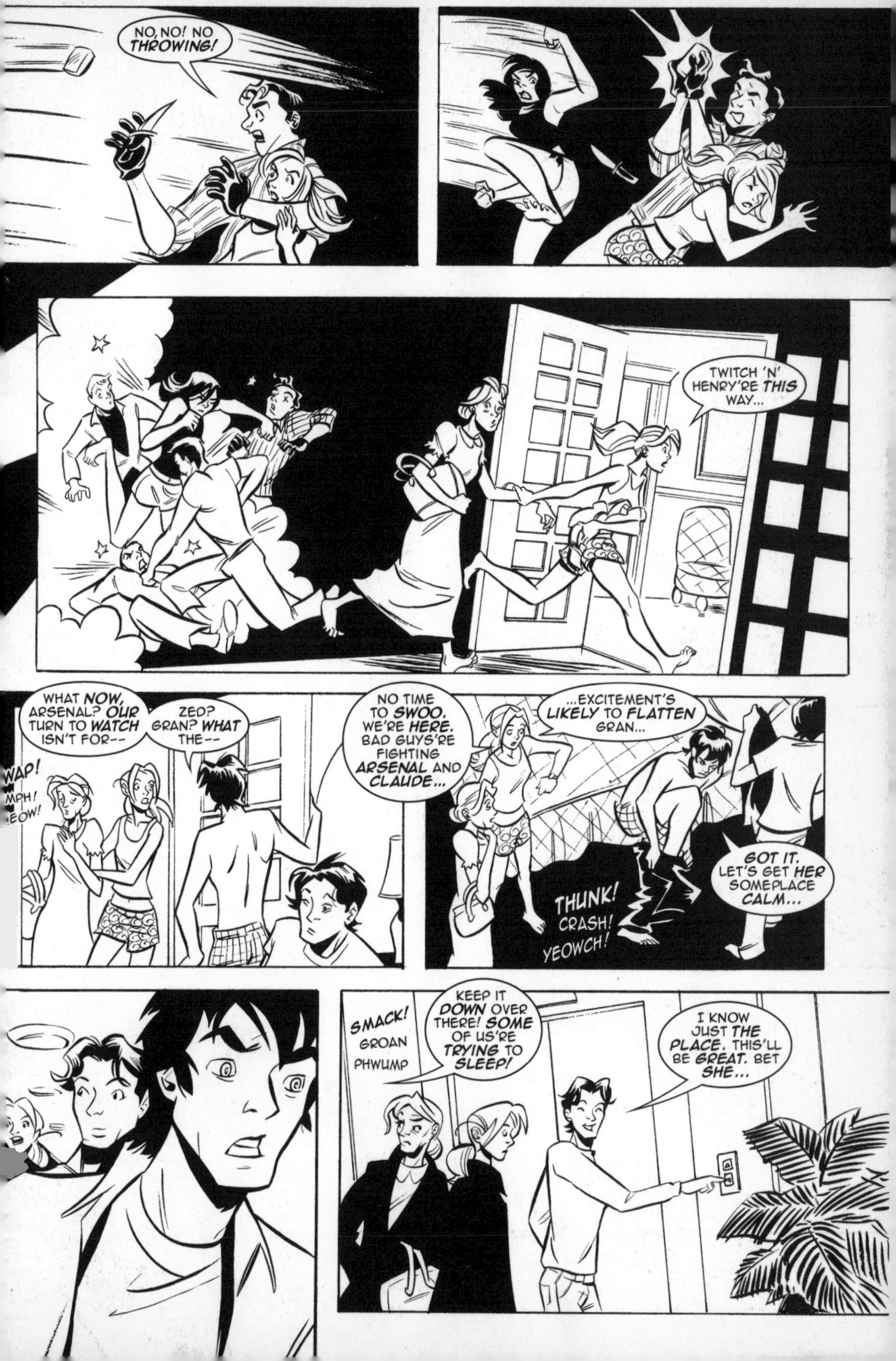

NO, NO! NO THROWING!
TWITCH 'N' HENRY'RE THIS WAY...
WHAT NOW, ARSENAL? OUR TURN TO WATCH ISN'T FOR--
ZED? GRAN? WHAT THE--
WAP!
MPH!
EOW!
NO TIME TO SWOO. WE'RE HERE. BAD GUYS'RE FIGHTING ARSENAL AND CLAUDE...
...EXCITEMENT'S LIKELY TO FLATTEN GRAN...
THUNK!
CRASH!
YEOWCH!
GOT IT. LET'S GET HER SOMEPLACE CALM...
SMACK!
GROAN
PHWUMP
KEEP IT DOWN OVER THERE! SOME OF US'RE TRYING TO SLEEP!
I KNOW JUST THE PLACE. THIS'LL BE GREAT. BET SHE...

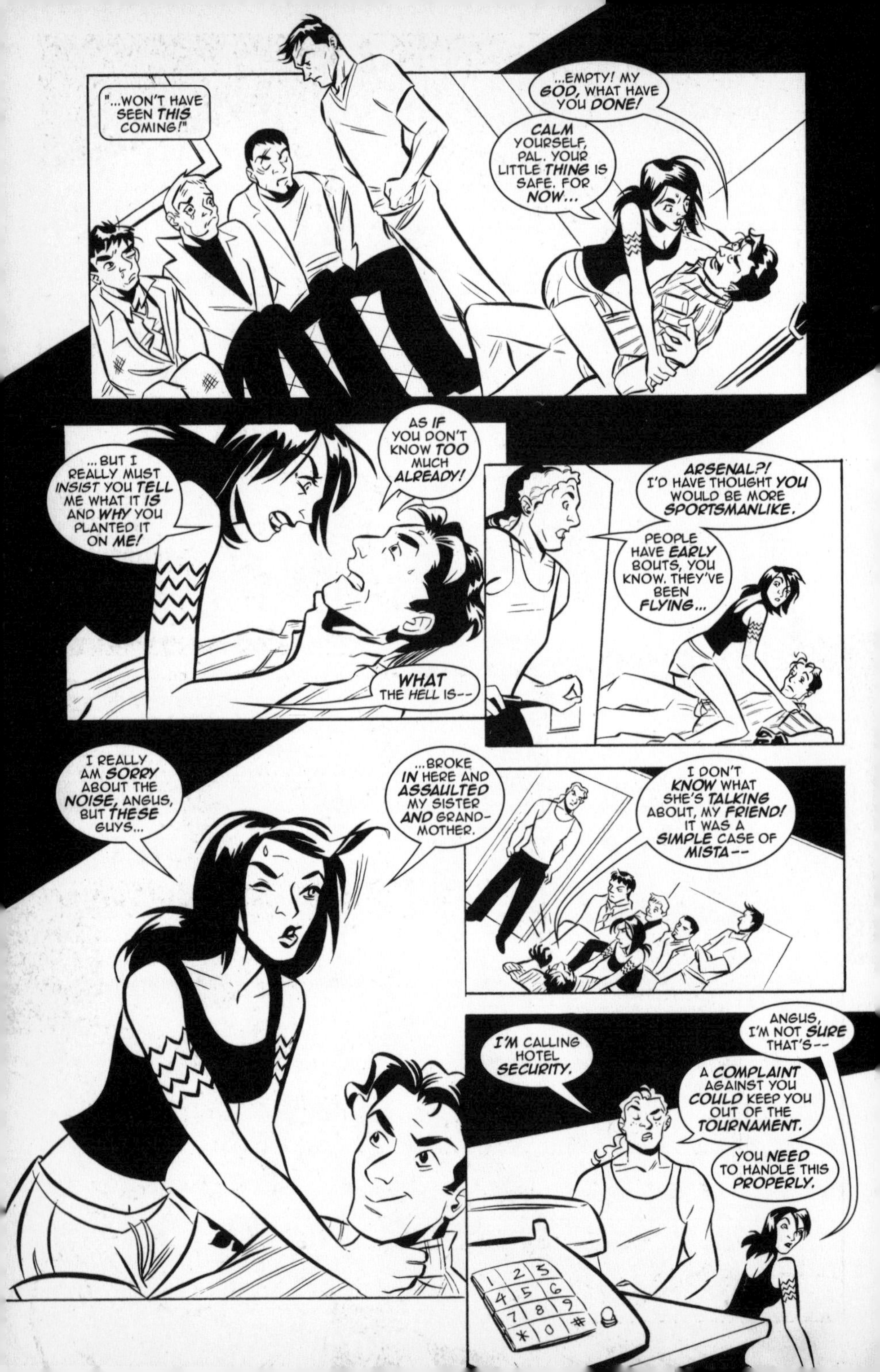
"...WON'T HAVE SEEN THIS COMING!"
...EMPTY! MY GOD, WHAT HAVE YOU DONE!
CALM YOURSELF, PAL. YOUR LITTLE THING IS SAFE. FOR NOW...
...BUT I REALLY MUST INSIST YOU TELL ME WHAT IT IS AND WHY YOU PLANTED IT ON ME!
AS IF YOU DON'T KNOW TOO MUCH ALREADY!
WHAT THE HELL IS--
ARSENAL?! I'D HAVE THOUGHT YOU WOULD BE MORE SPORTSMANLIKE.
PEOPLE HAVE EARLY BOUTS, YOU KNOW. THEY'VE BEEN FLYING...
I REALLY AM SORRY ABOUT THE NOISE, ANGUS, BUT THESE GUYS...
...BROKE IN HERE AND ASSAULTED MY SISTER AND GRAND-MOTHER.
I DON'T KNOW WHAT SHE'S TALKING ABOUT, MY FRIEND! IT WAS A SIMPLE CASE OF MISTA--
I'M CALLING HOTEL SECURITY.
ANGUS, I'M NOT SURE THAT'S--
A COMPLAINT AGAINST YOU COULD KEEP YOU OUT OF THE TOURNAMENT.
YOU NEED TO HANDLE THIS PROPERLY.

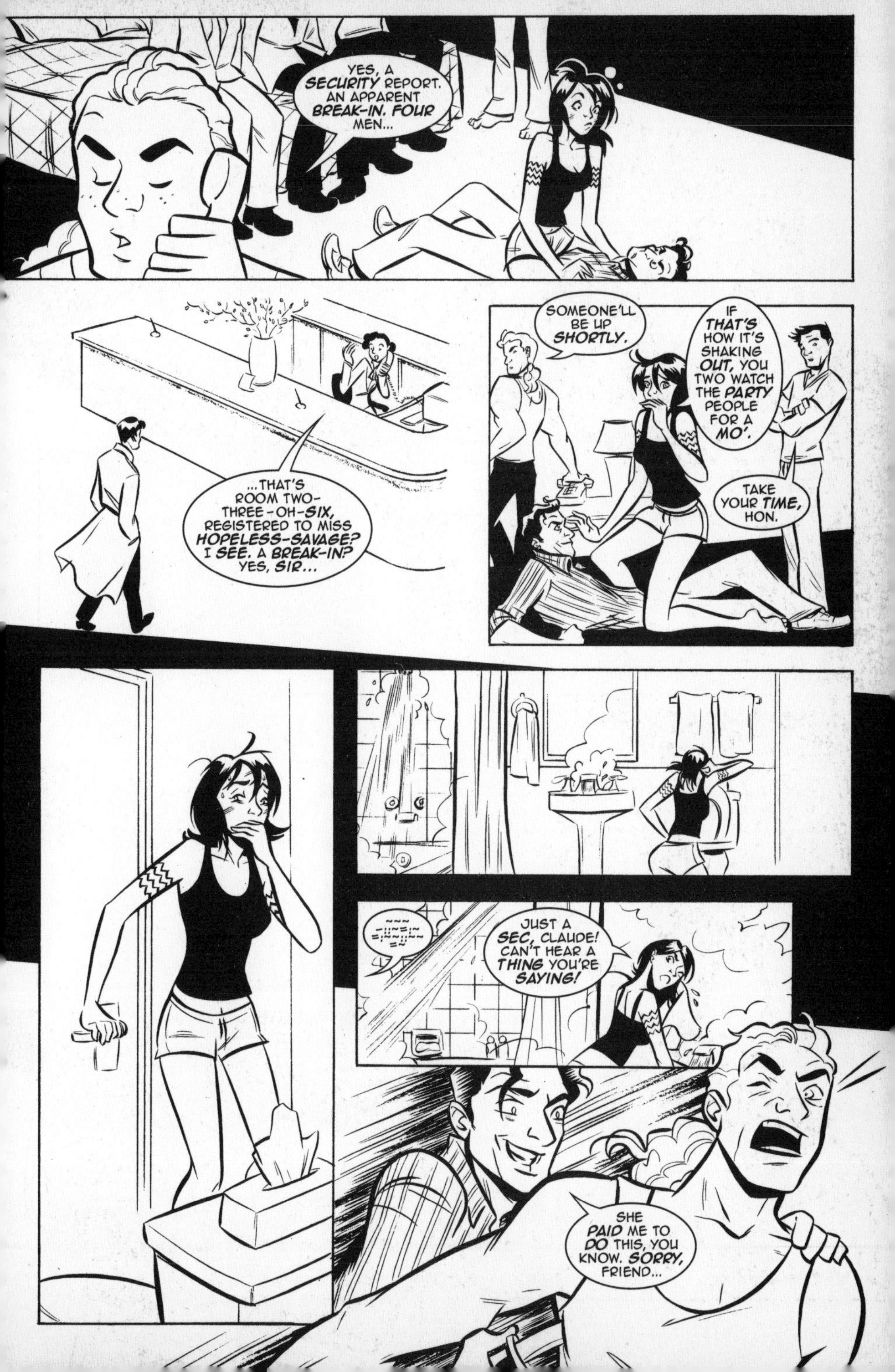
YES, A SECURITY REPORT. AN APPARENT BREAK-IN. FOUR MEN...
...THAT'S ROOM TWO-THREE-OH-SIX, REGISTERED TO MISS HOPELESS-SAVAGE? I SEE. A BREAK-IN? YES, SIR...
SOMEONE'LL BE UP SHORTLY.
IF THAT'S HOW IT'S SHAKING OUT, YOU TWO WATCH THE PARTY PEOPLE FOR A MO'.
TAKE YOUR TIME, HON.
JUST A SEC, CLAUDE! CAN'T HEAR A THING YOU'RE SAYING!
SHE PAID ME TO DO THIS, YOU KNOW. SORRY, FRIEND...

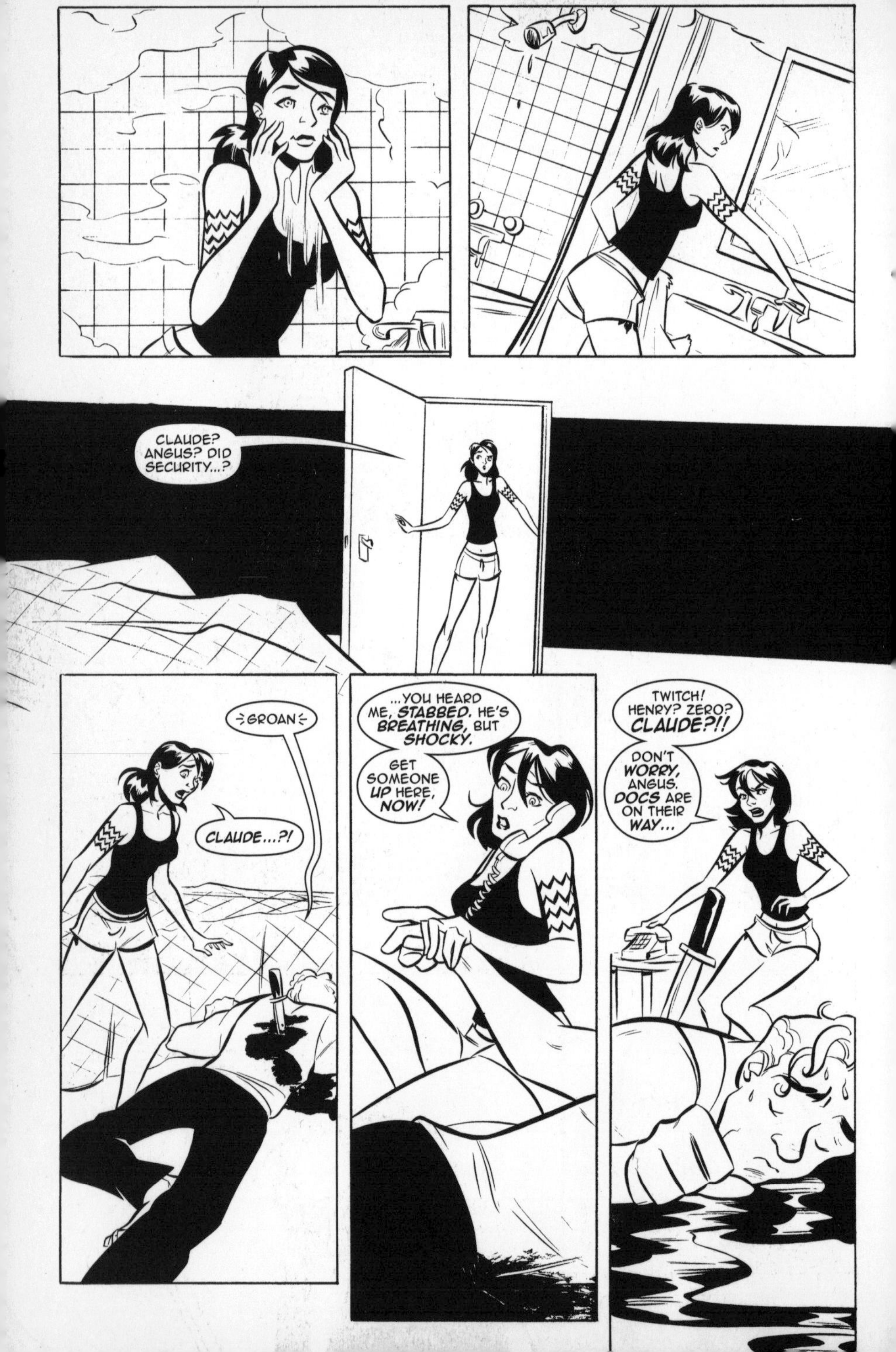
CLAUDE? ANGUS? DID SECURITY...?
GROAN
CLAUDE...?!
...YOU HEARD ME, STABBED. HE'S BREATHING, BUT SHOCKY.
GET SOMEONE UP HERE, NOW!
TWITCH! HENRY? ZERO? CLAUDE?!!
DON'T WORRY, ANGUS. DOCS ARE ON THEIR WAY...

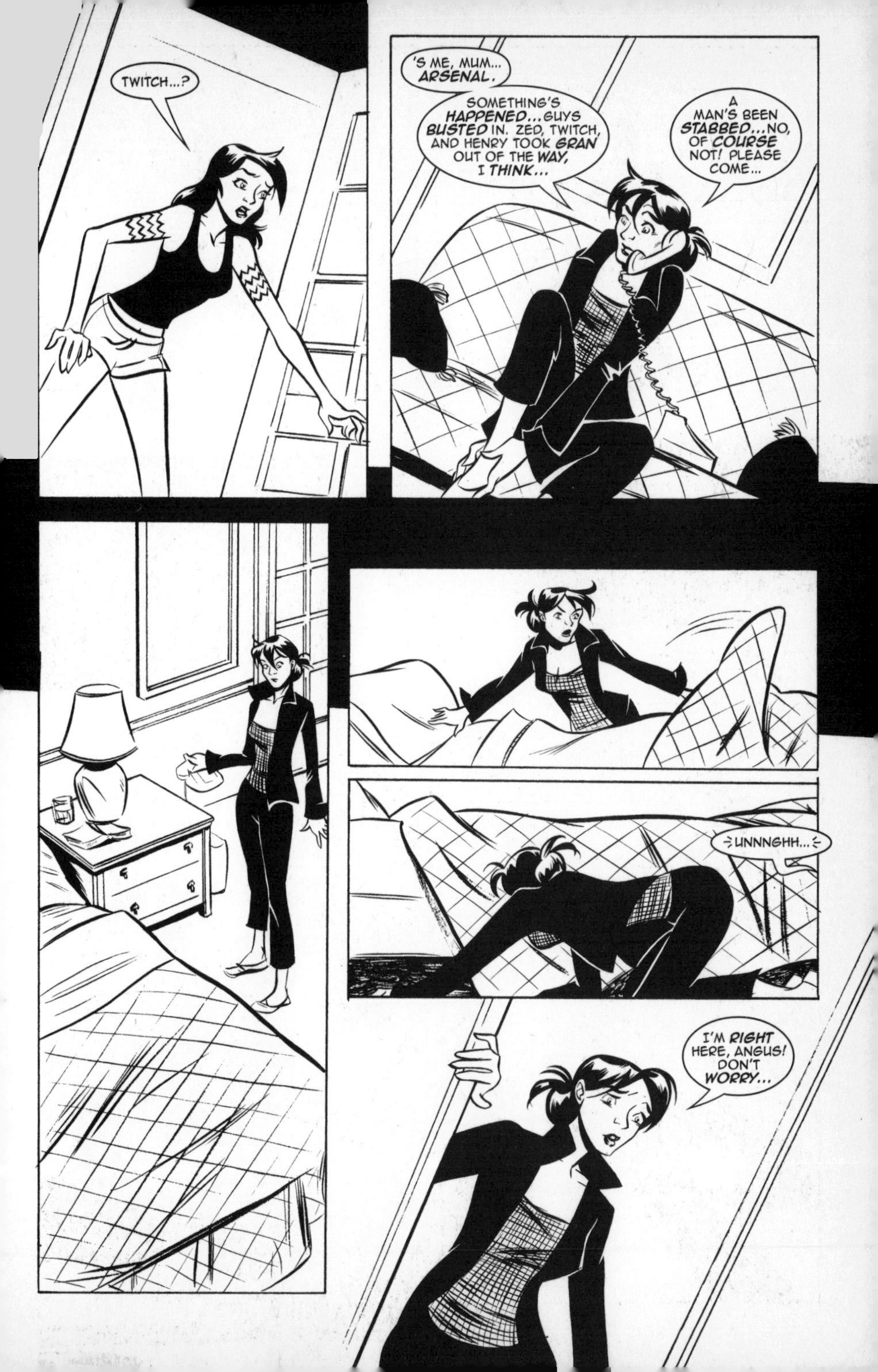
TWITCH...?
'S ME, MUM... ARSENAL.
SOMETHING'S HAPPENED... GUYS BUSTED IN. ZED, TWITCH, AND HENRY TOOK GRAN OUT OF THE WAY, I THINK...
A MAN'S BEEN STABBED... NO, OF COURSE NOT! PLEASE COME...
UNNNGHH...
I'M RIGHT HERE, ANGUS! DON'T WORRY...

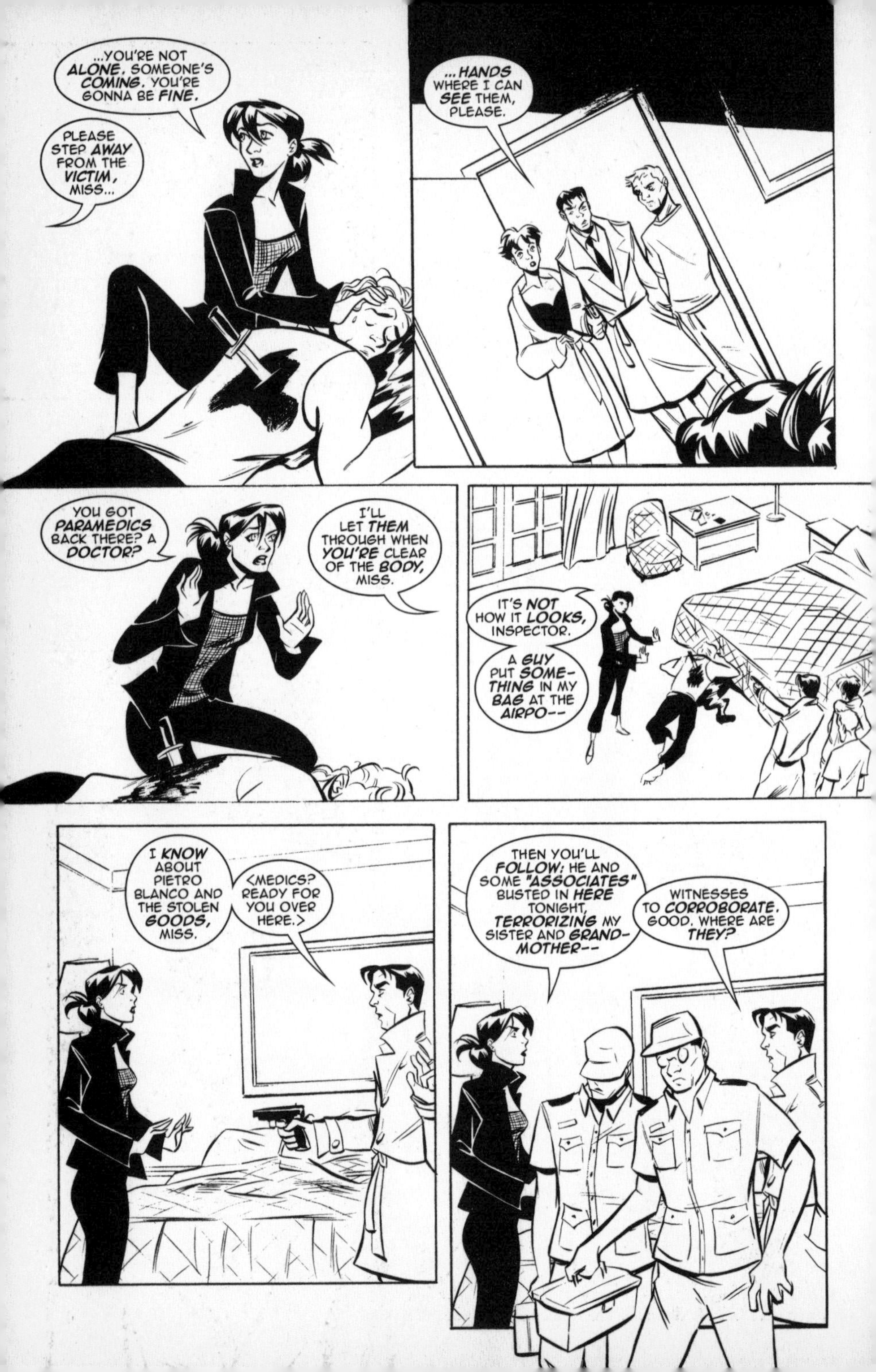
...YOU'RE NOT ALONE. SOMEONE'S COMING. YOU'RE GONNA BE FINE.
PLEASE STEP AWAY FROM THE VICTIM, MISS...
...HANDS WHERE I CAN SEE THEM, PLEASE.
YOU GOT PARAMEDICS BACK THERE? A DOCTOR?
I'LL LET THEM THROUGH WHEN YOU'RE CLEAR OF THE BODY, MISS.
IT'S NOT HOW IT LOOKS, INSPECTOR.
A GUY PUT SOME-THING IN MY BAG AT THE AIRPO--
I KNOW ABOUT PIETRO BLANCO AND THE STOLEN GOODS, MISS.
<MEDICS? READY FOR YOU OVER HERE.>
THEN YOU'LL FOLLOW: HE AND SOME "ASSOCIATES" BUSTED IN HERE TONIGHT, TERRORIZING MY SISTER AND GRAND-MOTHER--
WITNESSES TO CORROBORATE. GOOD. WHERE ARE THEY?

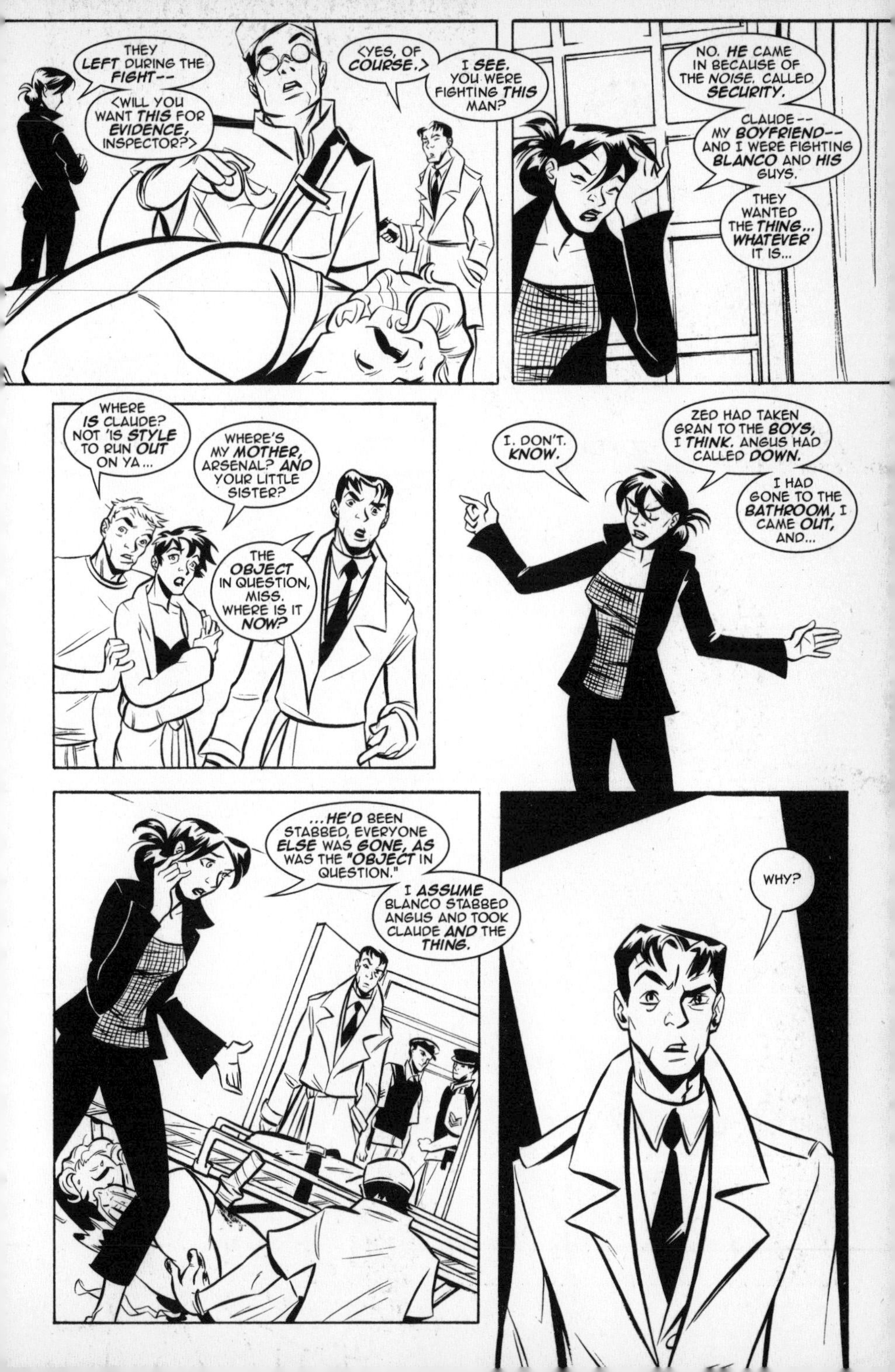
THEY LEFT DURING THE FIGHT--
<WILL YOU WANT THIS FOR EVIDENCE, INSPECTOR?>
<YES, OF COURSE.>
I SEE. YOU WERE FIGHTING THIS MAN?
NO. HE CAME IN BECAUSE OF THE NOISE. CALLED SECURITY.
CLAUDE -- MY BOYFRIEND-- AND I WERE FIGHTING BLANCO AND HIS GUYS.
THEY WANTED THE THING... WHATEVER IT IS...
WHERE IS CLAUDE? NOT 'IS STYLE TO RUN OUT ON YA...
WHERE'S MY MOTHER, ARSENAL? AND YOUR LITTLE SISTER?
THE OBJECT IN QUESTION, MISS. WHERE IS IT NOW?
I. DON'T. KNOW.
ZED HAD TAKEN GRAN TO THE BOYS, I THINK. ANGUS HAD CALLED DOWN.
I HAD GONE TO THE BATHROOM, I CAME OUT, AND...
...HE'D BEEN STABBED, EVERYONE ELSE WAS GONE, AS WAS THE "OBJECT IN QUESTION."
I ASSUME BLANCO STABBED ANGUS AND TOOK CLAUDE AND THE THING.
WHY?

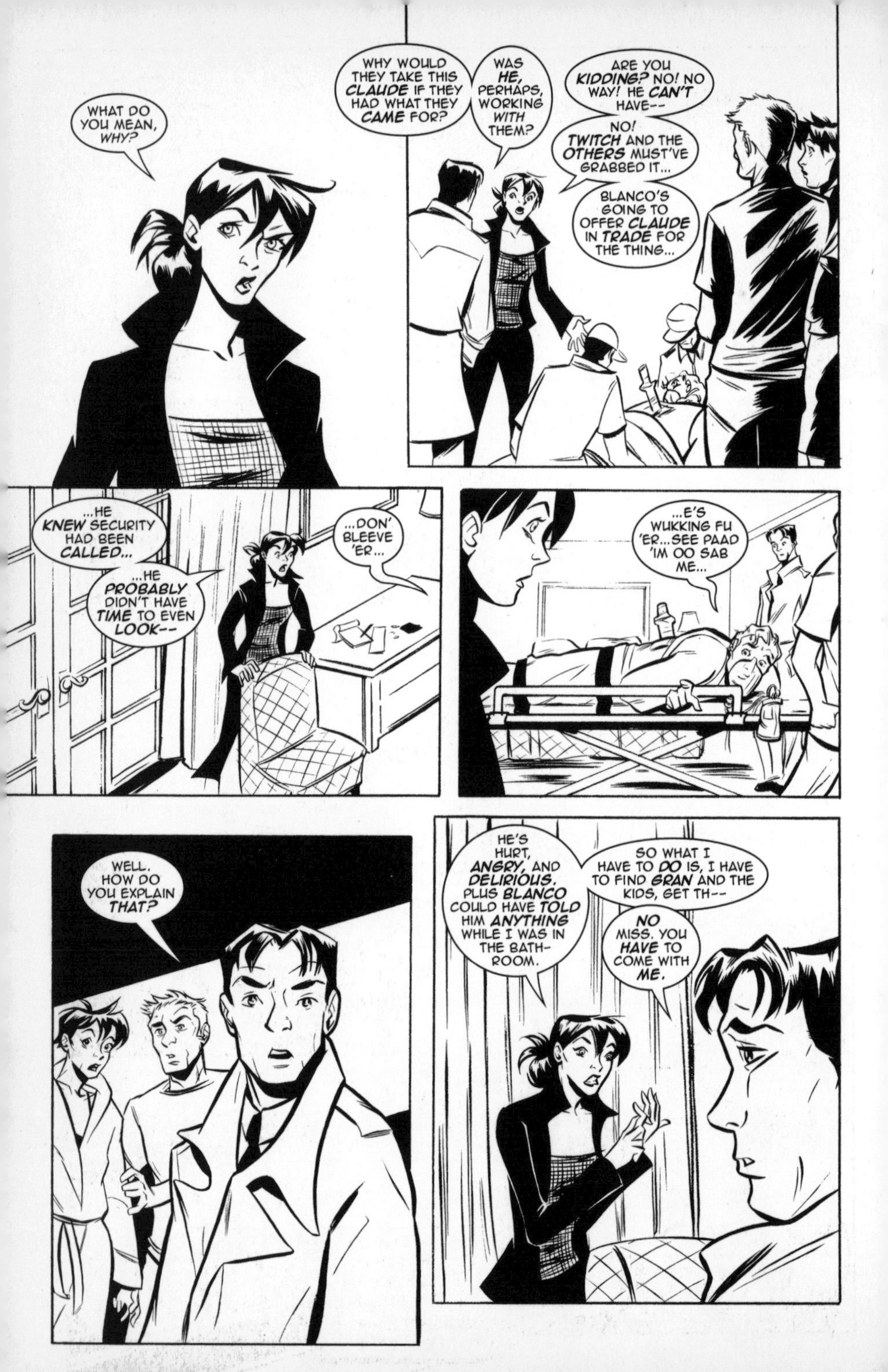
WHAT DO YOU MEAN, WHY?
WHY WOULD THEY TAKE THIS CLAUDE IF THEY HAD WHAT THEY CAME FOR?
WAS HE, PERHAPS, WORKING WITH THEM?
ARE YOU KIDDING? NO! NO WAY! HE CAN'T HAVE--
NO! TWITCH AND THE OTHERS MUST'VE GRABBED IT...
BLANCO'S GOING TO OFFER CLAUDE IN TRADE FOR THE THING...
...HE KNEW SECURITY HAD BEEN CALLED...
...HE PROBABLY DIDN'T HAVE TIME TO EVEN LOOK--
...DON' BLEEVE 'ER...
...E'S WUKKING FU 'ER...SEE PAAD 'IM OO SAB ME...
WELL. HOW DO YOU EXPLAIN THAT?
HE'S HURT, ANGRY, AND DELIRIOUS. PLUS BLANCO COULD HAVE TOLD HIM ANYTHING WHILE I WAS IN THE BATH-ROOM.
SO WHAT I HAVE TO DO IS, I HAVE TO FIND GRAN AND THE KIDS, GET TH--
NO MISS. YOU HAVE TO COME WITH ME.

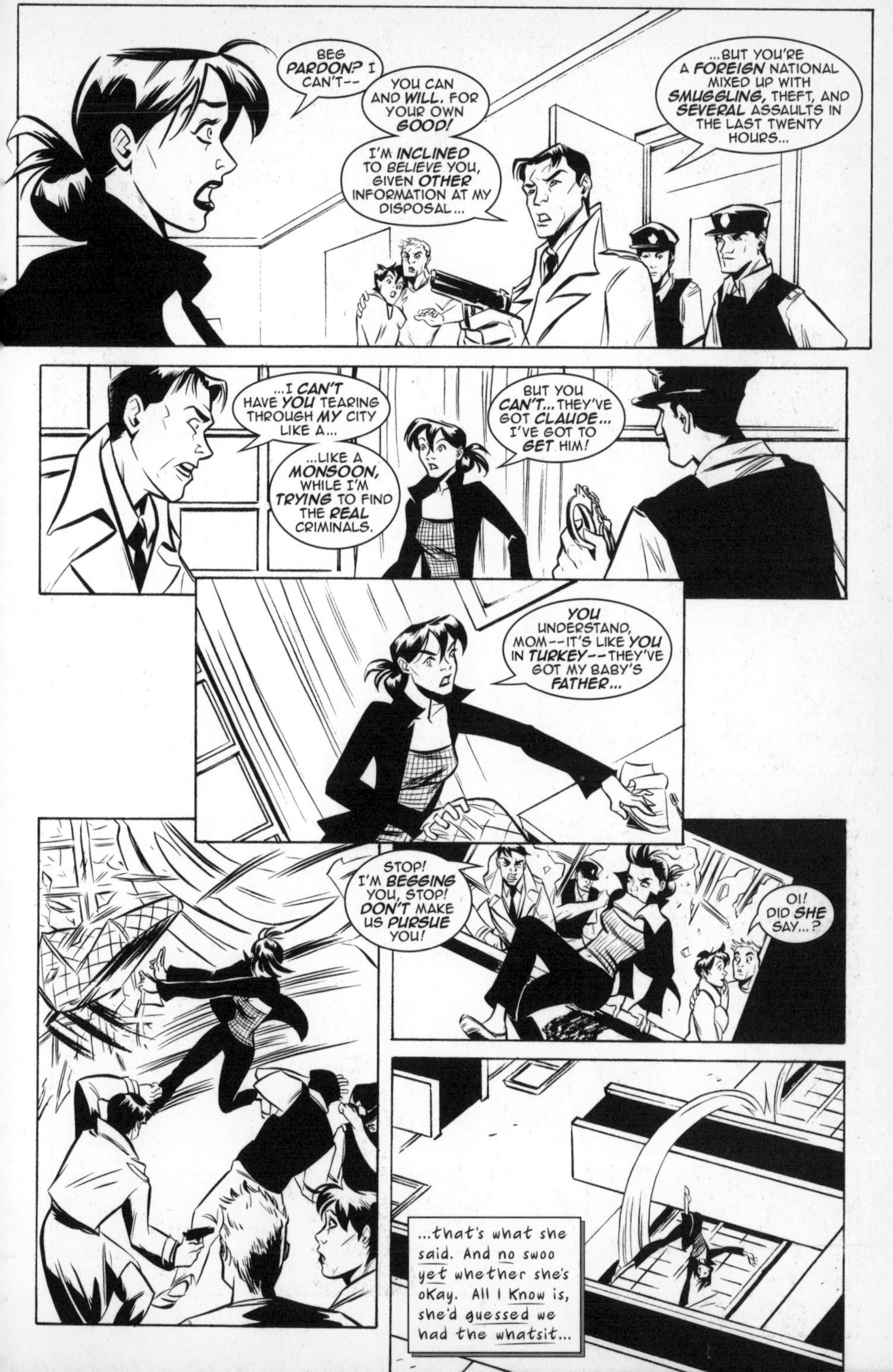
BEG PARDON? I CAN'T--
YOU CAN AND WILL. FOR YOUR OWN GOOD!
I'M INCLINED TO BELIEVE YOU, GIVEN OTHER INFORMATION AT MY DISPOSAL...
...BUT YOU'RE A FOREIGN NATIONAL MIXED UP WITH SMUGGLING, THEFT, AND SEVERAL ASSAULTS IN THE LAST TWENTY HOURS...
...I CAN'T HAVE YOU TEARING THROUGH MY CITY LIKE A...
...LIKE A MONSOON, WHILE I'M TRYING TO FIND THE REAL CRIMINALS.
BUT YOU CAN'T... THEY'VE GOT CLAUDE... I'VE GOT TO GET HIM!
YOU UNDERSTAND, MOM--IT'S LIKE YOU IN TURKEY--THEY'VE GOT MY BABY'S FATHER...
STOP! I'M BEGGING YOU, STOP! DON'T MAKE US PURSUE YOU!
OI! DID SHE SAY...?
...that's what she said. And no swoo yet whether she's okay. All I know is, she'd guessed we had the whatsit...

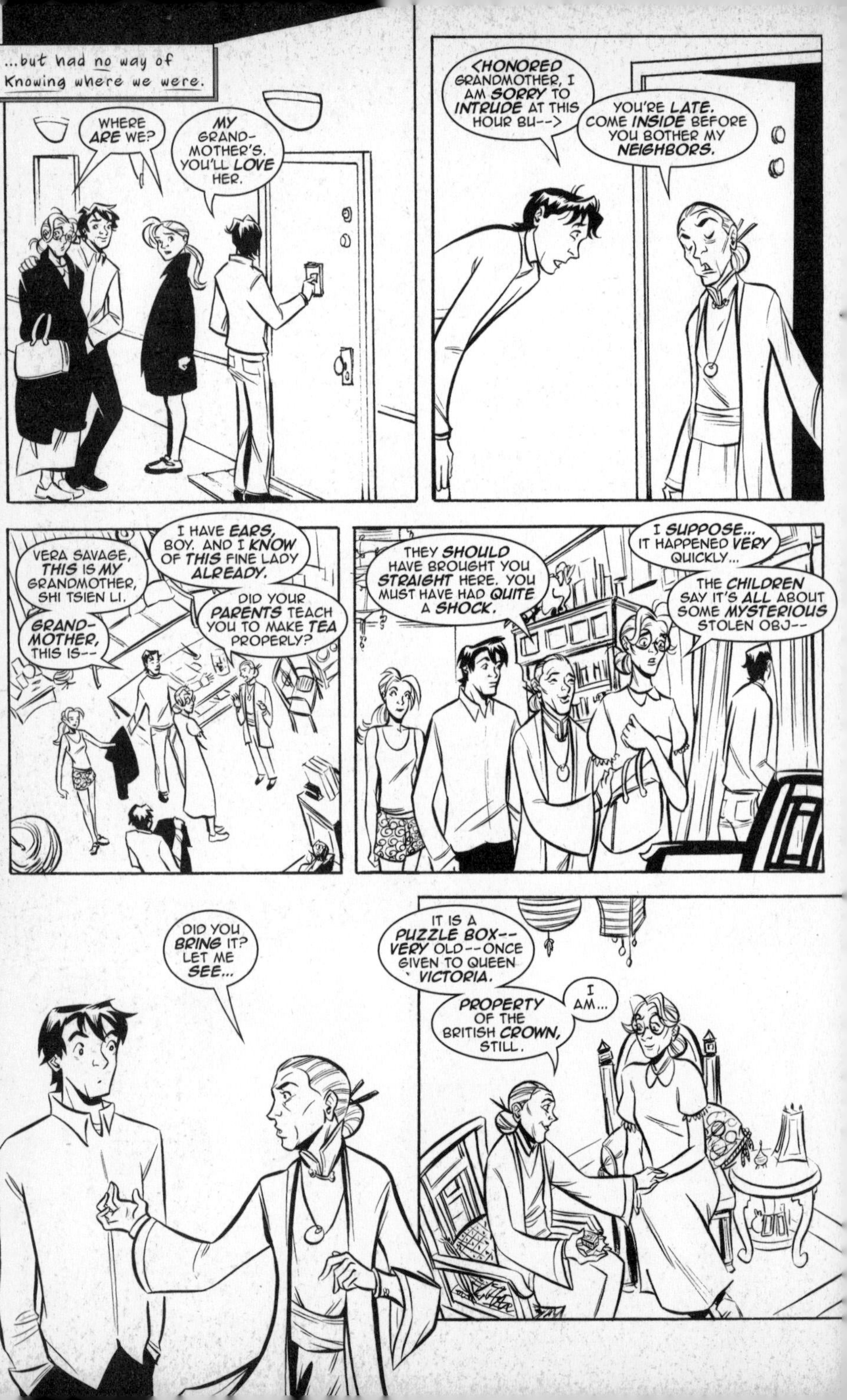

...but had no way of Knowing where we were.
WHERE ARE WE?
MY GRAND-MOTHER'S. YOU'LL LOVE HER.
<HONORED GRANDMOTHER, I AM SORRY TO INTRUDE AT THIS HOUR BU-->
YOU'RE LATE. COME INSIDE BEFORE YOU BOTHER MY NEIGHBORS.
VERA SAVAGE, THIS IS MY GRANDMOTHER, SHI TSIEN LI.
GRAND-MOTHER, THIS IS--
I HAVE EARS, BOY. AND I KNOW OF THIS FINE LADY ALREADY.
DID YOUR PARENTS TEACH YOU TO MAKE TEA PROPERLY?
THEY SHOULD HAVE BROUGHT YOU STRAIGHT HERE. YOU MUST HAVE HAD QUITE A SHOCK.
I SUPPOSE... IT HAPPENED VERY QUICKLY...
THE CHILDREN SAY IT'S ALL ABOUT SOME MYSTERIOUS STOLEN OBJ--
DID YOU BRING IT? LET ME SEE...
IT IS A PUZZLE BOX--VERY OLD--ONCE GIVEN TO QUEEN VICTORIA.
PROPERTY OF THE BRITISH CROWN, STILL.
I AM...

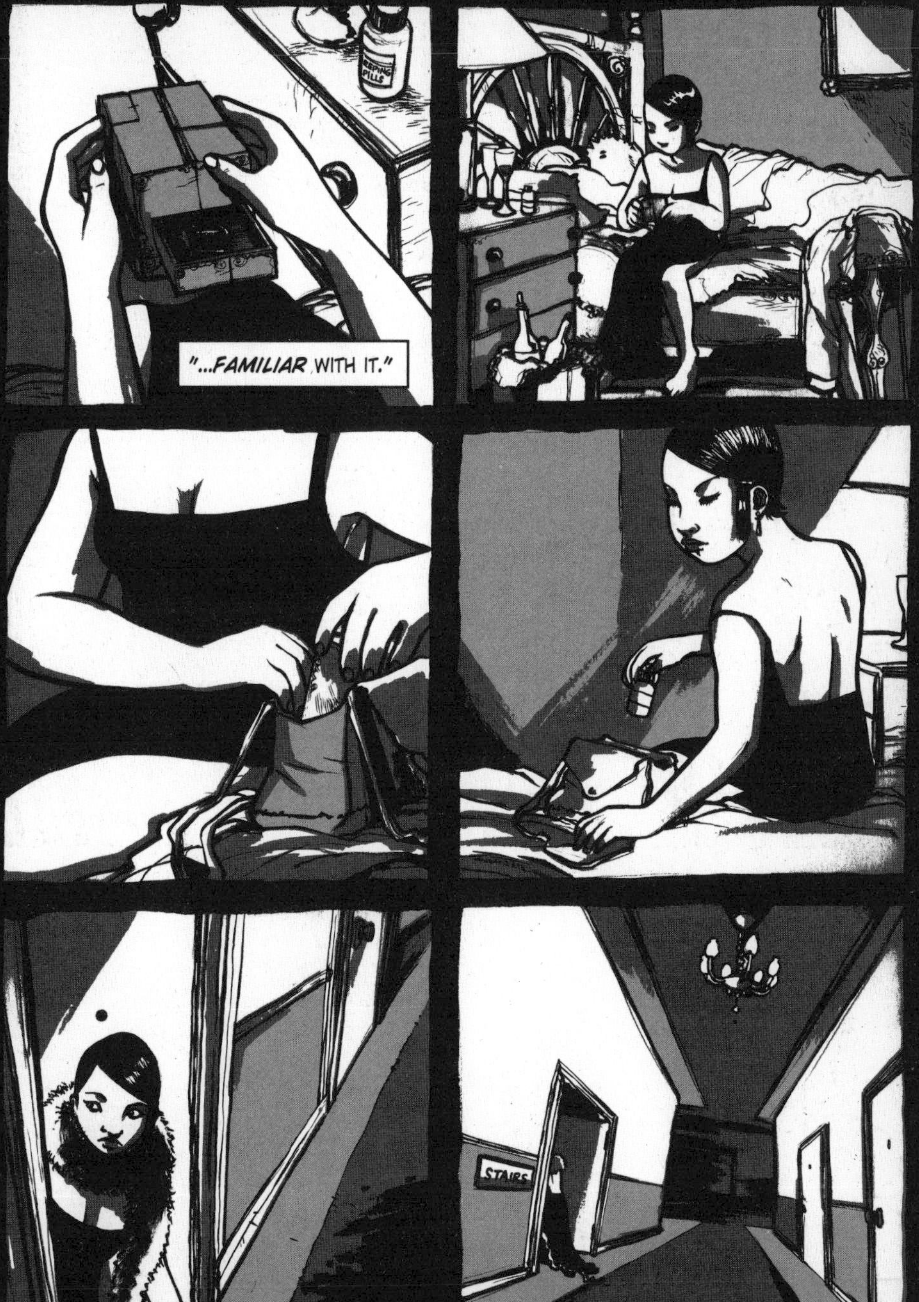

SLEEPING PILLS
"...FAMILIAR WITH IT."
STAIRS

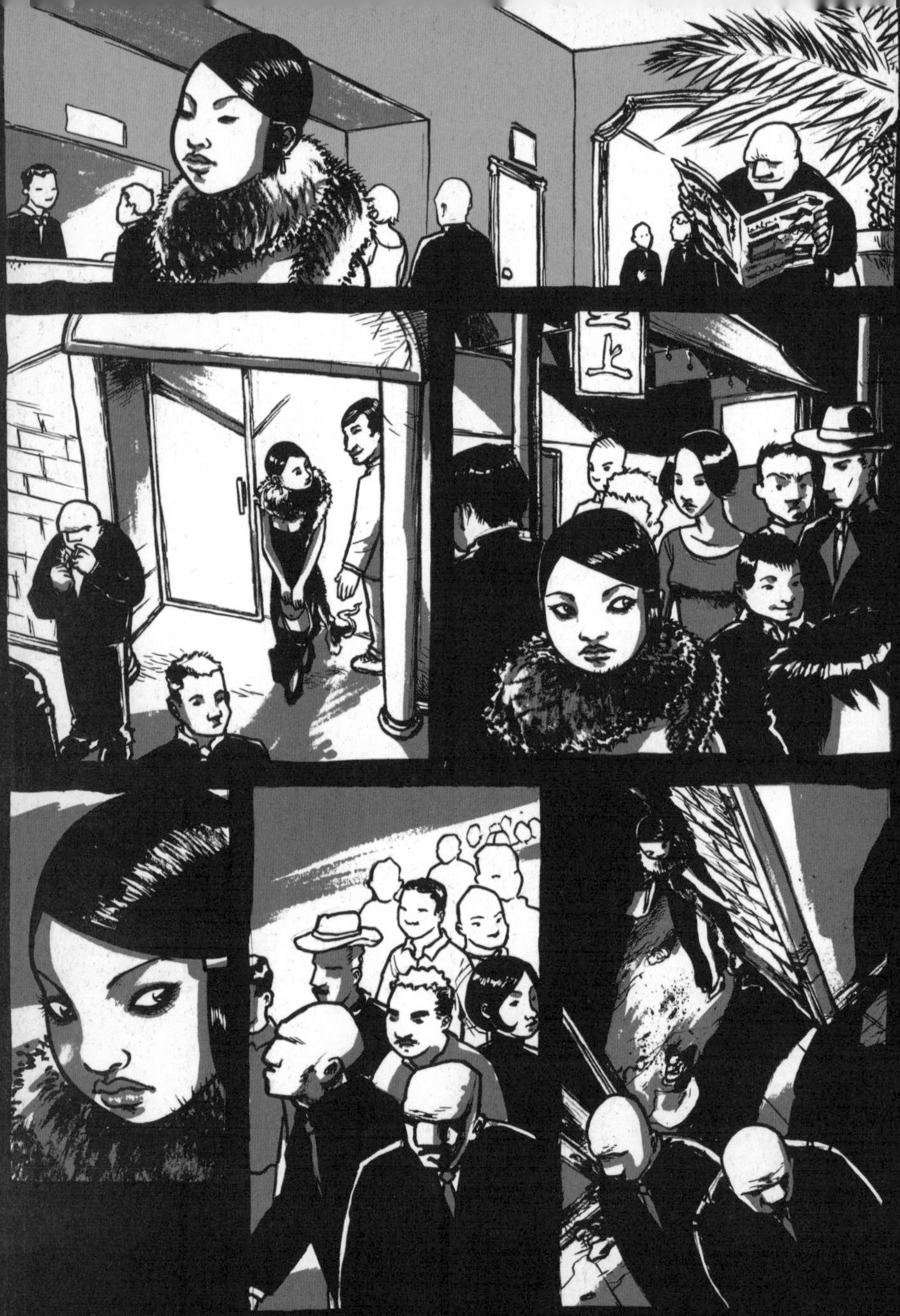

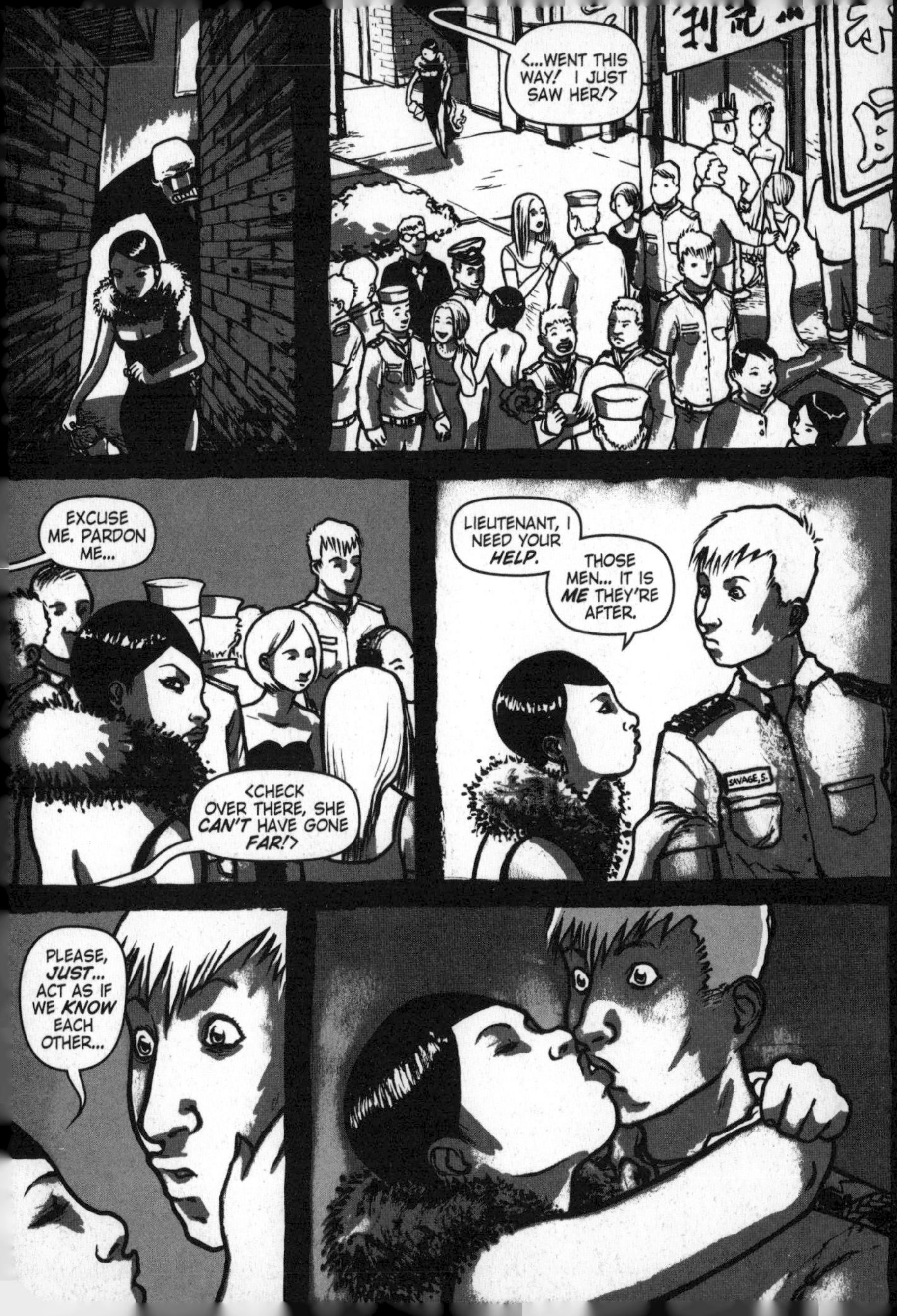
<...WENT THIS WAY! I JUST SAW HER!>
EXCUSE ME. PARDON ME...
<CHECK OVER THERE, SHE CAN'T HAVE GONE FAR!>
LIEUTENANT, I NEED YOUR HELP.
THOSE MEN... IT IS ME THEY'RE AFTER.
SAVAGE, S.
PLEASE, JUST... ACT AS IF WE KNOW EACH OTHER...

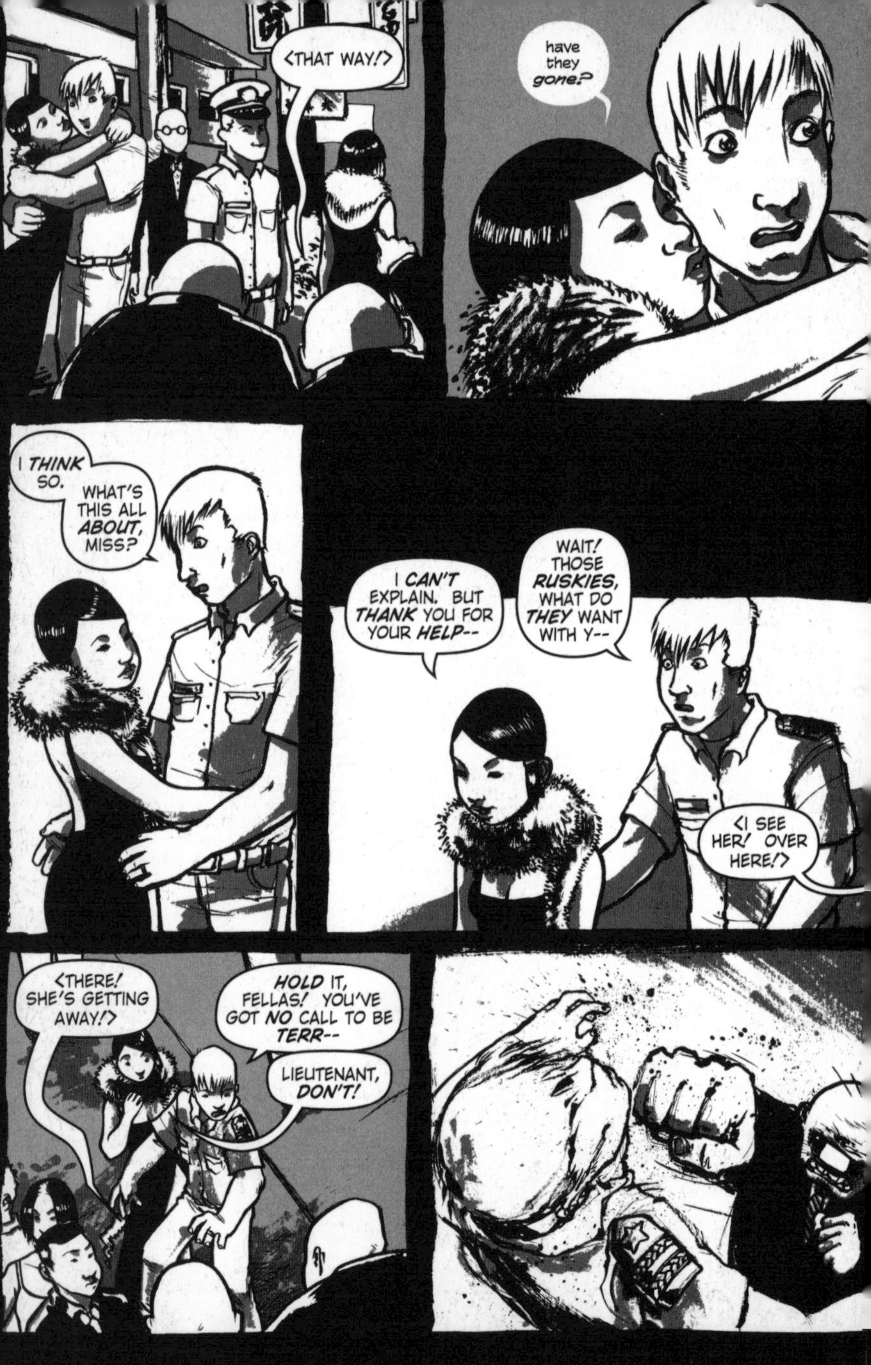
<THAT WAY!>
have they gone?
I THINK SO.
WHAT'S THIS ALL ABOUT, MISS?
I CAN'T EXPLAIN. BUT THANK YOU FOR YOUR HELP--
WAIT! THOSE RUSKIES, WHAT DO THEY WANT WITH Y--
<I SEE HER! OVER HERE!>
<THERE! SHE'S GETTING AWAY!>
HOLD IT, FELLAS! YOU'VE GOT NO CALL TO BE TERR--
LIEUTENANT, DON'T!

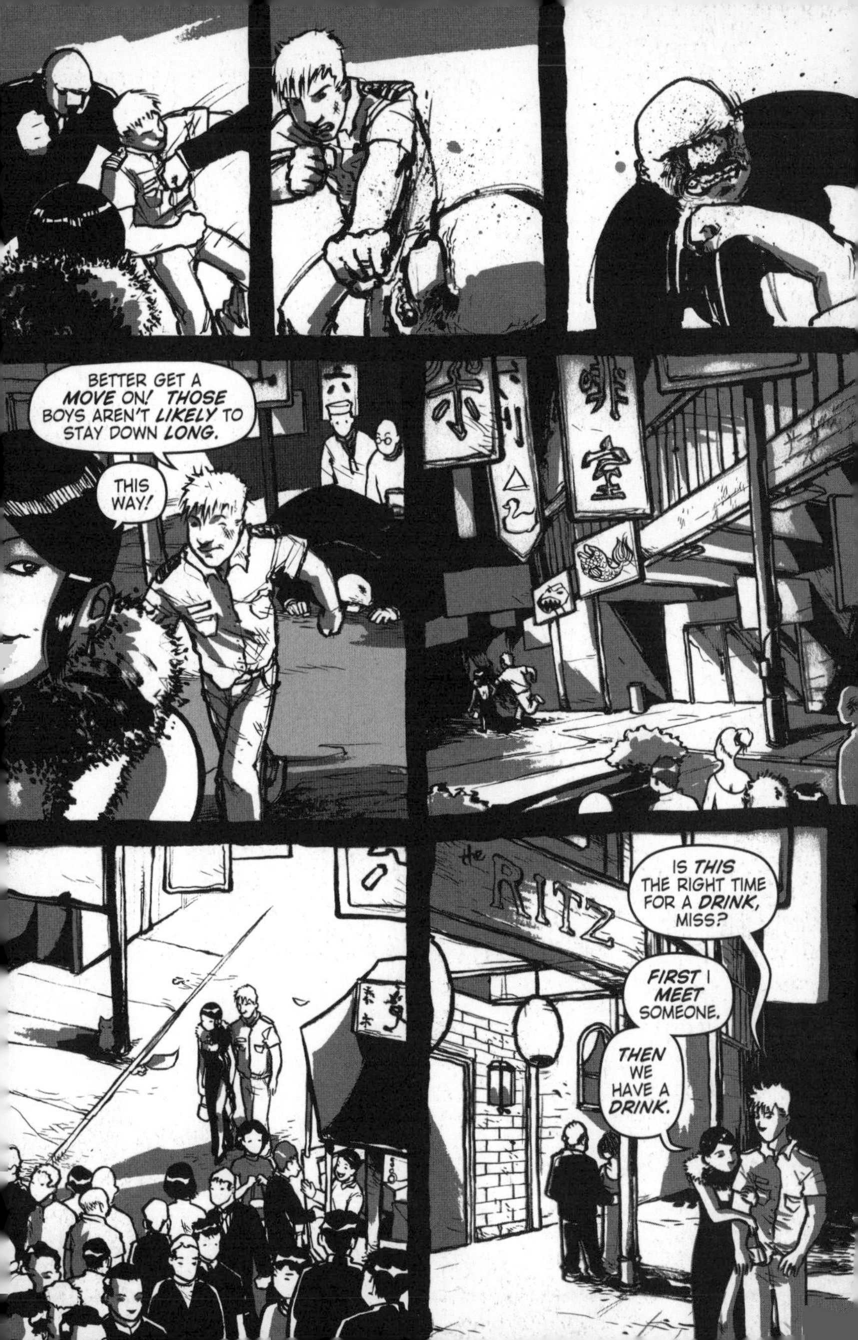
BETTER GET A MOVE ON! THOSE BOYS AREN'T LIKELY TO STAY DOWN LONG.
THIS WAY!
the RITZ
IS THIS THE RIGHT TIME FOR A DRINK, MISS?
FIRST I MEET SOMEONE.
THEN WE HAVE A DRINK.

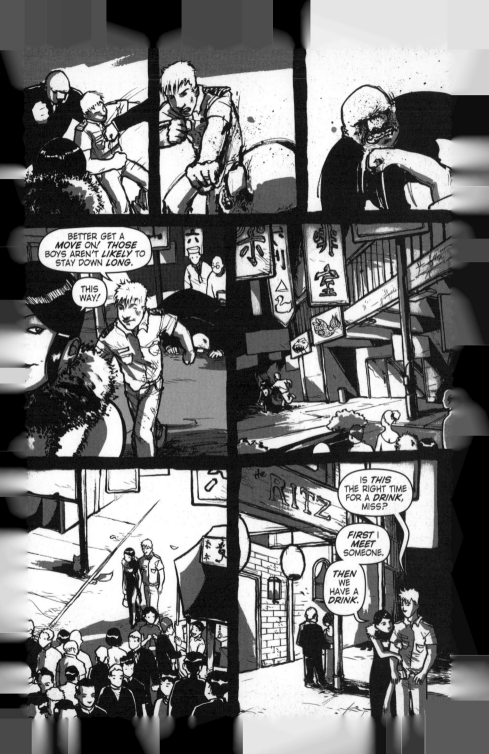

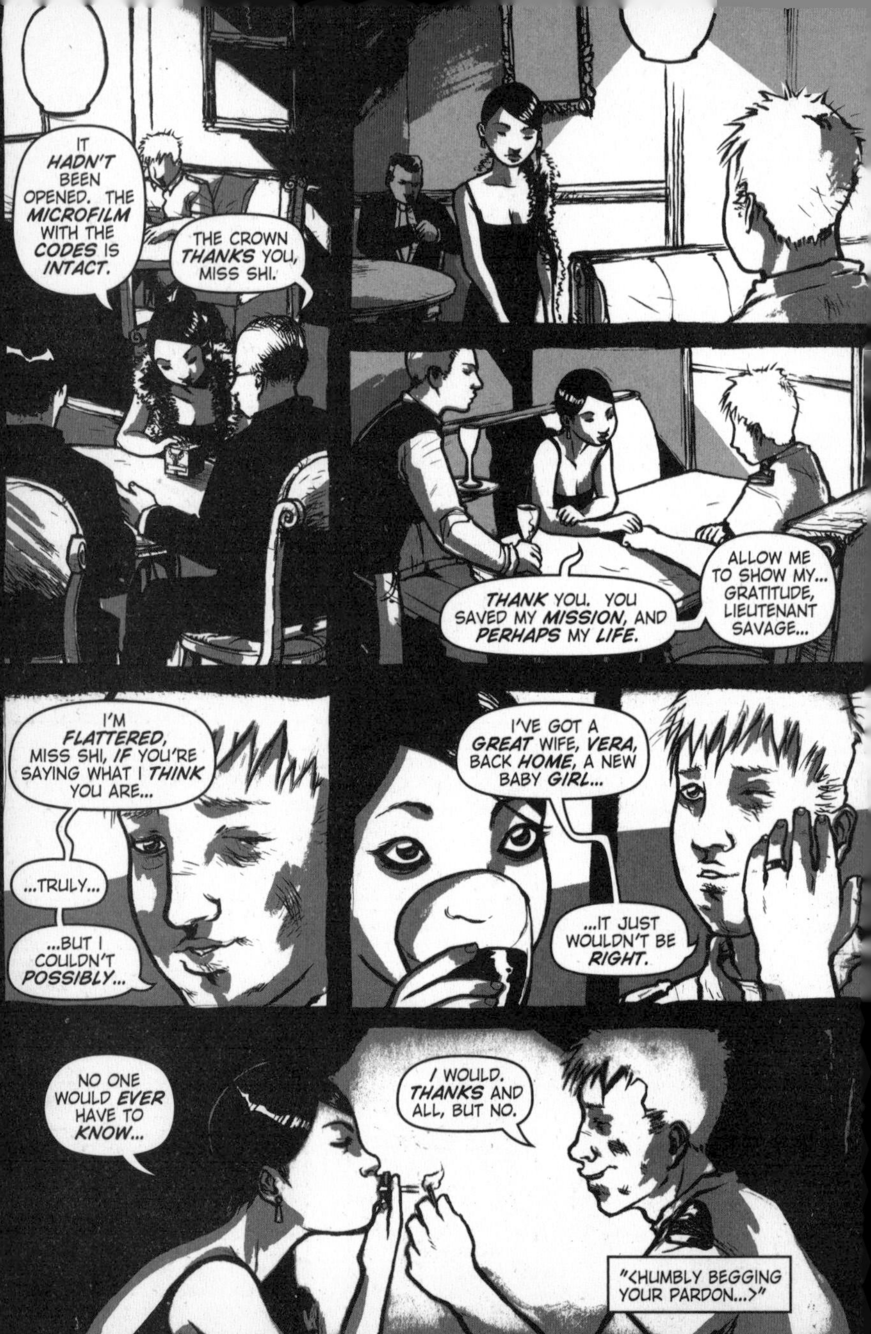
IT HADN'T BEEN OPENED. THE MICROFILM WITH THE CODES IS INTACT.
THE CROWN THANKS YOU, MISS SHI.
THANK YOU. YOU SAVED MY MISSION, AND PERHAPS MY LIFE.
ALLOW ME TO SHOW MY... GRATITUDE, LIEUTENANT SAVAGE...
I'M FLATTERED, MISS SHI, IF YOU'RE SAYING WHAT I THINK YOU ARE...
...TRULY...
...BUT I COULDN'T POSSIBLY...
I'VE GOT A GREAT WIFE, VERA, BACK HOME, A NEW BABY GIRL...
...IT JUST WOULDN'T BE RIGHT.
NO ONE WOULD EVER HAVE TO KNOW...
I WOULD. THANKS AND ALL, BUT NO.
"<HUMBLY BEGGING YOUR PARDON...>"

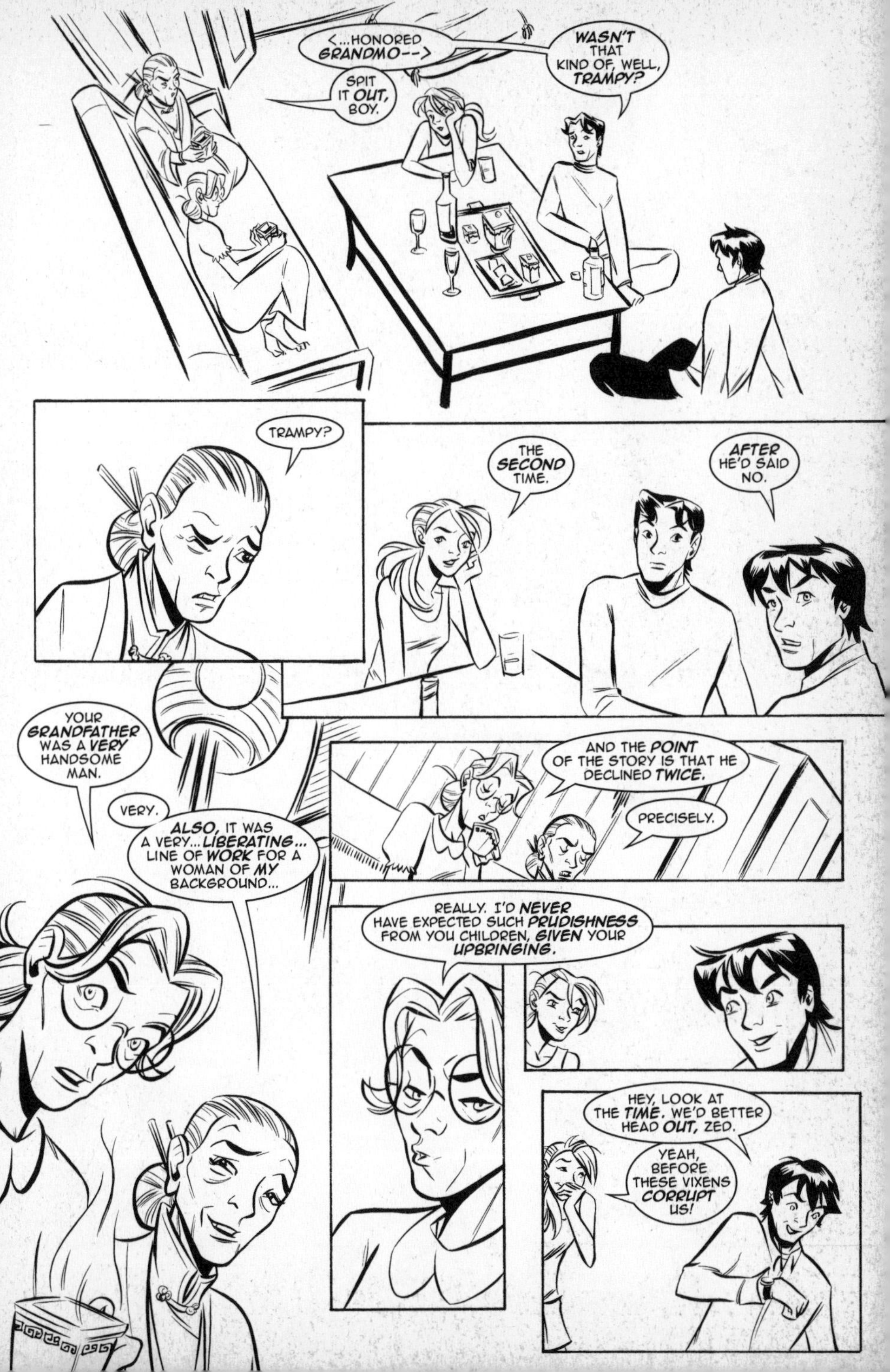
<...HONORED GRANDMO-->
SPIT IT OUT, BOY.
WASN'T THAT KIND OF, WELL, TRAMPY?
TRAMPY?
THE SECOND TIME.
AFTER HE'D SAID NO.
YOUR GRANDFATHER WAS A VERY HANDSOME MAN.
VERY.
ALSO, IT WAS A VERY... LIBERATING... LINE OF WORK FOR A WOMAN OF MY BACKGROUND...
AND THE POINT OF THE STORY IS THAT HE DECLINED TWICE.
PRECISELY.
REALLY. I'D NEVER HAVE EXPECTED SUCH PRUDISHNESS FROM YOU CHILDREN, GIVEN YOUR UPBRINGING.
HEY, LOOK AT THE TIME. WE'D BETTER HEAD OUT, ZED.
YEAH, BEFORE THESE VIXENS CORRUPT US!

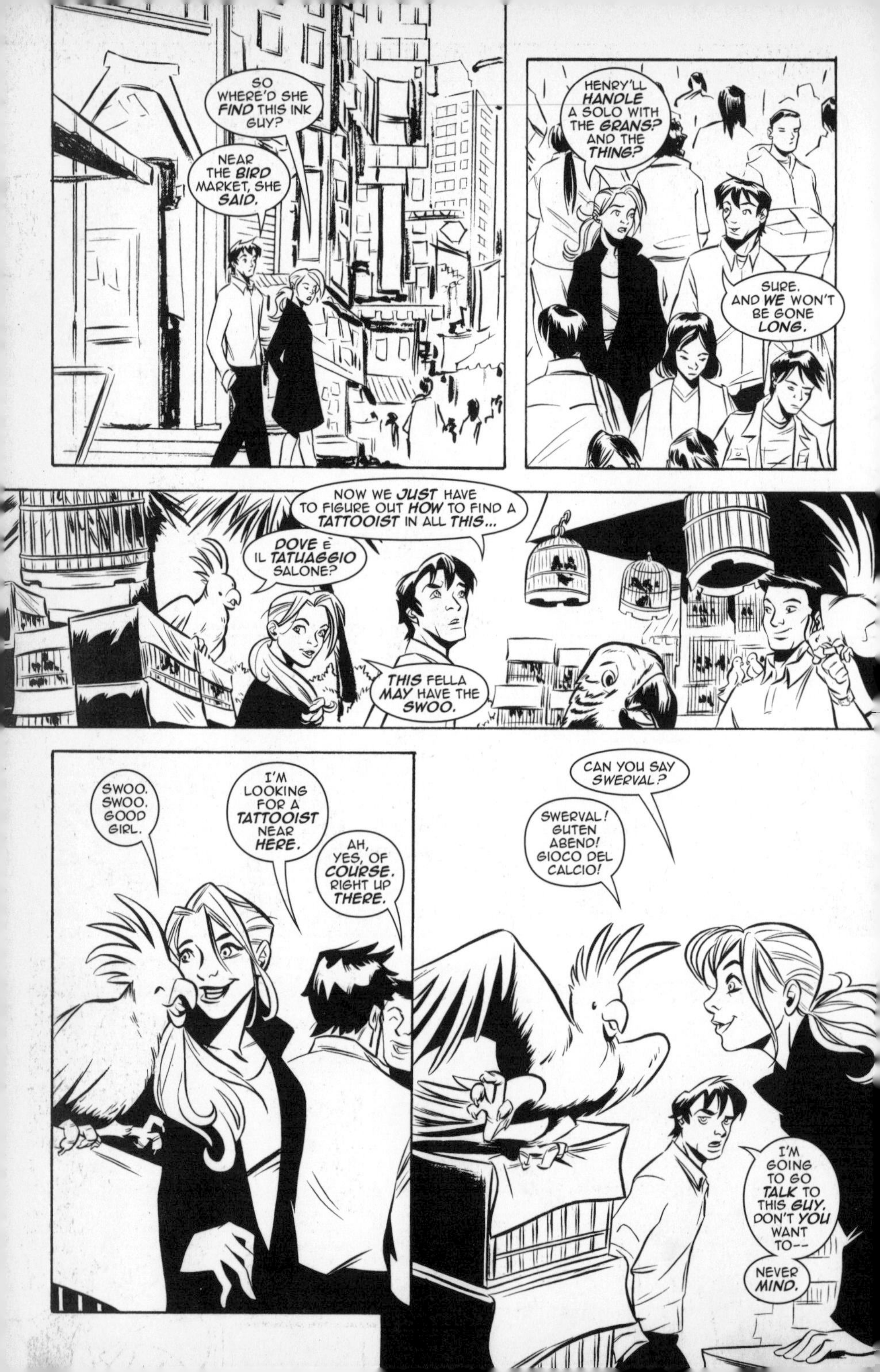
SO WHERE'D SHE FIND THIS INK GUY?
NEAR THE BIRD MARKET, SHE SAID.
HENRY'LL HANDLE A SOLO WITH THE GRANS? AND THE THING?
SURE. AND WE WON'T BE GONE LONG.
NOW WE JUST HAVE TO FIGURE OUT HOW TO FIND A TATTOOIST IN ALL THIS...
DOVE È IL TATUAGGIO SALONE?
THIS FELLA MAY HAVE THE SWOO.
SWOO. SWOO. GOOD GIRL.
I'M LOOKING FOR A TATTOOIST NEAR HERE.
AH, YES, OF COURSE. RIGHT UP THERE.
CAN YOU SAY SWERVAL?
SWERVAL! GUTEN ABEND! GIOCO DEL CALCIO!
I'M GOING TO GO TALK TO THIS GUY. DON'T YOU WANT TO--
NEVER MIND.

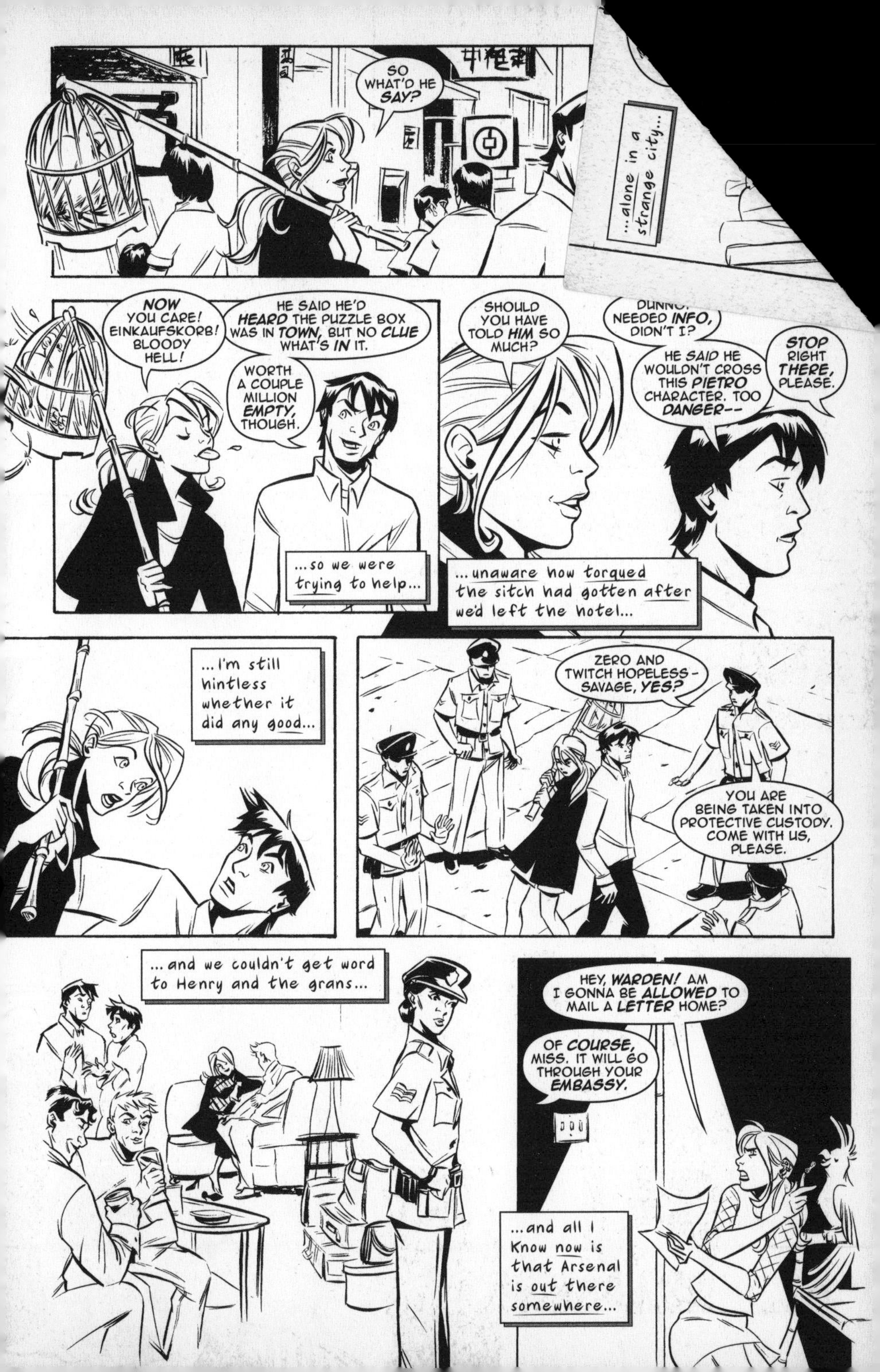
SO WHAT'D HE SAY?
...alone in a strange city...
NOW YOU CARE! EINKAUFSKORB! BLOODY HELL!
HE SAID HE'D HEARD THE PUZZLE BOX WAS IN TOWN, BUT NO CLUE WHAT'S IN IT.
WORTH A COUPLE MILLION EMPTY, THOUGH.
...so we were trying to help...
SHOULD YOU HAVE TOLD HIM SO MUCH?
NEEDED INFO, DIDN'T I?
HE SAID HE WOULDN'T CROSS THIS PIETRO CHARACTER. TOO DANGER--
STOP RIGHT THERE, PLEASE.
...unaware how torqued the sitch had gotten after we'd left the hotel...
...I'm still hintless whether it did any good...
ZERO AND TWITCH HOPELESS-SAVAGE, YES?
YOU ARE BEING TAKEN INTO PROTECTIVE CUSTODY. COME WITH US, PLEASE.
...and we couldn't get word to Henry and the grans...
HEY, WARDEN! AM I GONNA BE ALLOWED TO MAIL A LETTER HOME?
OF COURSE, MISS. IT WILL GO THROUGH YOUR EMBASSY.
...and all I Know now is that Arsenal is out there somewhere...

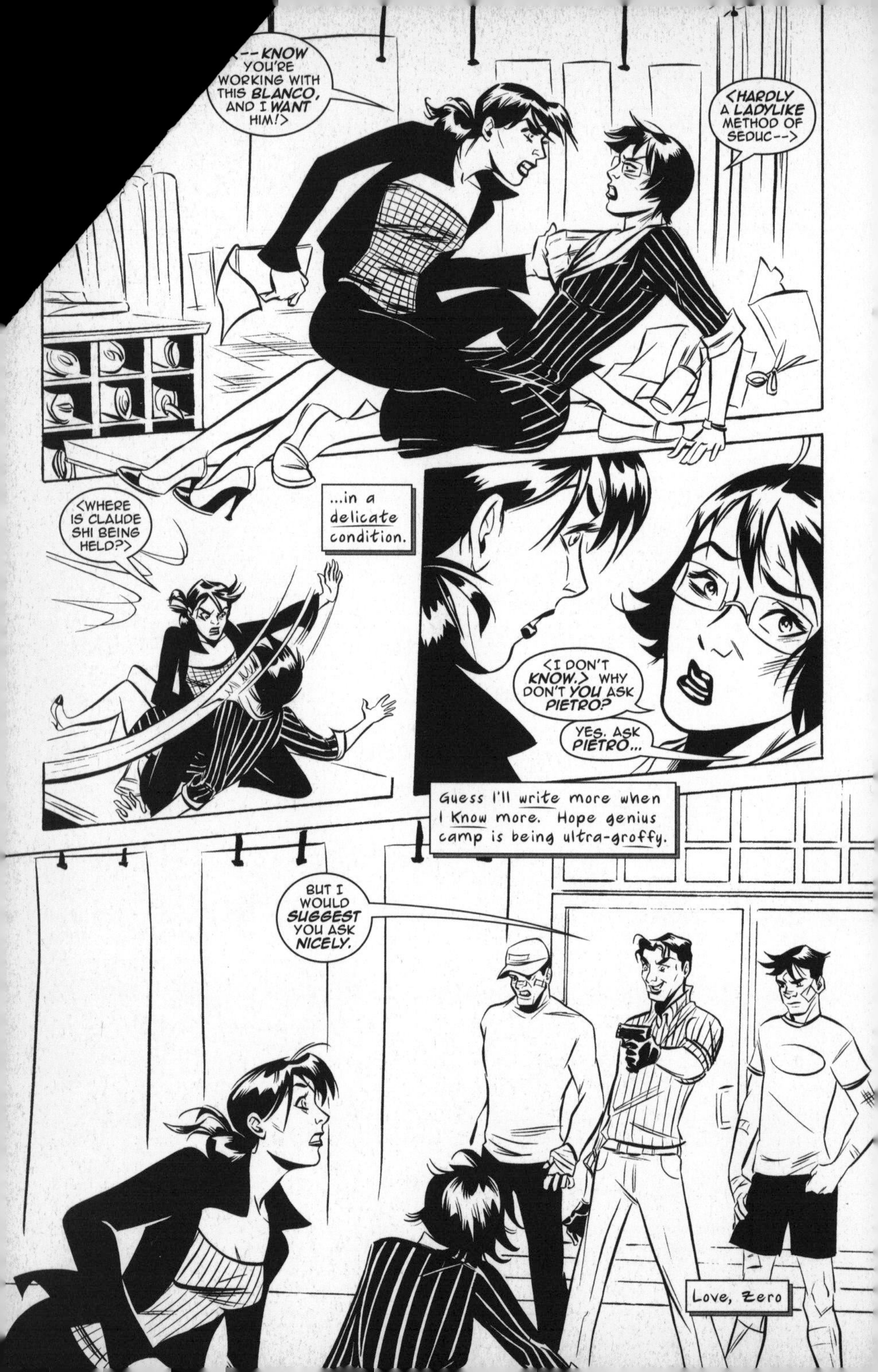
--KNOW YOU'RE WORKING WITH THIS BLANCO, AND I WANT HIM!>
<HARDLY A LADYLIKE METHOD OF SEDUC-->
...in a delicate condition.
<WHERE IS CLAUDE SHI BEING HELD?>
<I DON'T KNOW.> WHY DON'T YOU ASK PIETRO?
YES. ASK PIETRO...
Guess I'll write more when I Know more. Hope genius camp is being ultra-groffy.
BUT I WOULD SUGGEST YOU ASK NICELY.
Love, Zero

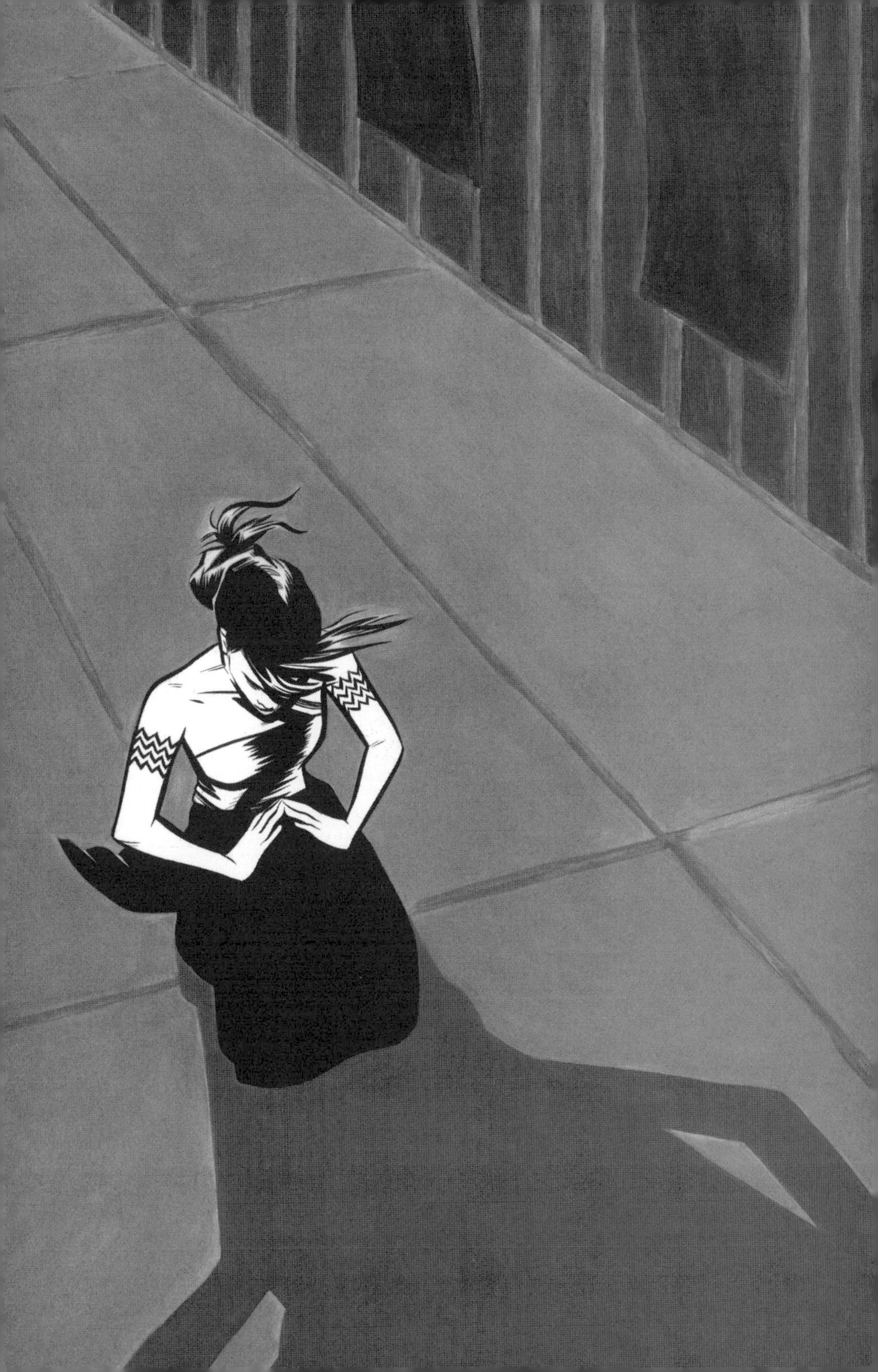

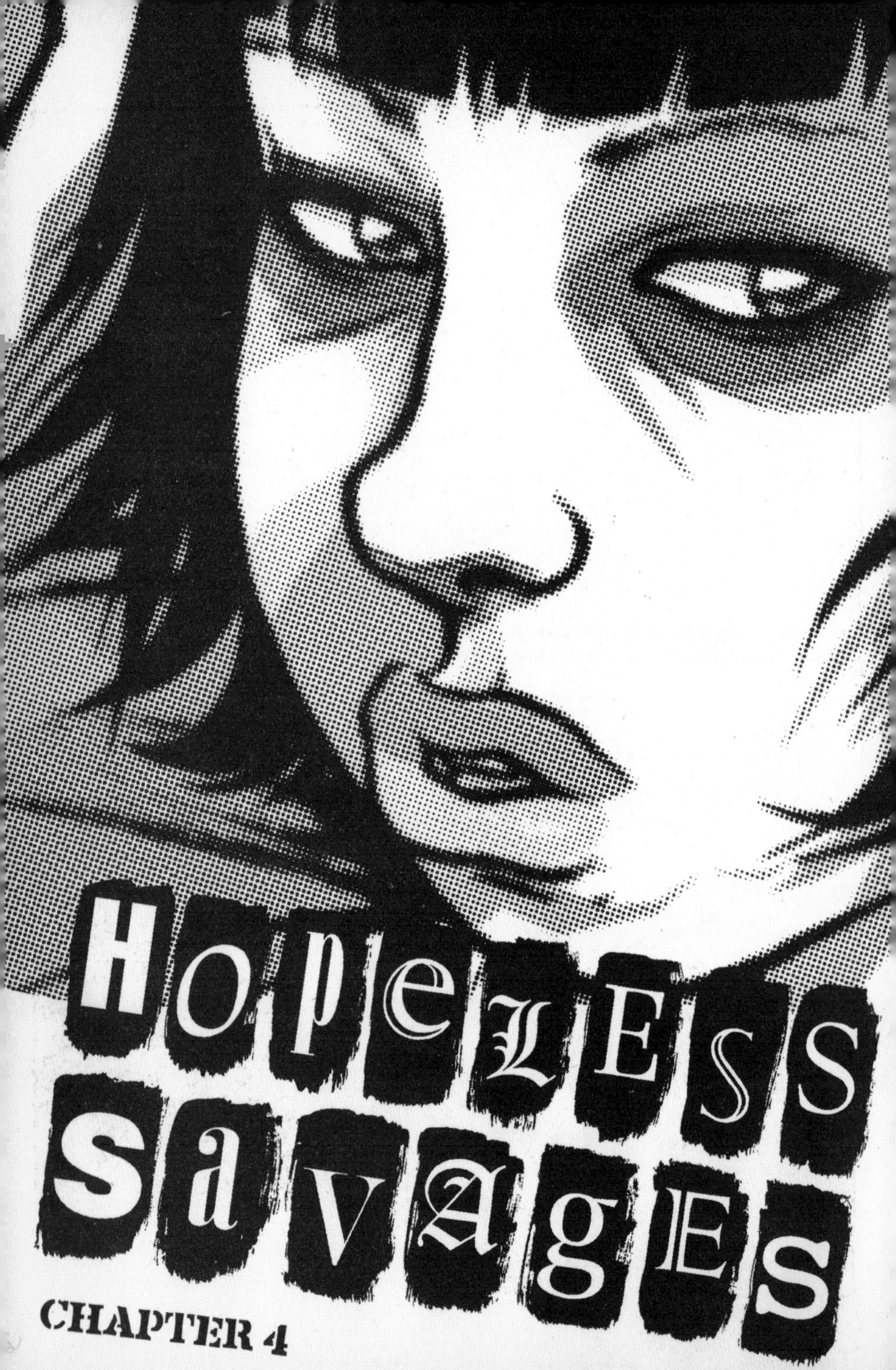

Hopeless Savages

CHAPTER 4

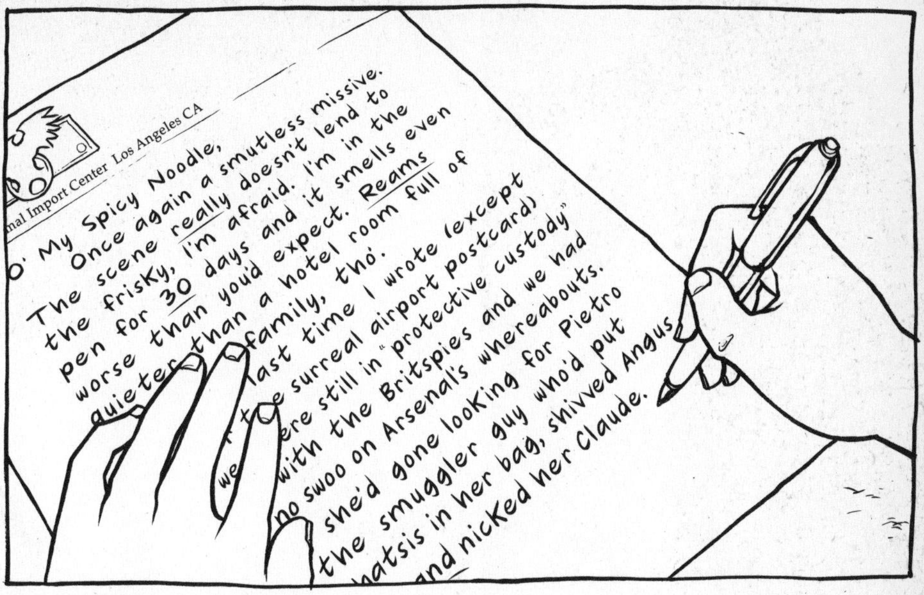
Import Center Los Angeles CA
My Spicy Noodle,
Once again a smutless missive.
The scene really doesn't lend to
the frisky, I'm afraid. I'm in the
pen for 30 days and it smells even
worse than you'd expect. Reams
quieter than a hotel room full of
family, tho.
last time I wrote (except
surreal airport postcard)
ere still in "protective custody"
with the Britspies and we had
no swoo on Arsenal's whereabouts.
she'd gone looking for Pietro
the smuggler guy who'd put
natsis in her bag, shivved Angus
and nicked her Claude.

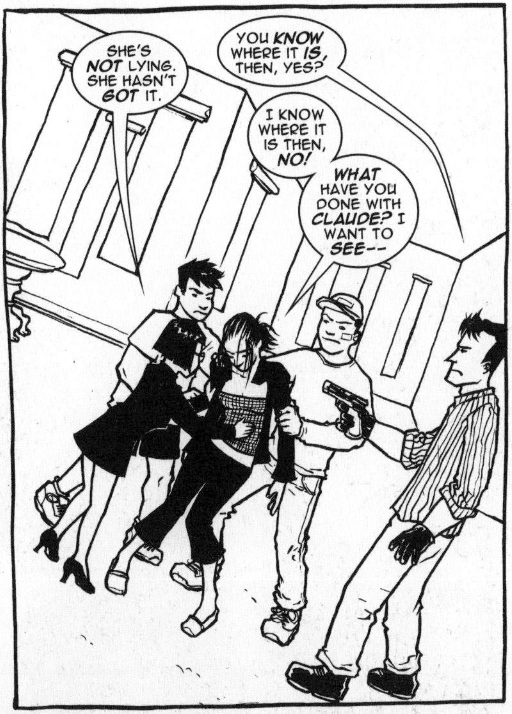
SHE'S NOT LYING. SHE HASN'T GOT IT.
YOU KNOW WHERE IT IS, THEN, YES?
I KNOW WHERE IT IS THEN, NO!
WHAT HAVE YOU DONE WITH CLAUDE? I WANT TO SEE--

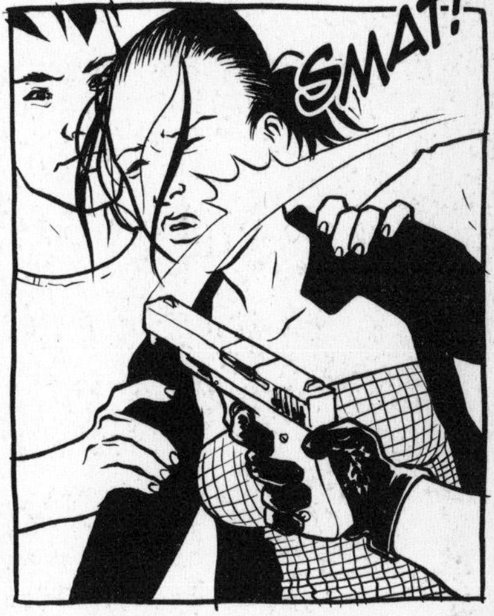
SMAT!

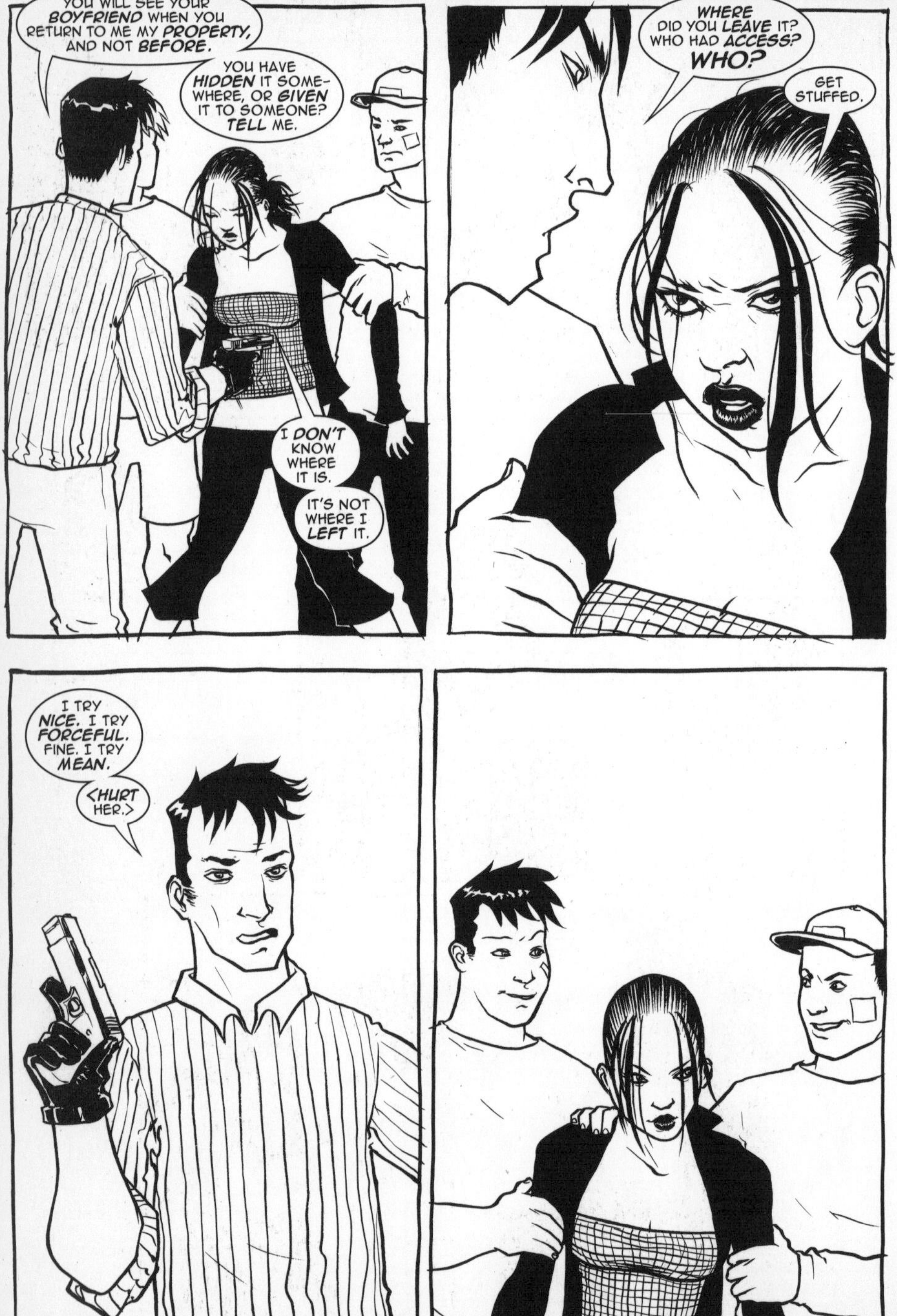
YOU WILL SEE YOUR BOYFRIEND WHEN YOU RETURN TO ME MY PROPERTY, AND NOT BEFORE.
YOU HAVE HIDDEN IT SOMEWHERE, OR GIVEN IT TO SOMEONE? TELL ME.
I DON'T KNOW WHERE IT IS.
IT'S NOT WHERE I LEFT IT.
WHERE DID YOU LEAVE IT? WHO HAD ACCESS? WHO?
GET STUFFED.
I TRY NICE. I TRY FORCEFUL. FINE. I TRY MEAN.
<HURT HER.>

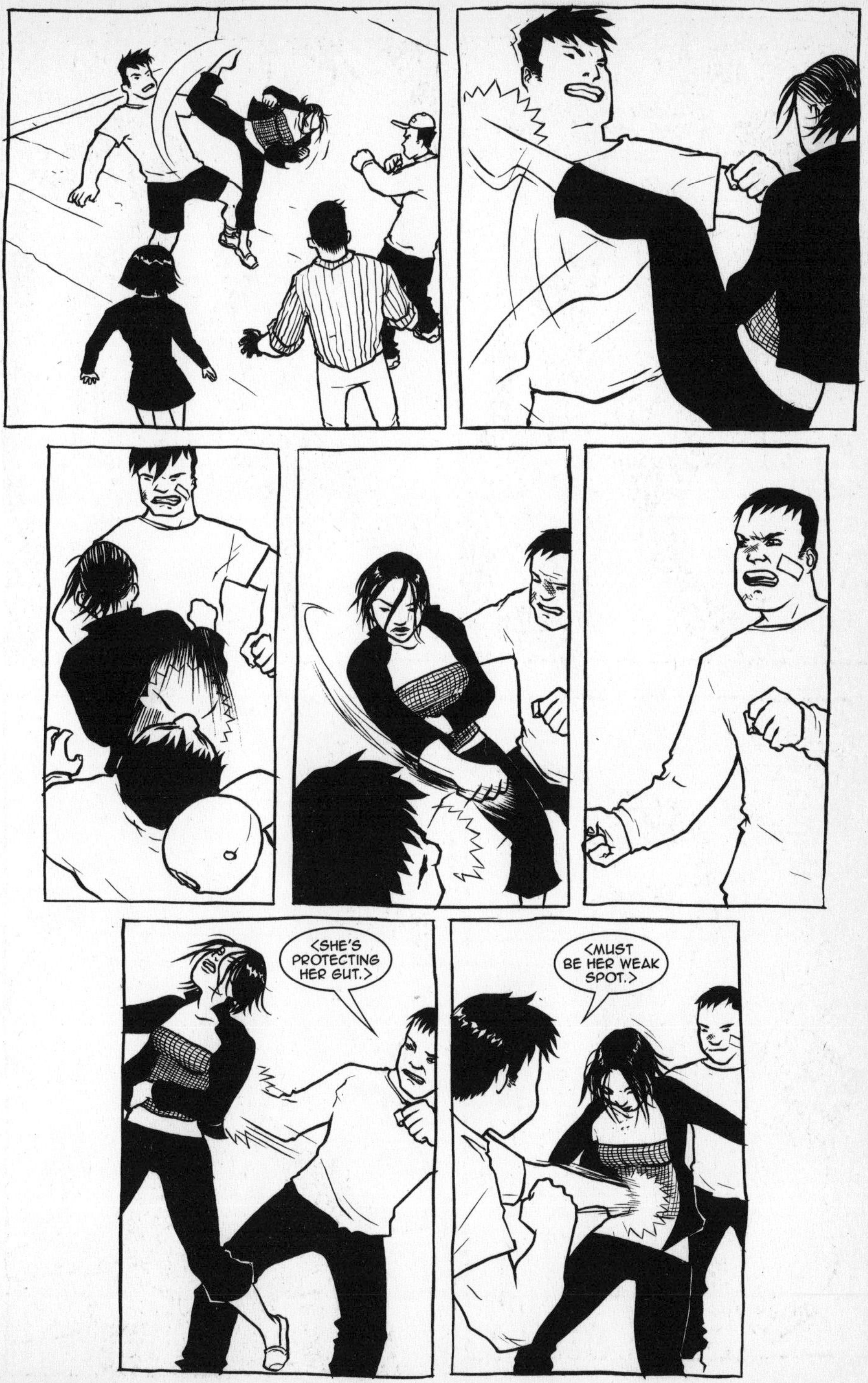
<SHE'S PROTECTING HER GUT.>
<MUST BE HER WEAK SPOT.>

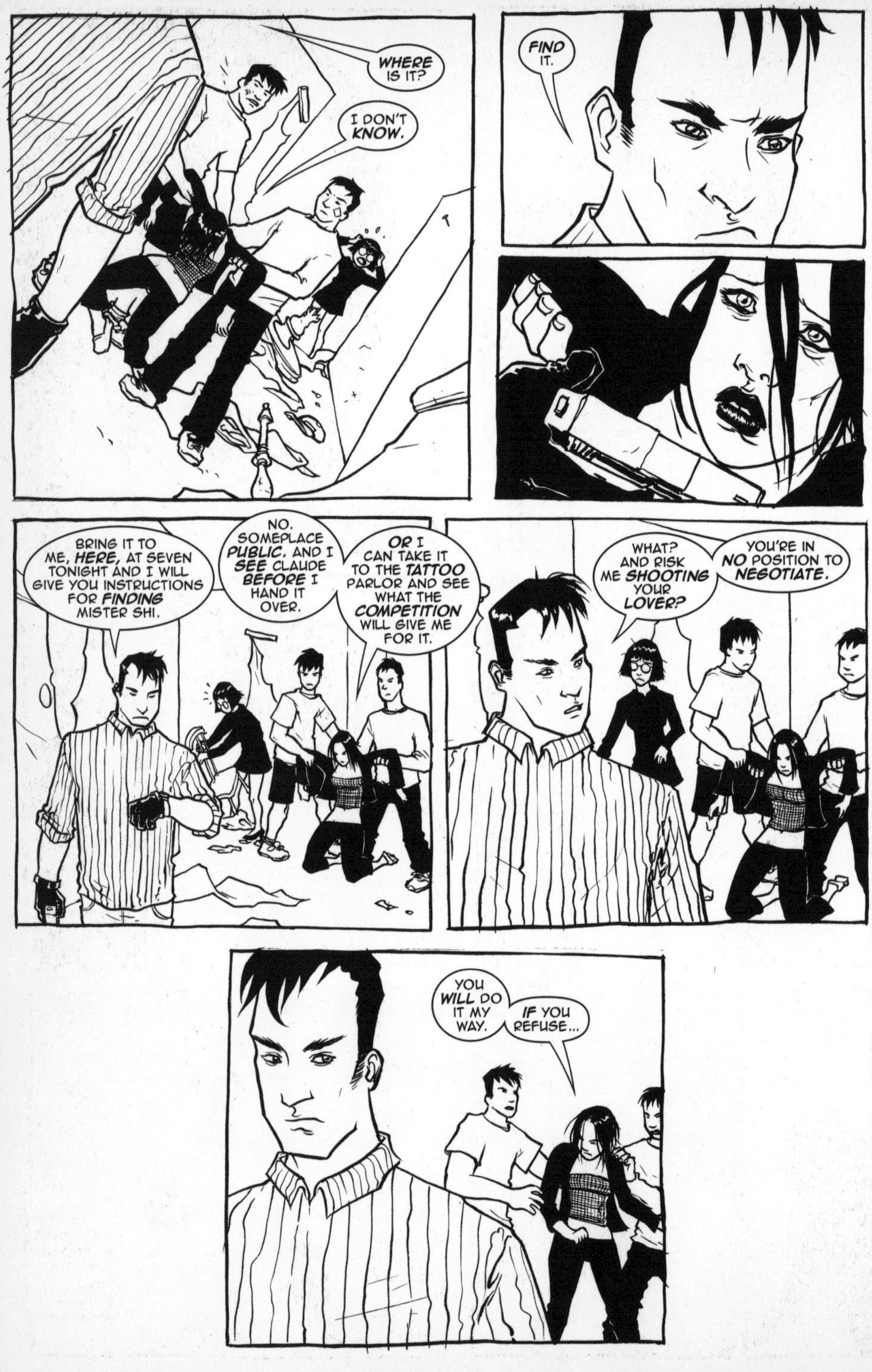
WHERE IS IT?
I DON'T KNOW.
FIND IT.
BRING IT TO ME, HERE, AT SEVEN TONIGHT AND I WILL GIVE YOU INSTRUCTIONS FOR FINDING MISTER SHI.
NO. SOMEPLACE PUBLIC. AND I SEE CLAUDE BEFORE I HAND IT OVER.
OR I CAN TAKE IT TO THE TATTOO PARLOR AND SEE WHAT THE COMPETITION WILL GIVE ME FOR IT.
WHAT? AND RISK ME SHOOTING YOUR LOVER?
YOU'RE IN NO POSITION TO NEGOTIATE.
YOU WILL DO IT MY WAY.
IF YOU REFUSE...

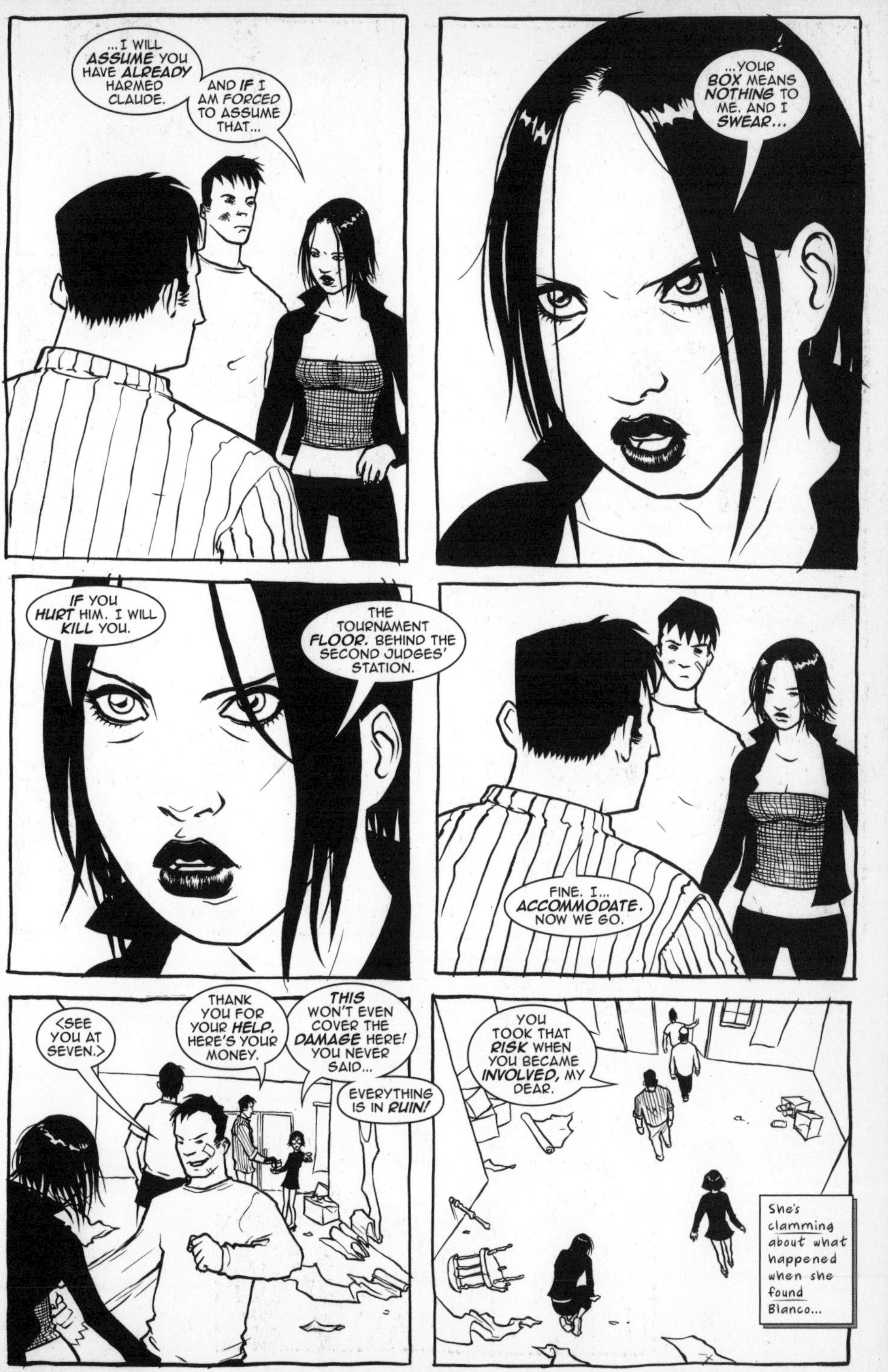
...I WILL ASSUME YOU HAVE ALREADY HARMED CLAUDE.
AND IF I AM FORCED TO ASSUME THAT...
...YOUR BOX MEANS NOTHING TO ME. AND I SWEAR...
IF YOU HURT HIM, I WILL KILL YOU.
THE TOURNAMENT FLOOR. BEHIND THE SECOND JUDGES' STATION.
FINE. I... ACCOMMODATE. NOW WE GO.
<SEE YOU AT SEVEN.>
THANK YOU FOR YOUR HELP. HERE'S YOUR MONEY.
THIS WON'T EVEN COVER THE DAMAGE HERE! YOU NEVER SAID...
EVERYTHING IS IN RUIN!
YOU TOOK THAT RISK WHEN YOU BECAME INVOLVED, MY DEAR.
She's clamming about what happened when she found Blanco...

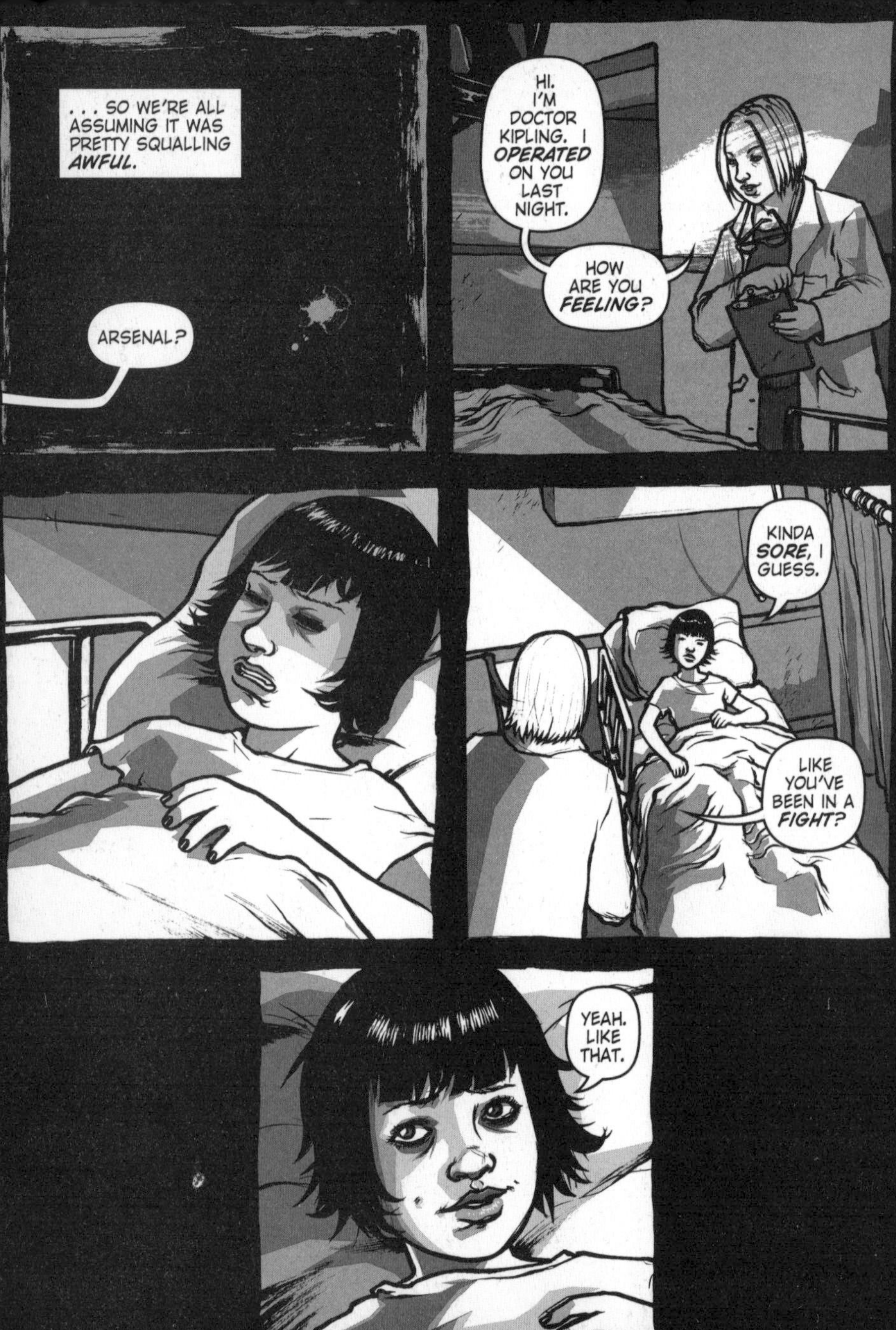
. . . SO WE'RE ALL ASSUMING IT WAS PRETTY SQUALLING AWFUL.
ARSENAL?
HI. I'M DOCTOR KIPLING. I OPERATED ON YOU LAST NIGHT.
HOW ARE YOU FEELING?
KINDA SORE, I GUESS.
LIKE YOU'VE BEEN IN A FIGHT?
YEAH. LIKE THAT.

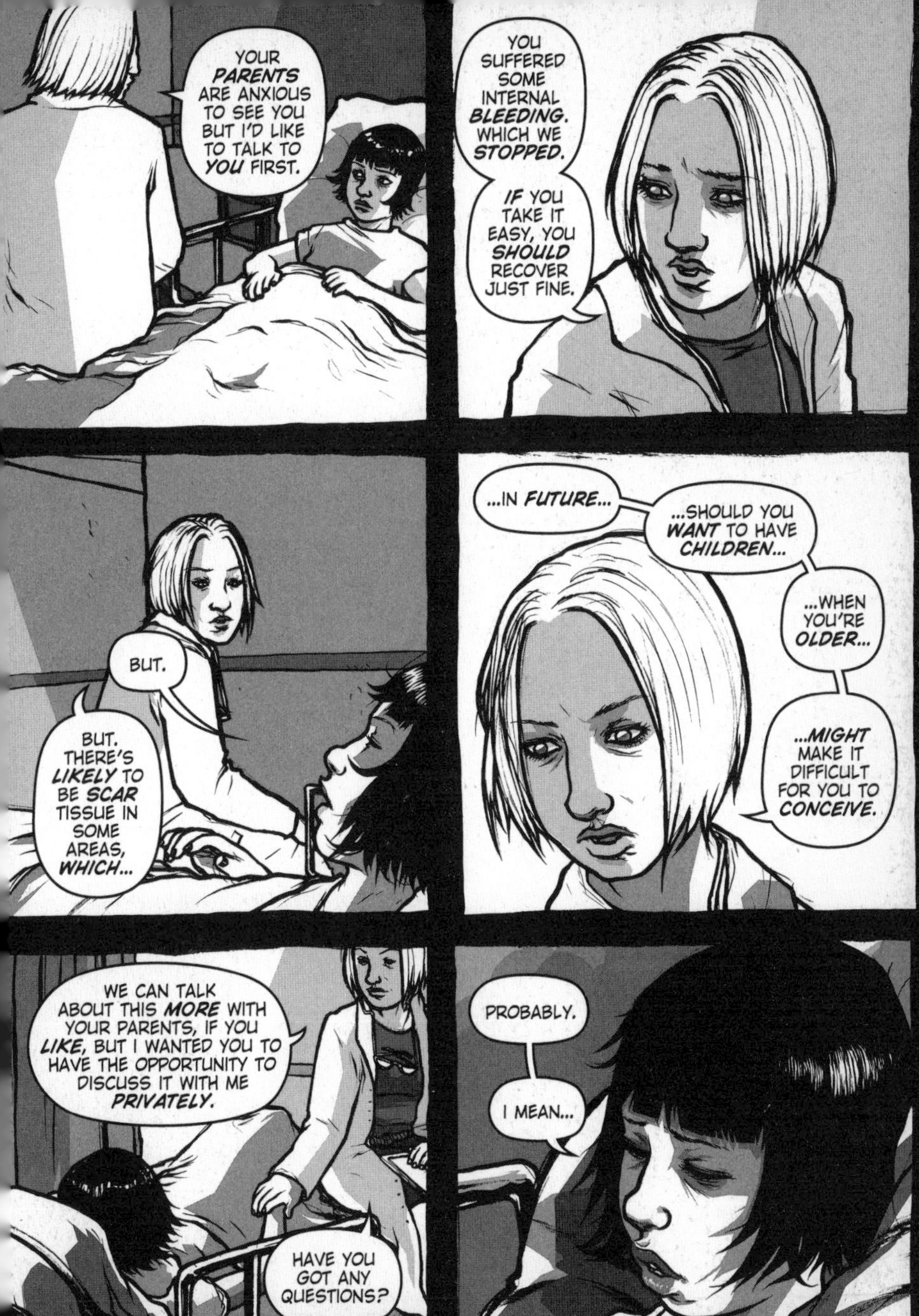
YOUR PARENTS ARE ANXIOUS TO SEE YOU BUT I'D LIKE TO TALK TO YOU FIRST.
YOU SUFFERED SOME INTERNAL BLEEDING. WHICH WE STOPPED.
IF YOU TAKE IT EASY, YOU SHOULD RECOVER JUST FINE.
BUT.
BUT. THERE'S LIKELY TO BE SCAR TISSUE IN SOME AREAS, WHICH...
...IN FUTURE...
...SHOULD YOU WANT TO HAVE CHILDREN...
...WHEN YOU'RE OLDER...
...MIGHT MAKE IT DIFFICULT FOR YOU TO CONCEIVE.
WE CAN TALK ABOUT THIS MORE WITH YOUR PARENTS, IF YOU LIKE, BUT I WANTED YOU TO HAVE THE OPPORTUNITY TO DISCUSS IT WITH ME PRIVATELY.
HAVE YOU GOT ANY QUESTIONS?
PROBABLY.
I MEAN...

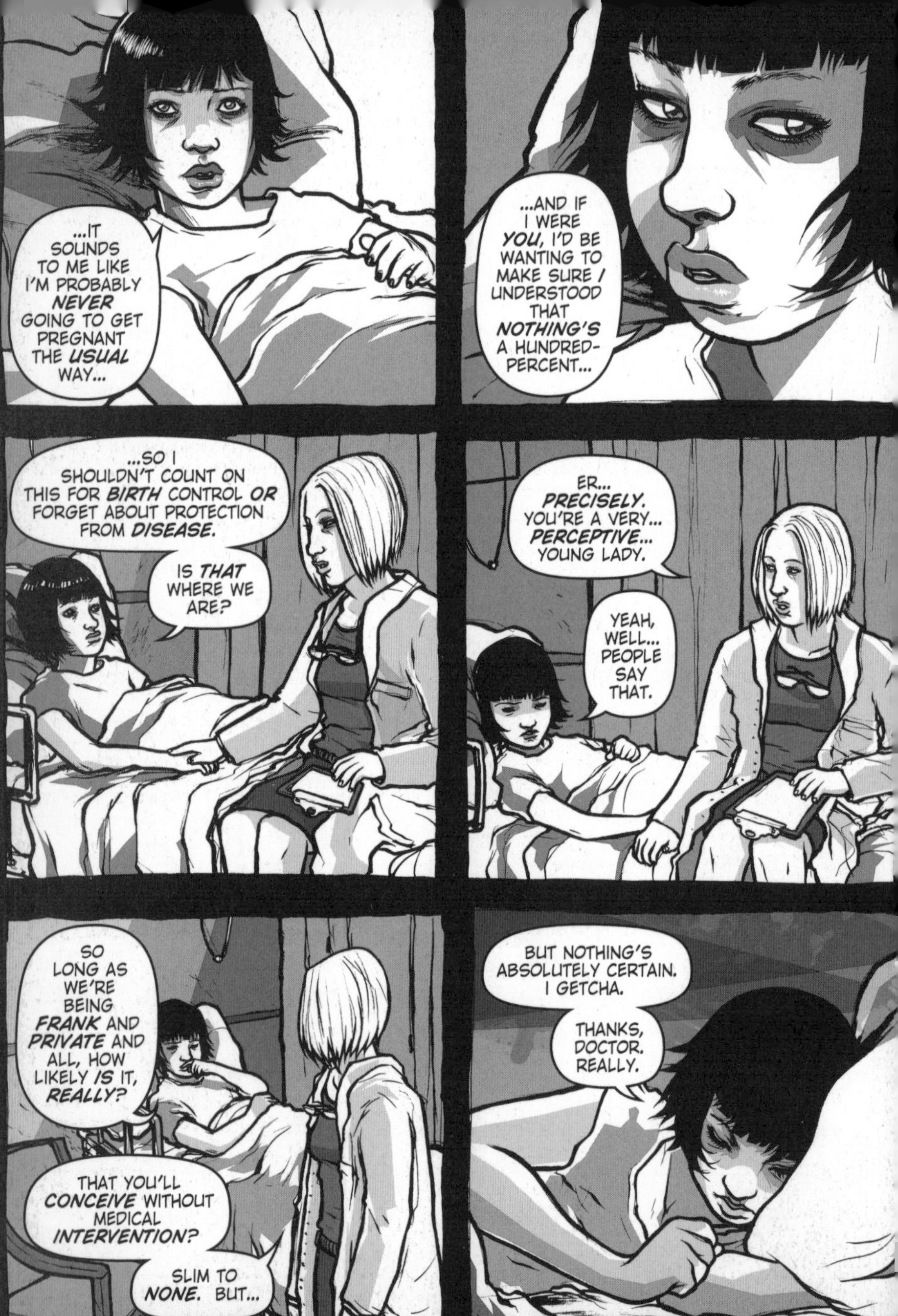
...IT SOUNDS TO ME LIKE I'M PROBABLY NEVER GOING TO GET PREGNANT THE USUAL WAY...
...AND IF I WERE YOU, I'D BE WANTING TO MAKE SURE I UNDERSTOOD THAT NOTHING'S A HUNDRED-PERCENT...
...SO I SHOULDN'T COUNT ON THIS FOR BIRTH CONTROL OR FORGET ABOUT PROTECTION FROM DISEASE.
IS THAT WHERE WE ARE?
ER... PRECISELY. YOU'RE A VERY... PERCEPTIVE... YOUNG LADY.
YEAH, WELL... PEOPLE SAY THAT.
SO LONG AS WE'RE BEING FRANK AND PRIVATE AND ALL, HOW LIKELY IS IT, REALLY?
THAT YOU'LL CONCEIVE WITHOUT MEDICAL INTERVENTION?
SLIM TO NONE. BUT...
BUT NOTHING'S ABSOLUTELY CERTAIN. I GETCHA.
THANKS, DOCTOR. REALLY.

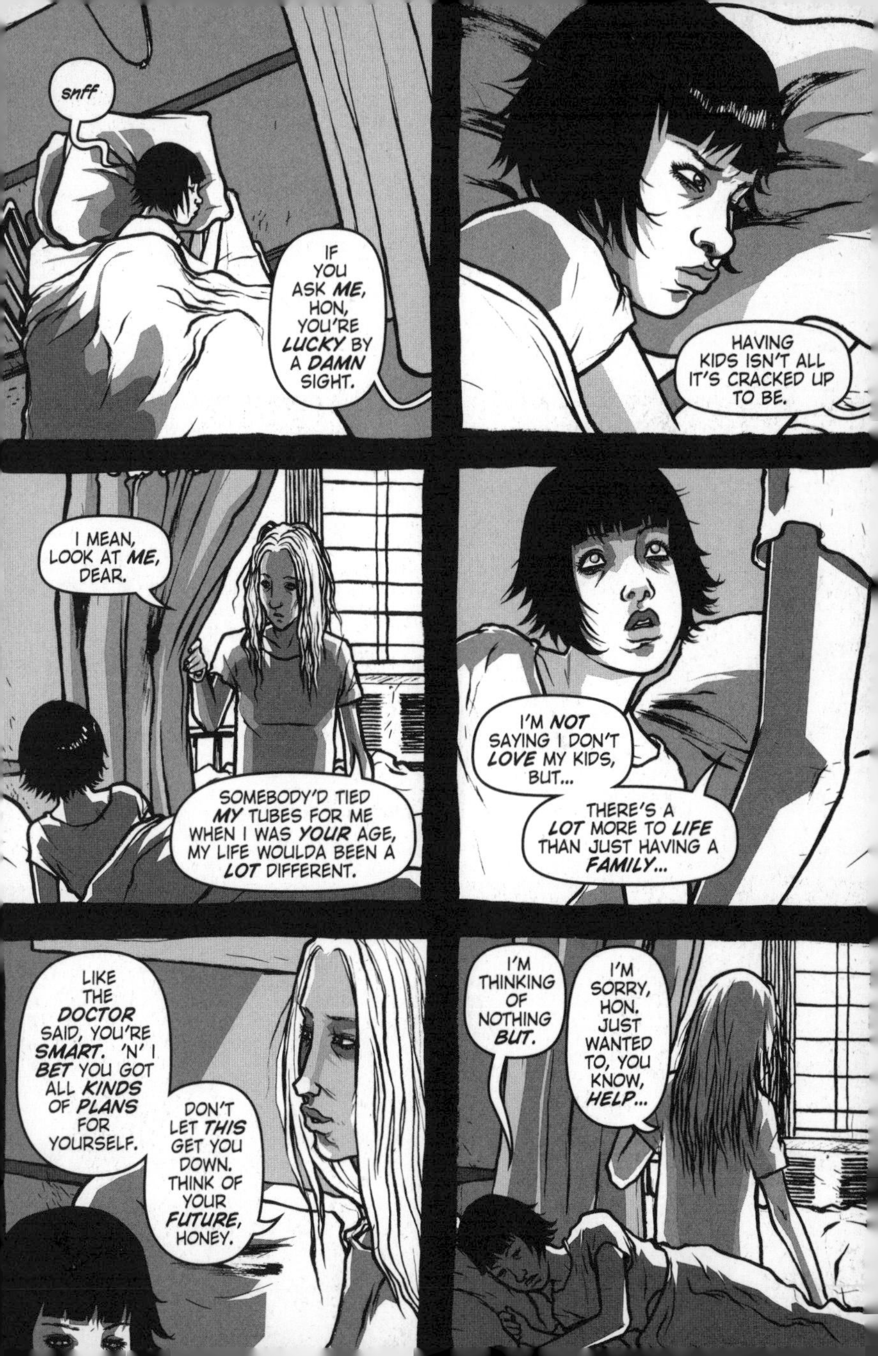
snff
IF YOU ASK ME, HON, YOU'RE LUCKY BY A DAMN SIGHT.
HAVING KIDS ISN'T ALL IT'S CRACKED UP TO BE.
I MEAN, LOOK AT ME, DEAR.
SOMEBODY'D TIED MY TUBES FOR ME WHEN I WAS YOUR AGE, MY LIFE WOULDA BEEN A LOT DIFFERENT.
I'M NOT SAYING I DON'T LOVE MY KIDS, BUT...
THERE'S A LOT MORE TO LIFE THAN JUST HAVING A FAMILY...
LIKE THE DOCTOR SAID, YOU'RE SMART. 'N' I BET YOU GOT ALL KINDS OF PLANS FOR YOURSELF.
DON'T LET THIS GET YOU DOWN. THINK OF YOUR FUTURE, HONEY.
I'M THINKING OF NOTHING BUT.
I'M SORRY, HON. JUST WANTED TO, YOU KNOW, HELP...

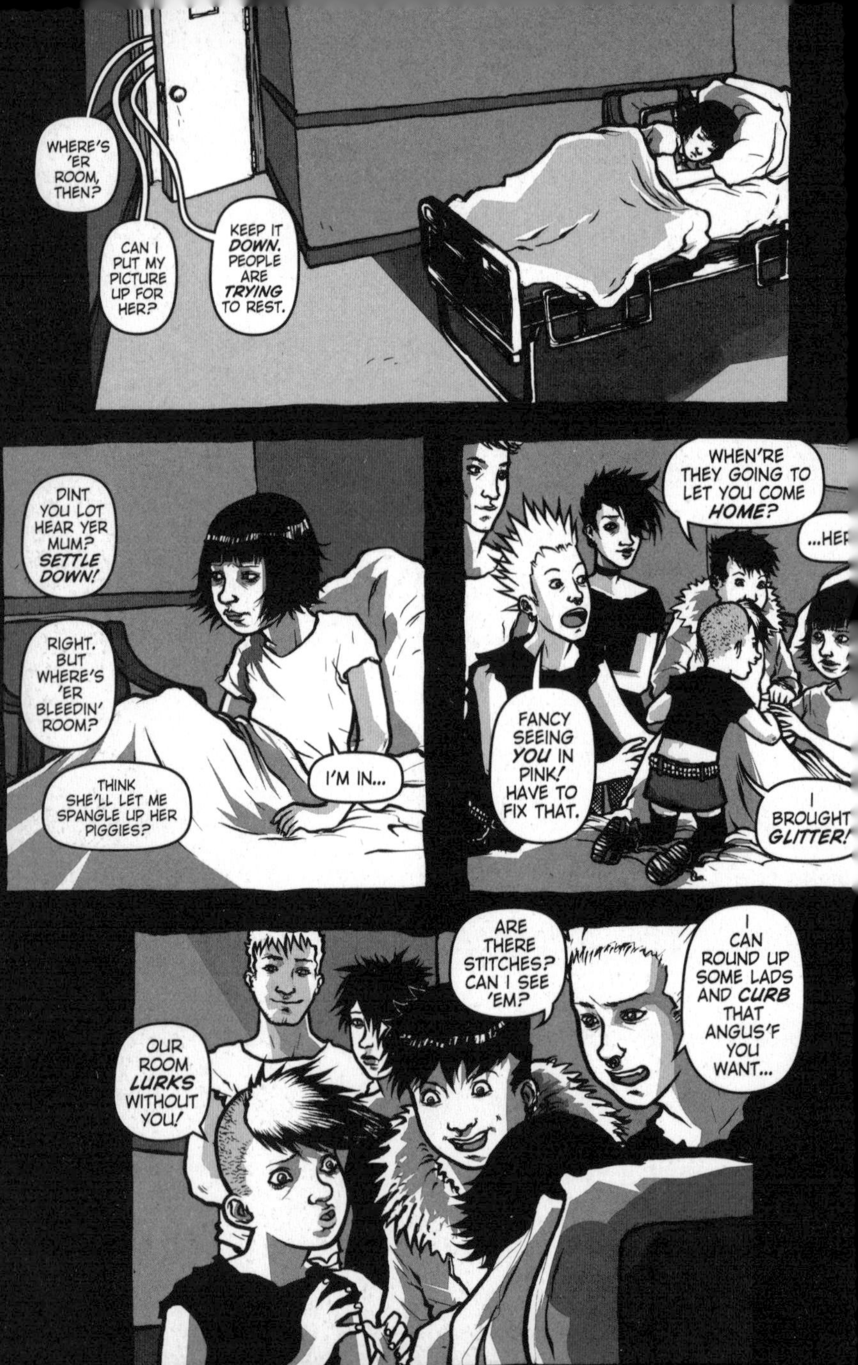

WHERE'S 'ER ROOM, THEN?
CAN I PUT MY PICTURE UP FOR HER?
KEEP IT DOWN. PEOPLE ARE TRYING TO REST.
DINT YOU LOT HEAR YER MUM? SETTLE DOWN!
RIGHT. BUT WHERE'S 'ER BLEEDIN' ROOM?
THINK SHE'LL LET ME SPANGLE UP HER PIGGIES?
I'M IN...
WHEN'RE THEY GOING TO LET YOU COME HOME?
...HEI
FANCY SEEING YOU IN PINK! HAVE TO FIX THAT.
I BROUGHT GLITTER!
ARE THERE STITCHES? CAN I SEE 'EM?
I CAN ROUND UP SOME LADS AND CURB THAT ANGUS'F YOU WANT...
OUR ROOM LURKS WITHOUT YOU!

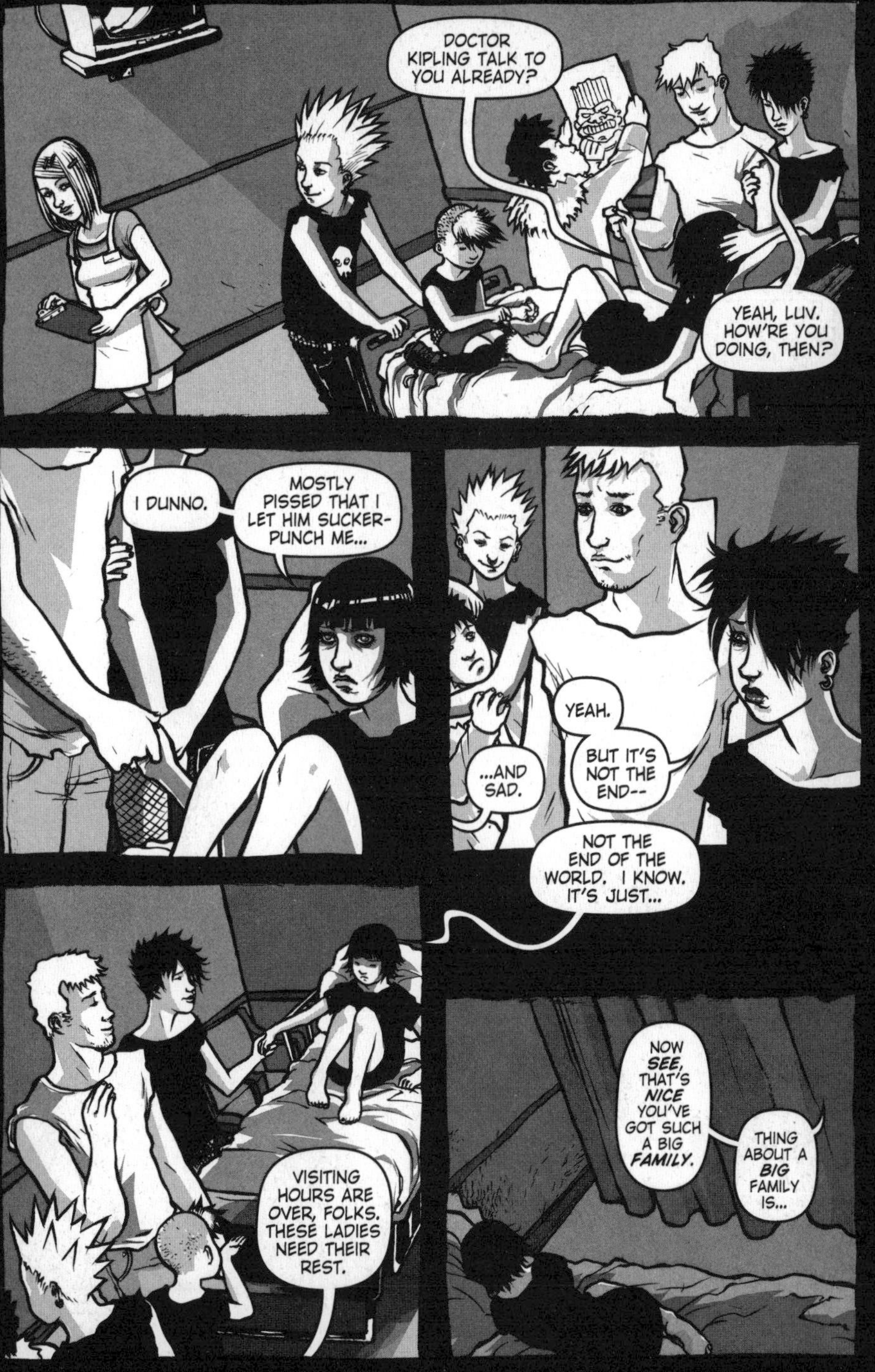
DOCTOR KIPLING TALK TO YOU ALREADY?
YEAH, LUV. HOW'RE YOU DOING, THEN?
I DUNNO.
MOSTLY PISSED THAT I LET HIM SUCKER-PUNCH ME...
...AND SAD.
YEAH.
BUT IT'S NOT THE END--
NOT THE END OF THE WORLD. I KNOW. IT'S JUST...
VISITING HOURS ARE OVER, FOLKS. THESE LADIES NEED THEIR REST.
NOW SEE, THAT'S NICE YOU'VE GOT SUCH A BIG FAMILY.
THING ABOUT A BIG FAMILY IS...

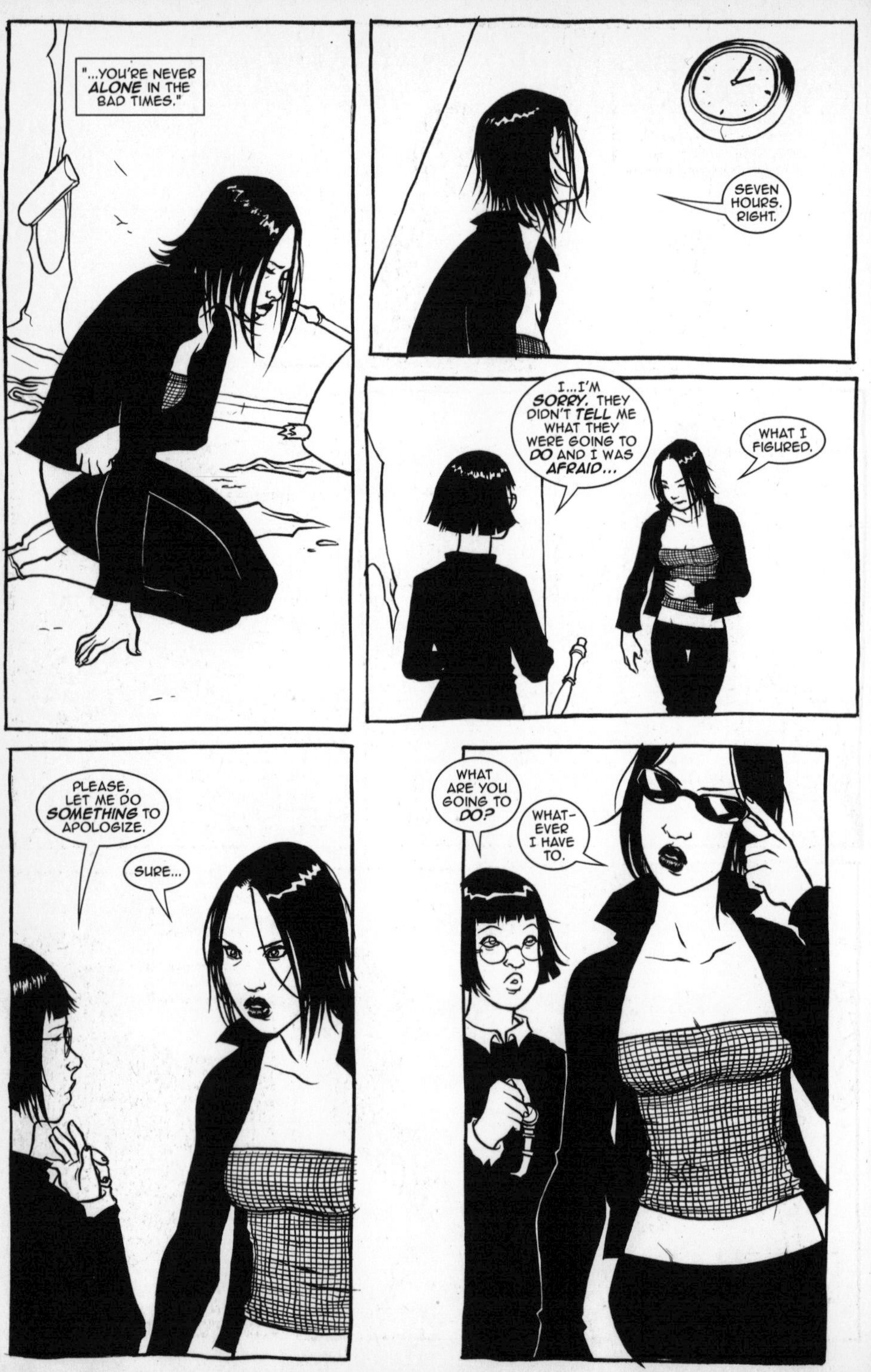
"...YOU'RE NEVER ALONE IN THE BAD TIMES."
SEVEN HOURS. RIGHT.
I...I'M SORRY. THEY DIDN'T TELL ME WHAT THEY WERE GOING TO DO AND I WAS AFRAID...
WHAT I FIGURED.
PLEASE, LET ME DO SOMETHING TO APOLOGIZE.
SURE...
WHAT ARE YOU GOING TO DO?
WHAT-EVER I HAVE TO.

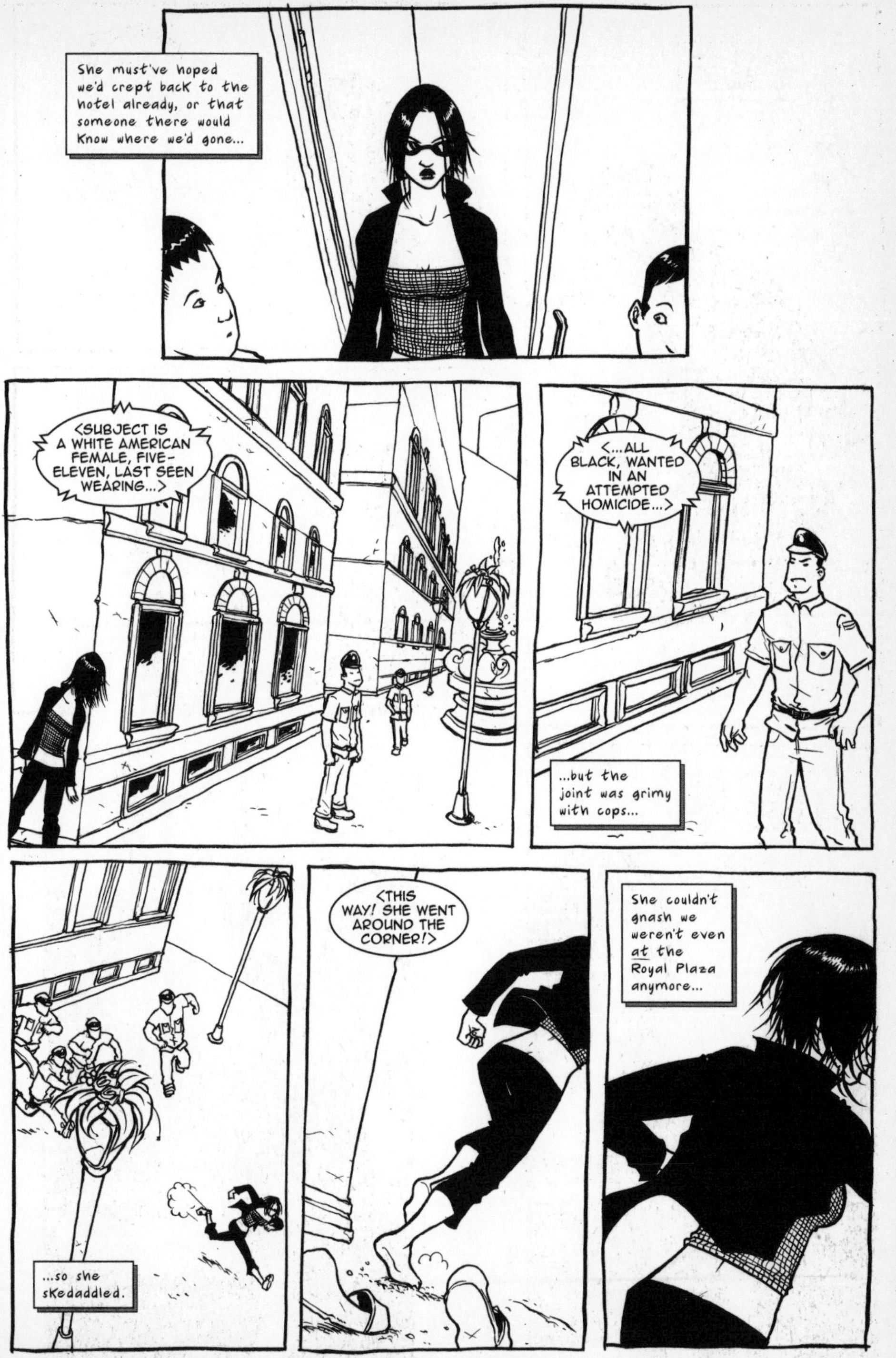
She must've hoped we'd crept back to the hotel already, or that someone there would Know where we'd gone...
<SUBJECT IS A WHITE AMERICAN FEMALE, FIVE-ELEVEN, LAST SEEN WEARING...>
<...ALL BLACK, WANTED IN AN ATTEMPTED HOMICIDE...>
...but the joint was grimy with cops...
...so she sKedaddled.
<THIS WAY! SHE WENT AROUND THE CORNER!>
She couldn't gnash we weren't even at the Royal Plaza anymore...

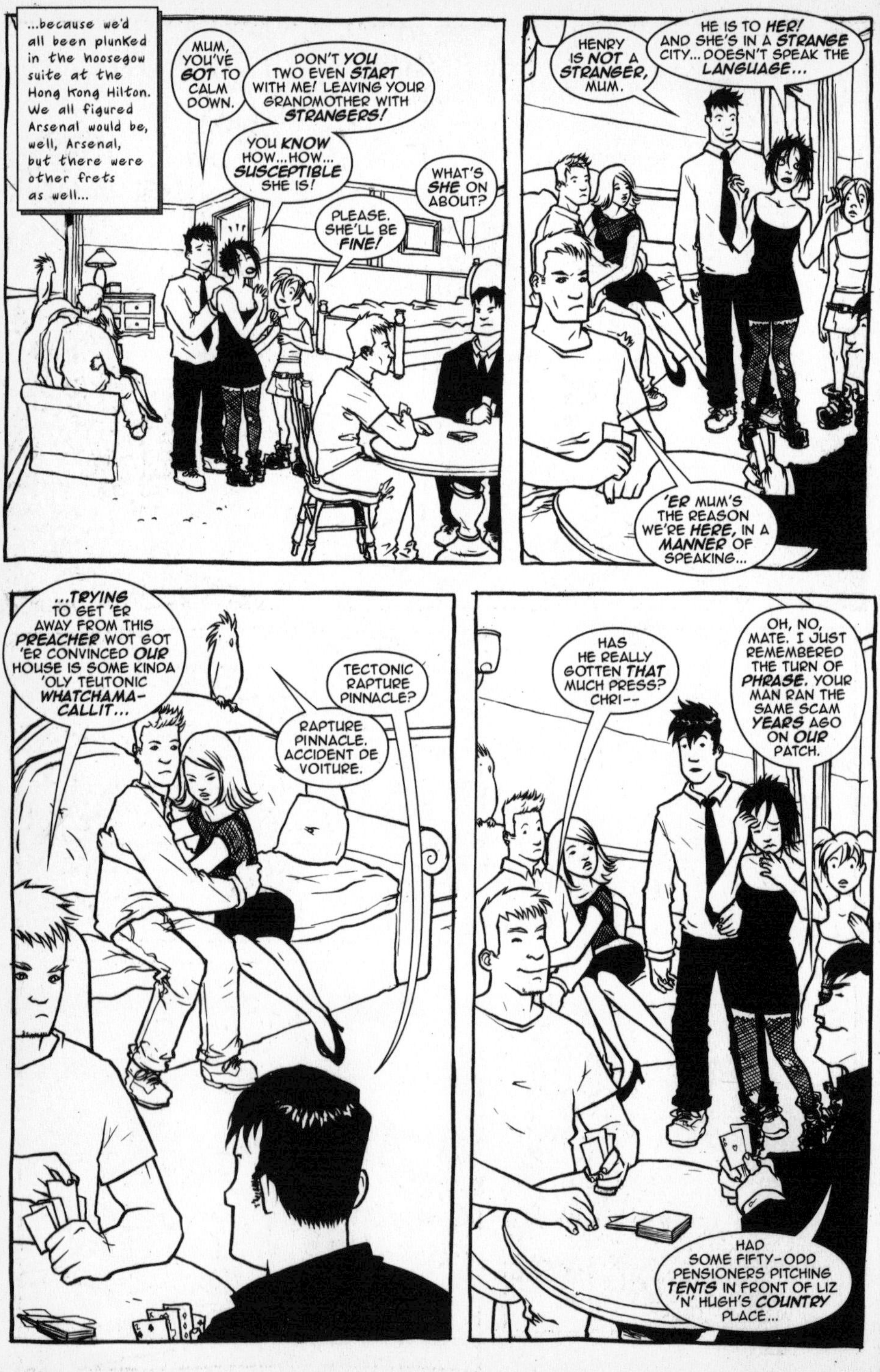
...because we'd all been plunked in the hoosegow suite at the Hong Kong Hilton. We all figured Arsenal would be, well, Arsenal, but there were other frets as well...
MUM, YOU'VE GOT TO CALM DOWN.
DON'T YOU TWO EVEN START WITH ME! LEAVING YOUR GRANDMOTHER WITH STRANGERS!
YOU KNOW HOW...HOW... SUSCEPTIBLE SHE IS!
PLEASE. SHE'LL BE FINE!
WHAT'S SHE ON ABOUT?
HENRY IS NOT A STRANGER, MUM.
HE IS TO HER! AND SHE'S IN A STRANGE CITY... DOESN'T SPEAK THE LANGUAGE...
'ER MUM'S THE REASON WE'RE HERE, IN A MANNER OF SPEAKING...
...TRYING TO GET 'ER AWAY FROM THIS PREACHER WOT GOT 'ER CONVINCED OUR HOUSE IS SOME KINDA 'OLY TEUTONIC WHATCHAMA-CALLIT...
RAPTURE PINNACLE. ACCIDENT DE VOITURE.
TECTONIC RAPTURE PINNACLE?
HAS HE REALLY GOTTEN THAT MUCH PRESS? CHRI--
OH, NO, MATE. I JUST REMEMBERED THE TURN OF PHRASE. YOUR MAN RAN THE SAME SCAM YEARS AGO ON OUR PATCH.
HAD SOME FIFTY-ODD PENSIONERS PITCHING TENTS IN FRONT OF LIZ 'N' HUGH'S COUNTRY PLACE...

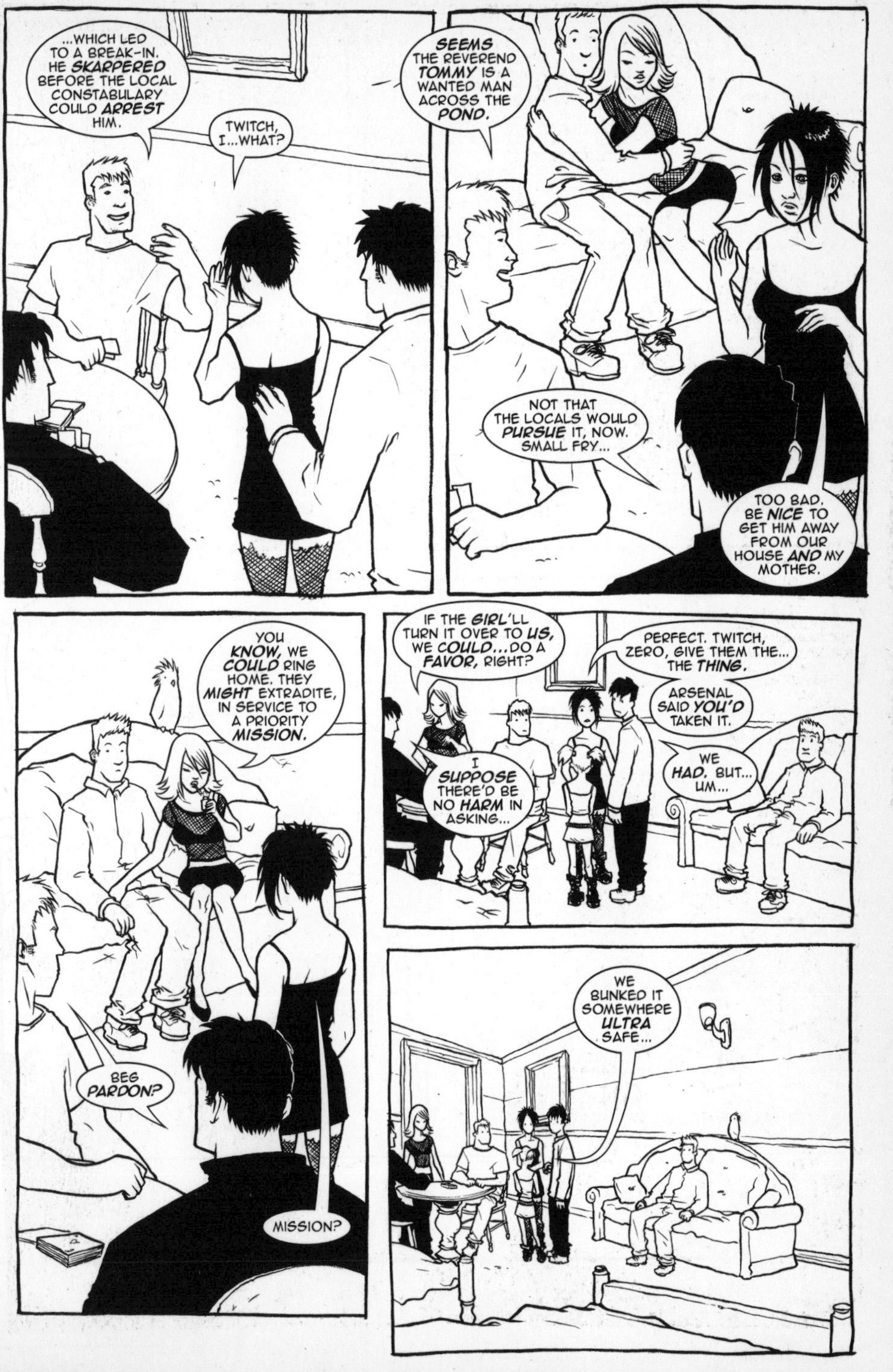
...WHICH LED TO A BREAK-IN. HE SKARPERED BEFORE THE LOCAL CONSTABULARY COULD ARREST HIM.
TWITCH, I...WHAT?
SEEMS THE REVEREND TOMMY IS A WANTED MAN ACROSS THE POND.
NOT THAT THE LOCALS WOULD PURSUE IT, NOW. SMALL FRY...
TOO BAD. BE NICE TO GET HIM AWAY FROM OUR HOUSE AND MY MOTHER.
YOU KNOW, WE COULD RING HOME. THEY MIGHT EXTRADITE, IN SERVICE TO A PRIORITY MISSION.
BEG PARDON?
MISSION?
IF THE GIRL'LL TURN IT OVER TO US, WE COULD...DO A FAVOR, RIGHT?
I SUPPOSE THERE'D BE NO HARM IN ASKING...
PERFECT. TWITCH, ZERO, GIVE THEM THE... THE THING.
ARSENAL SAID YOU'D TAKEN IT.
WE HAD. BUT... UM...
WE BUNKED IT SOMEWHERE ULTRA SAFE...

YOU LEFT IT WITH MY MOTHER?! THE TOP-SECRET THING KILLERS ARE LOOKING FOR, YOU LEFT WITH MY POOR DEFENSELESS WIDOWED MOTHER FROM NEBRASKA!? SHE MUST BE A WRECK!
LOVELY LITTLE THING. YOU WON'T SHOW ME HOW TO OPEN IT?
NO. IN MY DAY IT WAS USED TO SMUGGLE MOST DANGEROUS SECRETS.
IF IT IS STILL BEING USED FOR SUCH PURPOSES, BETTER WE DON'T KNOW.
YOU SAY THAT, BUT YOU STILL INSIST ON GOING OUT SIGHTSEEING?
YOU WORRY TOO MUCH.
VERA DESERVES TO SEE THE CITY AFTER COMING ALL THIS WAY.
AT LEAST LET ME LEAVE A NOTE FOR TWITCH AND ZERO, TELLING THEM WHERE WE'VE GONE...
AS YOU WISH. PUT DOWN THE FLOWER MARKET, THE SYMPHONY, THE OLD HARBOR--
YOU'RE GOING TO BRING IT WITH US?
IT'S PERFECTLY SAFE. WHO WOULD THINK TO LOOK FOR IT...

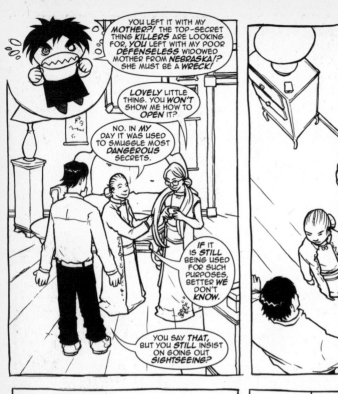

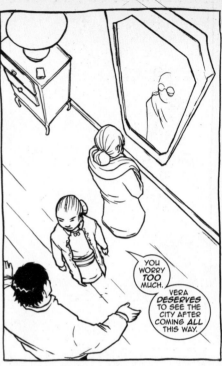

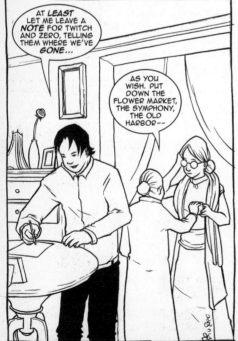

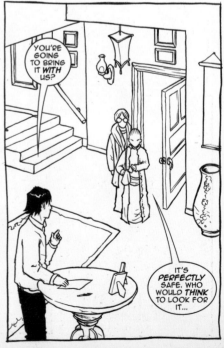

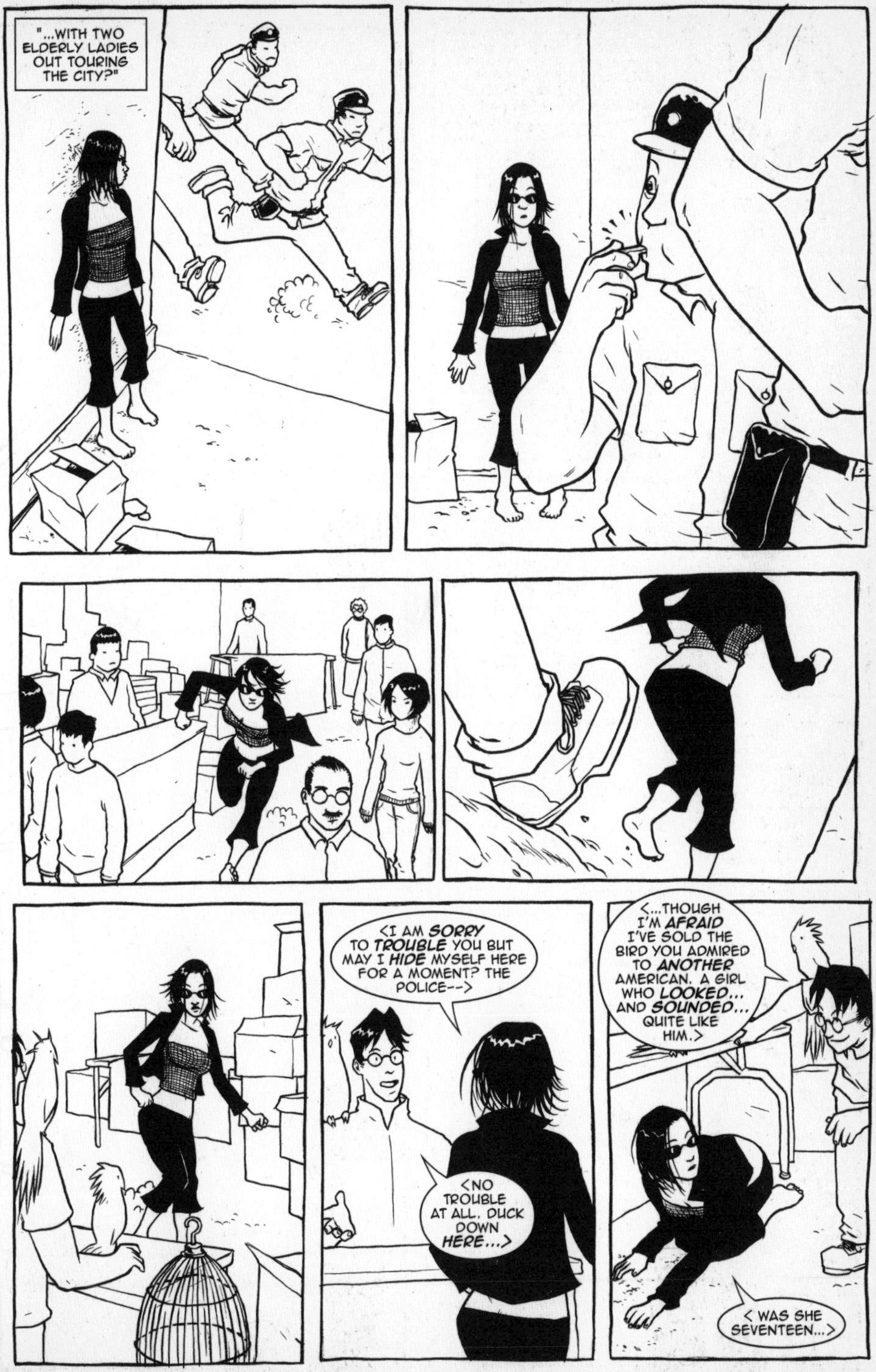
"...WITH TWO ELDERLY LADIES OUT TOURING THE CITY?"
<I AM SORRY TO TROUBLE YOU BUT MAY I HIDE MYSELF HERE FOR A MOMENT? THE POLICE-->
<NO TROUBLE AT ALL. DUCK DOWN HERE...>
<...THOUGH I'M AFRAID I'VE SOLD THE BIRD YOU ADMIRED TO ANOTHER AMERICAN. A GIRL WHO LOOKED... AND SOUNDED... QUITE LIKE HIM.>
< WAS SHE SEVENTEEN...>

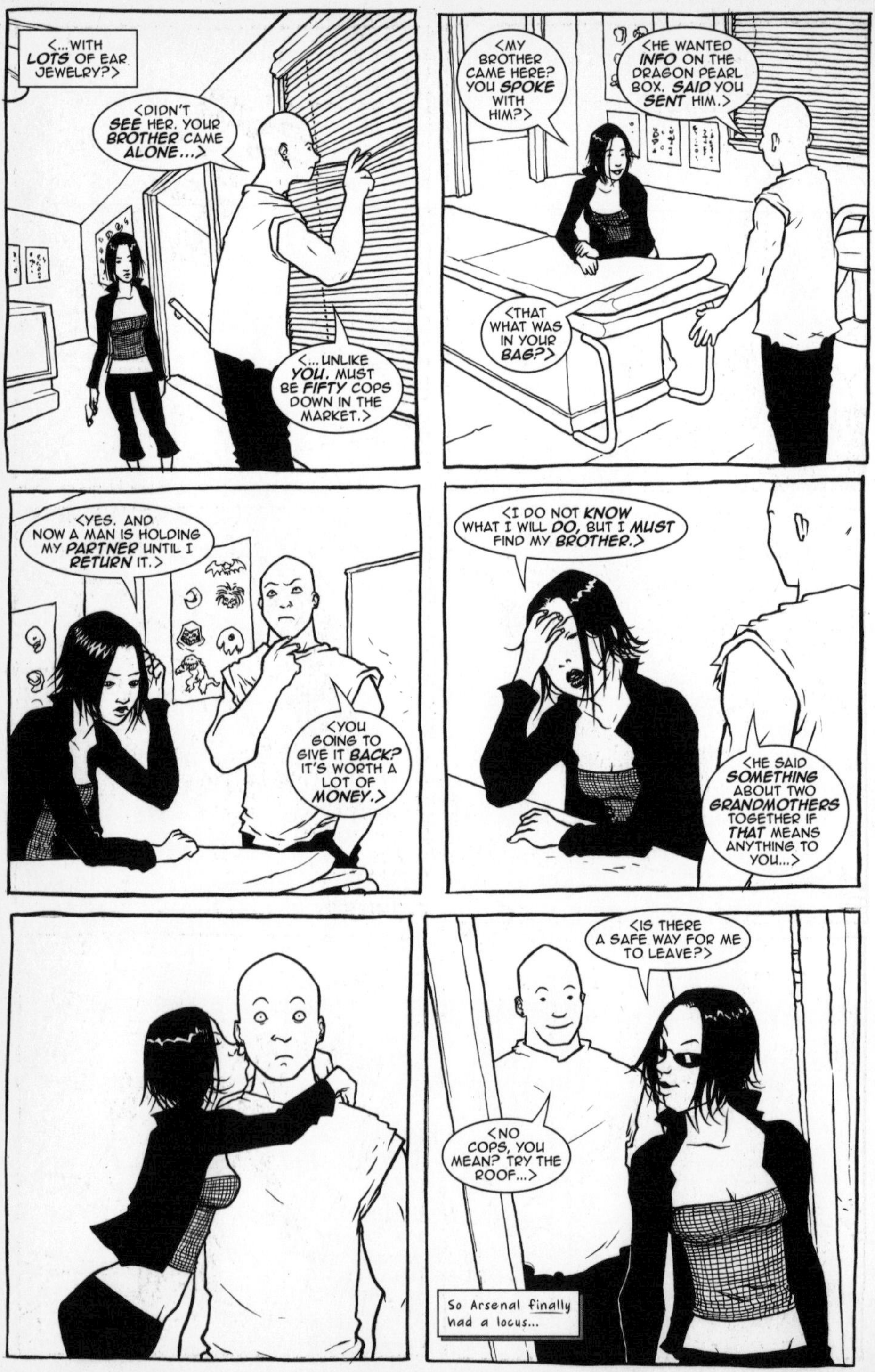
<...WITH LOTS OF EAR JEWELRY?>
<DIDN'T SEE HER. YOUR BROTHER CAME ALONE...>
<...UNLIKE YOU. MUST BE FIFTY COPS DOWN IN THE MARKET.>
<MY BROTHER CAME HERE? YOU SPOKE WITH HIM?>
<HE WANTED INFO ON THE DRAGON PEARL BOX. SAID YOU SENT HIM.>
<THAT WHAT WAS IN YOUR BAG?>
<YES. AND NOW A MAN IS HOLDING MY PARTNER UNTIL I RETURN IT.>
<YOU GOING TO GIVE IT BACK? IT'S WORTH A LOT OF MONEY.>
<I DO NOT KNOW WHAT I WILL DO, BUT I MUST FIND MY BROTHER.>
<HE SAID SOMETHING ABOUT TWO GRANDMOTHERS TOGETHER IF THAT MEANS ANYTHING TO YOU...>
<IS THERE A SAFE WAY FOR ME TO LEAVE?>
<NO COPS, YOU MEAN? TRY THE ROOF...>
So Arsenal finally had a locus...

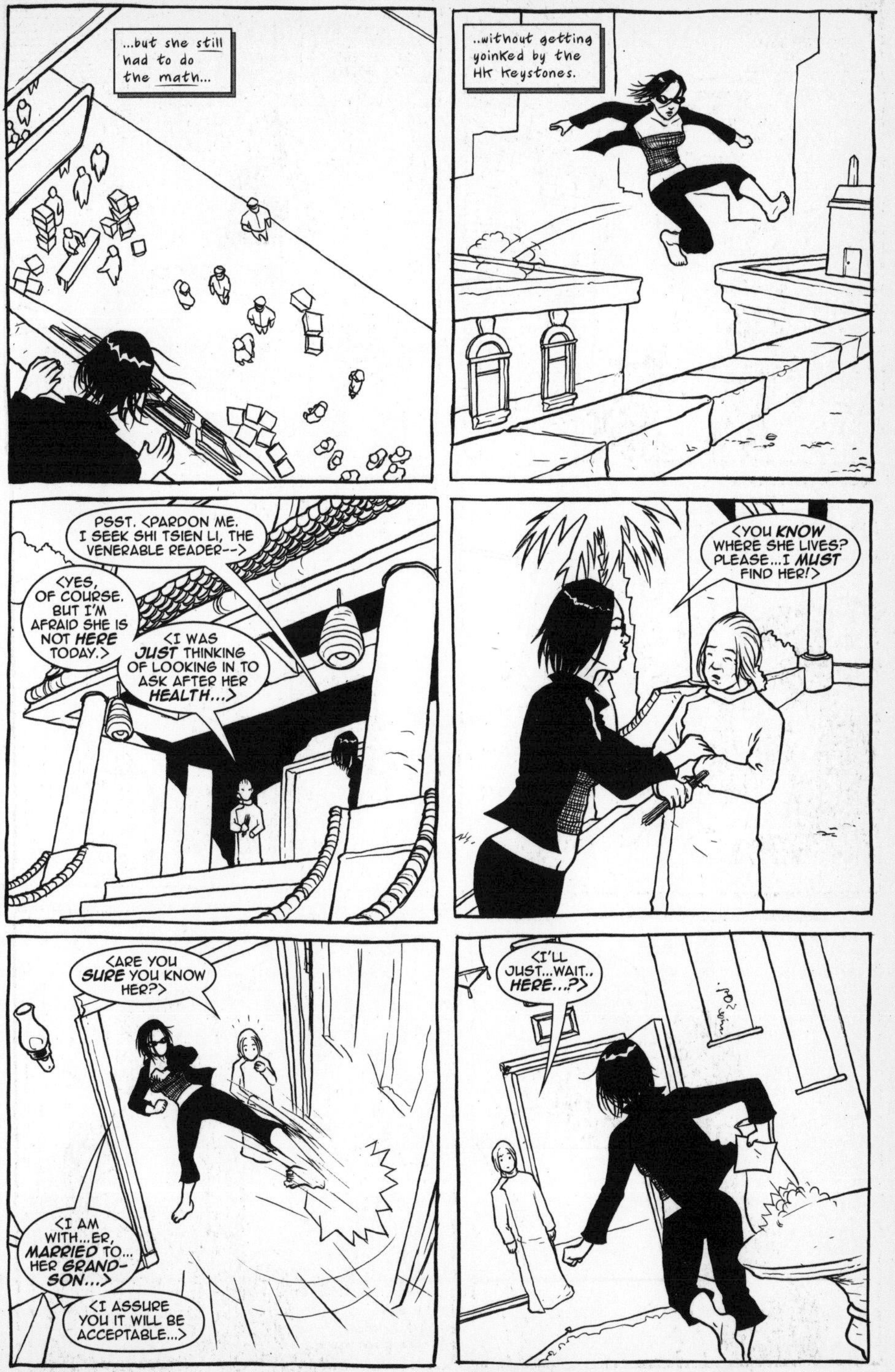
...but she still had to do the math...
..without getting yoinked by the HK Keystones.
PSST. <PARDON ME. I SEEK SHI TSIEN LI, THE VENERABLE READER-->
<YES, OF COURSE. BUT I'M AFRAID SHE IS NOT HERE TODAY.>
<I WAS JUST THINKING OF LOOKING IN TO ASK AFTER HER HEALTH...>
<YOU KNOW WHERE SHE LIVES? PLEASE...I MUST FIND HER!>
<ARE YOU SURE YOU KNOW HER?>
<I AM WITH...ER, MARRIED TO... HER GRAND-SON...>
<I ASSURE YOU IT WILL BE ACCEPTABLE...>
<I'LL JUST...WAIT.. HERE...?>

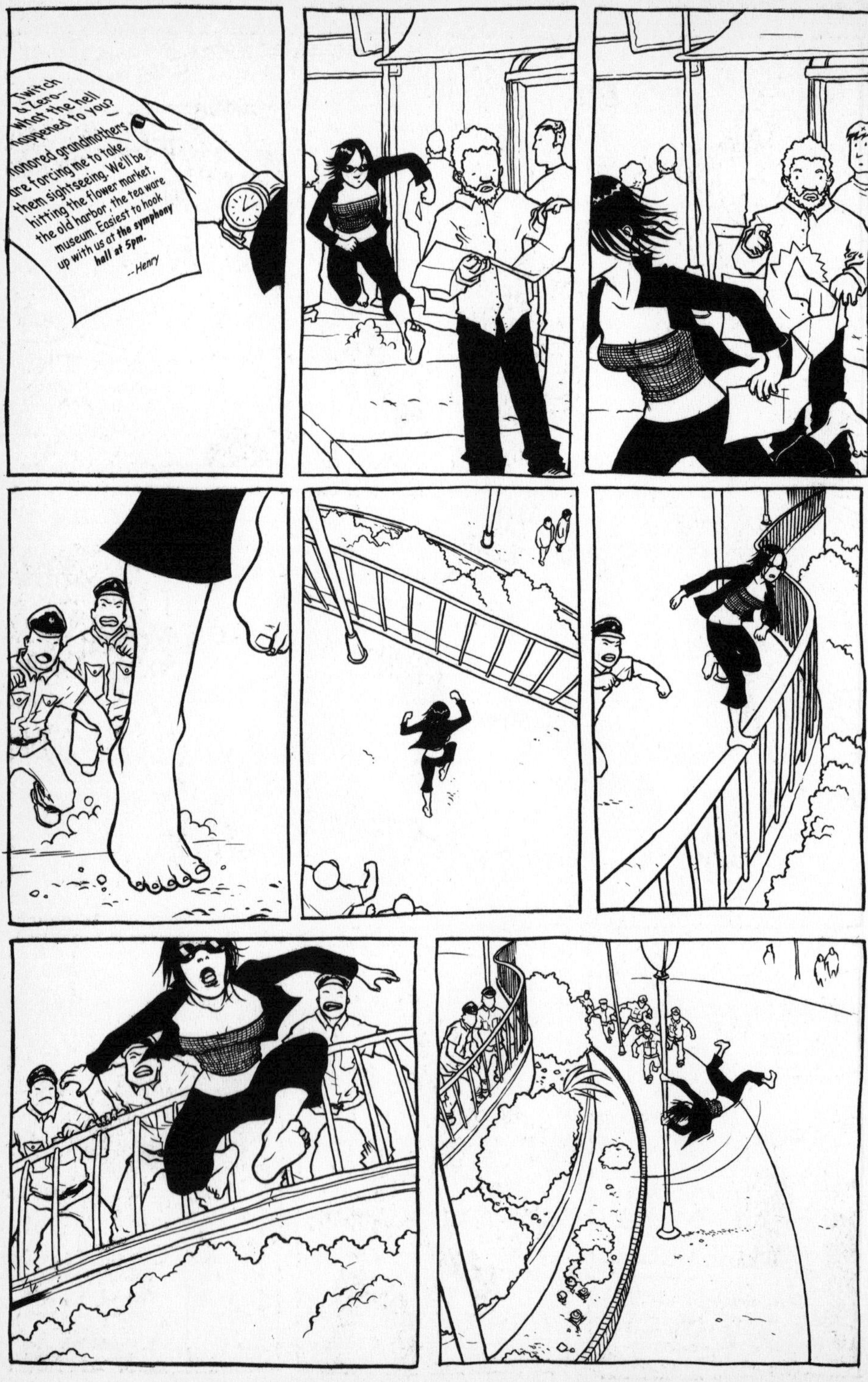
Twitch & Zero-- what the hell happened to you?
honored grandmothers are forcing me to take them sightseeing. We'll be hitting the flower market, the old harbor, the tea ware museum. Easiest to hook up with us at the symphony hall at 5pm.
--Henry

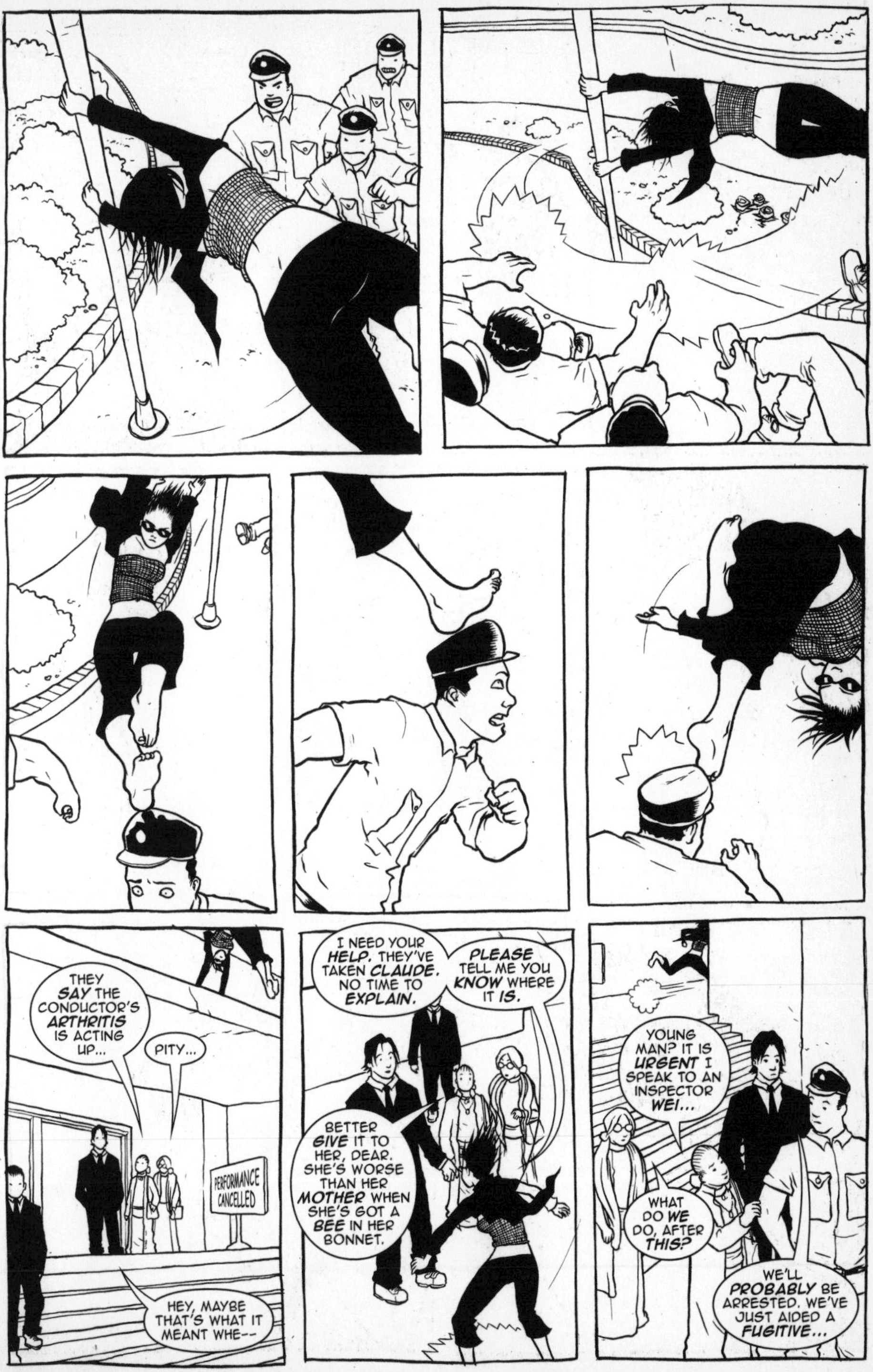
THEY SAY THE CONDUCTOR'S ARTHRITIS IS ACTING UP...
PITY...
PERFORMANCE CANCELLED
HEY, MAYBE THAT'S WHAT IT MEANT WHE--
I NEED YOUR HELP. THEY'VE TAKEN CLAUDE. NO TIME TO EXPLAIN.
PLEASE TELL ME YOU KNOW WHERE IT IS.
BETTER GIVE IT TO HER, DEAR. SHE'S WORSE THAN HER MOTHER WHEN SHE'S GOT A BEE IN HER BONNET.
YOUNG MAN? IT IS URGENT I SPEAK TO AN INSPECTOR WEI...
WHAT DO WE DO, AFTER THIS?
WE'LL PROBABLY BE ARRESTED. WE'VE JUST AIDED A FUGITIVE...

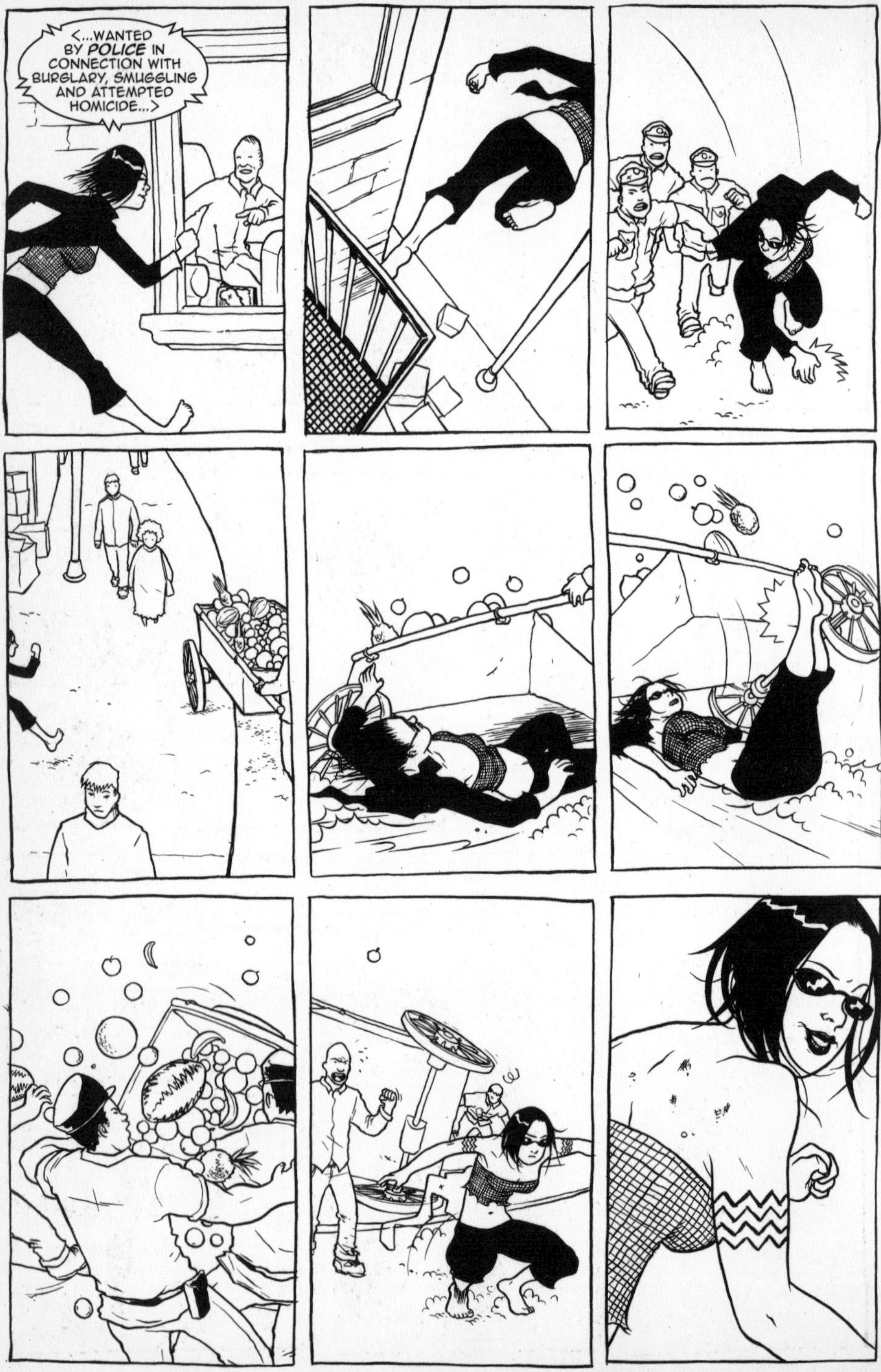
<...WANTED BY POLICE IN CONNECTION WITH BURGLARY, SMUGGLING AND ATTEMPTED HOMICIDE...>

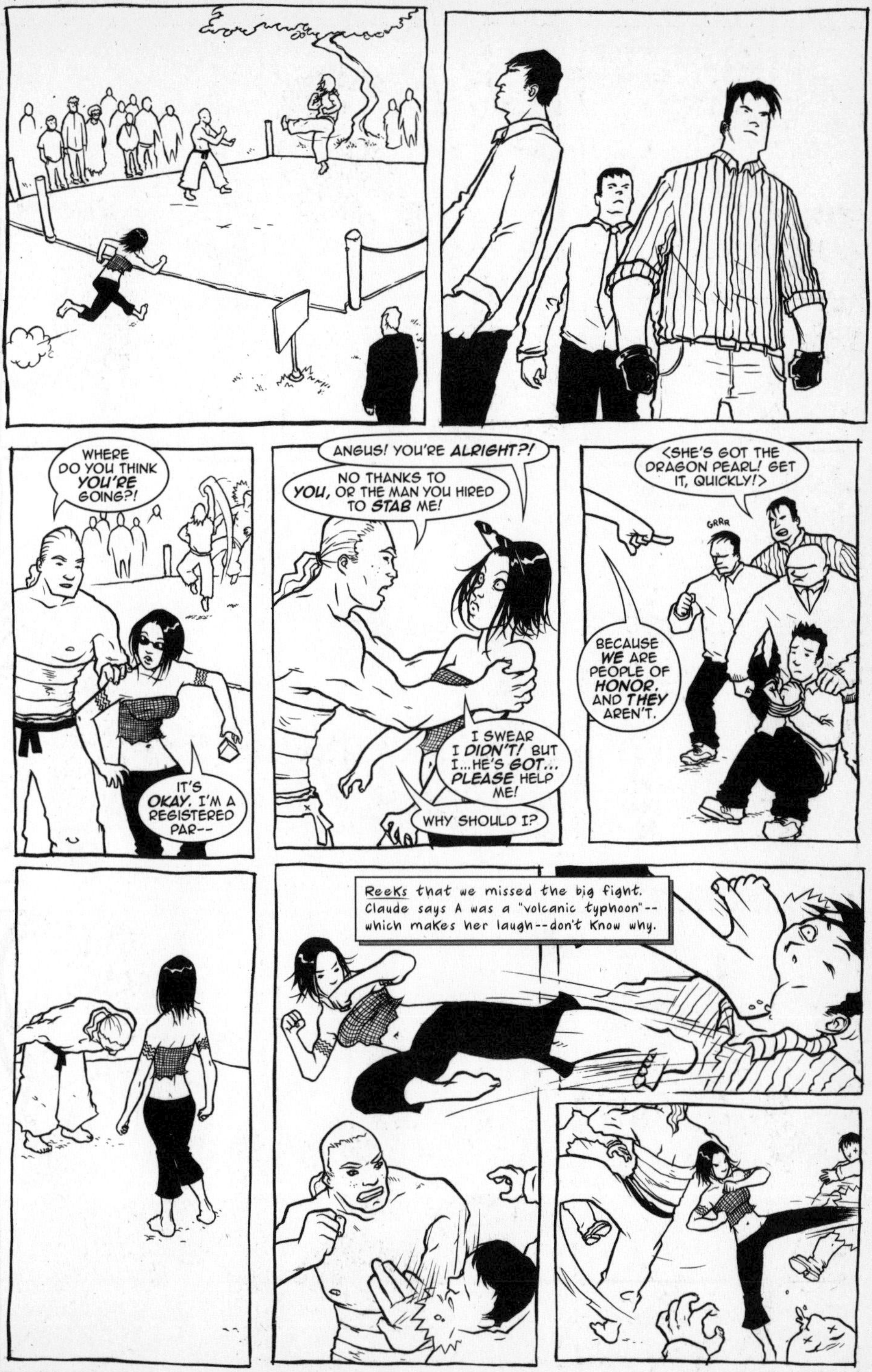
WHERE DO YOU THINK YOU'RE GOING?!
IT'S OKAY. I'M A REGISTERED PAR--
ANGUS! YOU'RE ALRIGHT?!
NO THANKS TO YOU, OR THE MAN YOU HIRED TO STAB ME!
I SWEAR I DIDN'T! BUT I...HE'S GOT... PLEASE HELP ME!
WHY SHOULD I?
<SHE'S GOT THE DRAGON PEARL! GET IT, QUICKLY!>
GRRR
BECAUSE WE ARE PEOPLE OF HONOR. AND THEY AREN'T.
Reeks that we missed the big fight. Claude says A was a "volcanic typhoon"--which makes her laugh--don't know why.

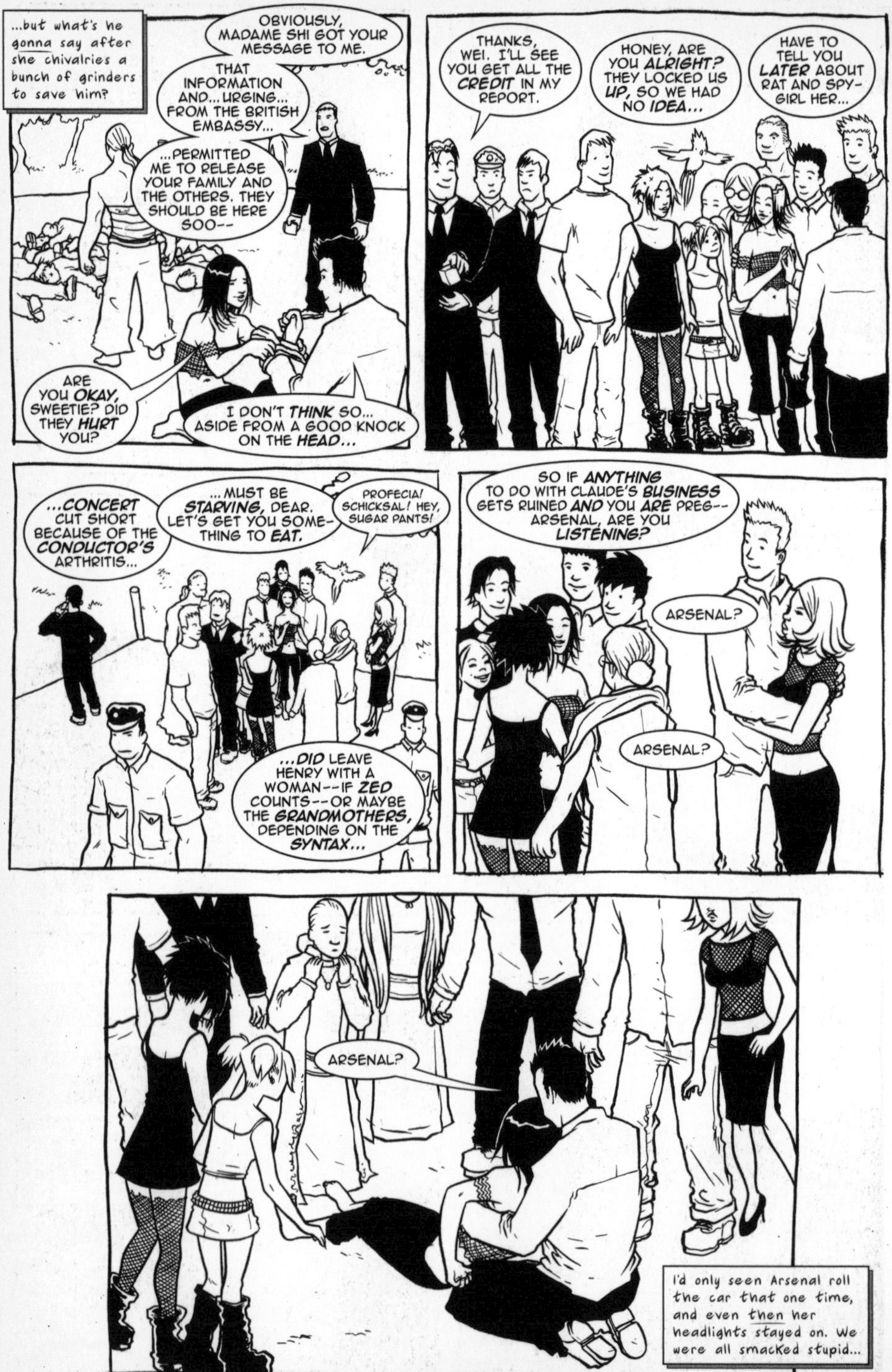
...but what's he gonna say after she chivalries a bunch of grinders to save him?
OBVIOUSLY, MADAME SHI GOT YOUR MESSAGE TO ME.
THAT INFORMATION AND... URGING... FROM THE BRITISH EMBASSY...
...PERMITTED ME TO RELEASE YOUR FAMILY AND THE OTHERS. THEY SHOULD BE HERE SOO--
ARE YOU OKAY, SWEETIE? DID THEY HURT YOU?
I DON'T THINK SO... ASIDE FROM A GOOD KNOCK ON THE HEAD...
THANKS, WEI. I'LL SEE YOU GET ALL THE CREDIT IN MY REPORT.
HONEY, ARE YOU ALRIGHT? THEY LOCKED US UP, SO WE HAD NO IDEA...
HAVE TO TELL YOU LATER ABOUT RAT AND SPY-GIRL HER...
...CONCERT CUT SHORT BECAUSE OF THE CONDUCTOR'S ARTHRITIS...
...MUST BE STARVING, DEAR. LET'S GET YOU SOME-THING TO EAT.
PROFECIA! SCHICKSAL! HEY, SUGAR PANTS!
...DID LEAVE HENRY WITH A WOMAN--IF ZED COUNTS--OR MAYBE THE GRANDMOTHERS, DEPENDING ON THE SYNTAX...
SO IF ANYTHING TO DO WITH CLAUDE'S BUSINESS GETS RUINED AND YOU ARE PREG-- ARSENAL, ARE YOU LISTENING?
ARSENAL?
ARSENAL?
ARSENAL?
I'd only seen Arsenal roll the car that one time, and even then her headlights stayed on. We were all smacked stupid...

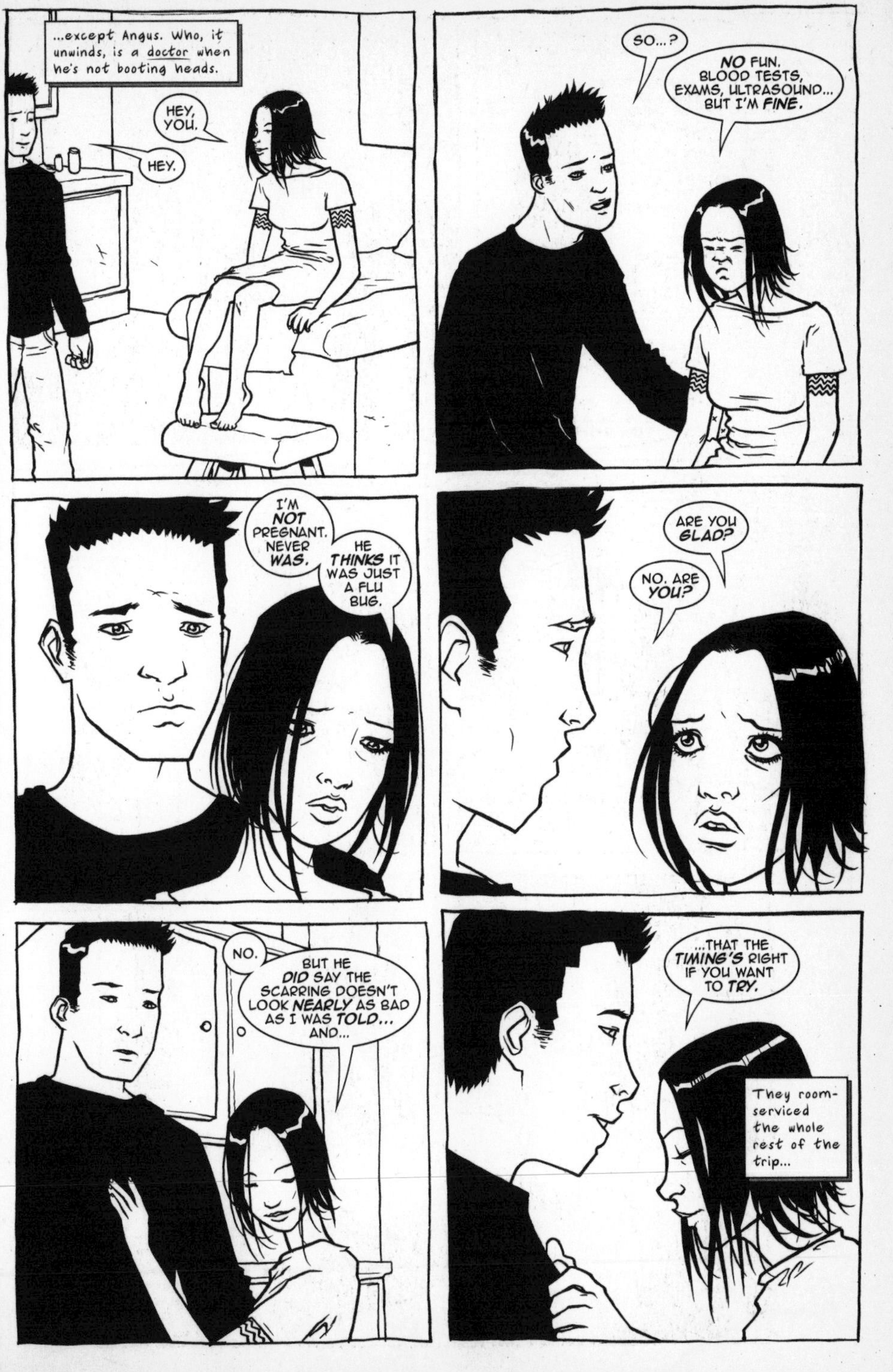

...except Angus. Who, it unwinds, is a doctor when he's not booting heads.
HEY, YOU.
HEY.
SO...?
NO FUN. BLOOD TESTS, EXAMS, ULTRASOUND... BUT I'M FINE.
I'M NOT PREGNANT. NEVER WAS.
HE THINKS IT WAS JUST A FLU BUG.
ARE YOU GLAD?
NO. ARE YOU?
NO.
BUT HE DID SAY THE SCARRING DOESN'T LOOK NEARLY AS BAD AS I WAS TOLD... AND...
...THAT THE TIMING'S RIGHT IF YOU WANT TO TRY.
They room-serviced the whole rest of the trip...

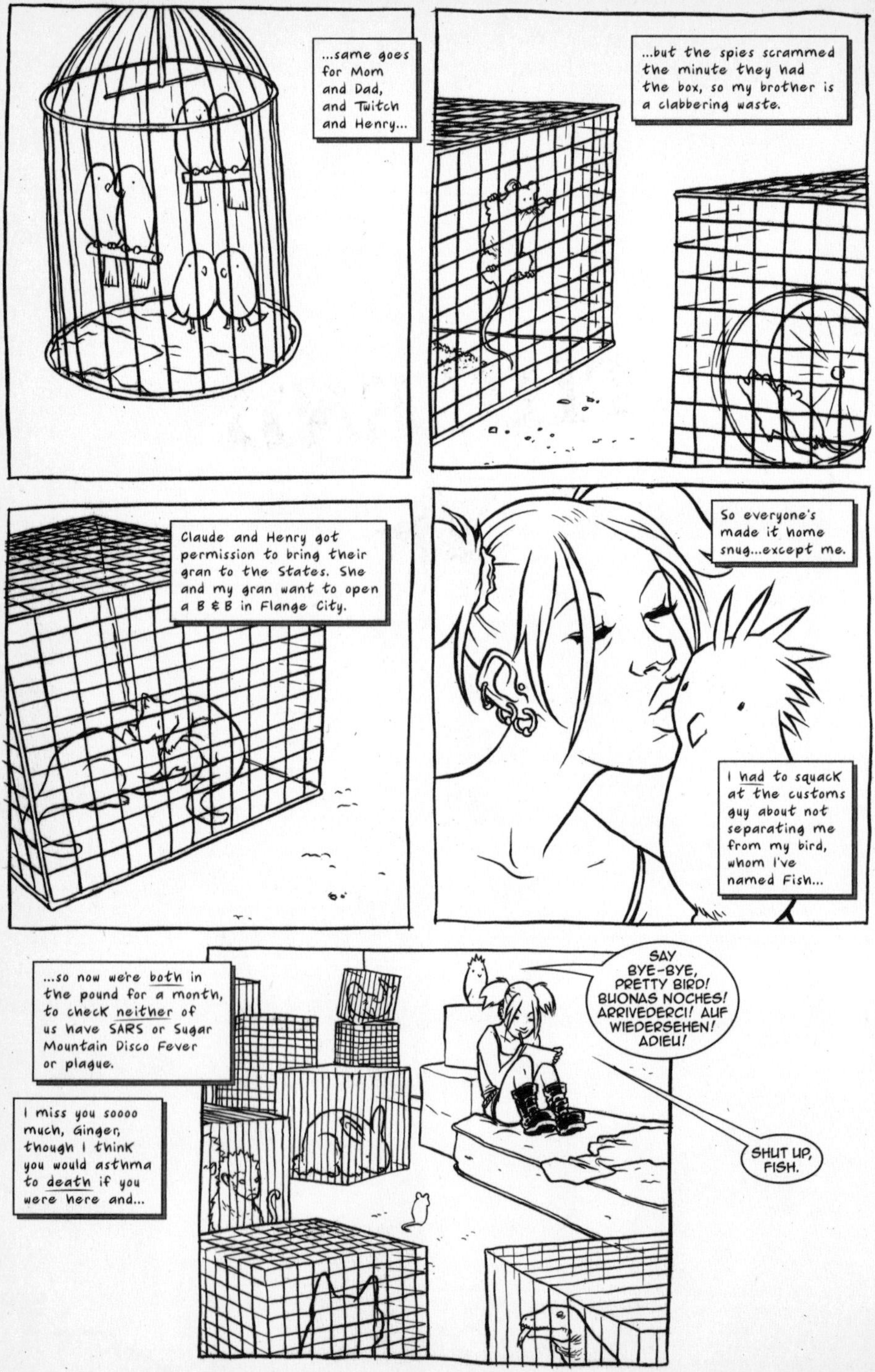
...same goes for Mom and Dad, and Twitch and Henry...
...but the spies scrammed the minute they had the box, so my brother is a clabbering waste.
Claude and Henry got permission to bring their gran to the States. She and my gran want to open a B & B in Flange City.
So everyone's made it home snug...except me.
I had to squack at the customs guy about not separating me from my bird, whom I've named Fish...
...so now we're both in the pound for a month, to check neither of us have SARS or Sugar Mountain Disco Fever or plague.
SAY BYE-BYE, PRETTY BIRD! BUONAS NOCHES! ARRIVEDERCI! AUF WIEDERSEHEN! ADIEU!
I miss you soooo much, Ginger, though I think you would asthma to death if you were here and...
SHUT UP, FISH.

THE END

★

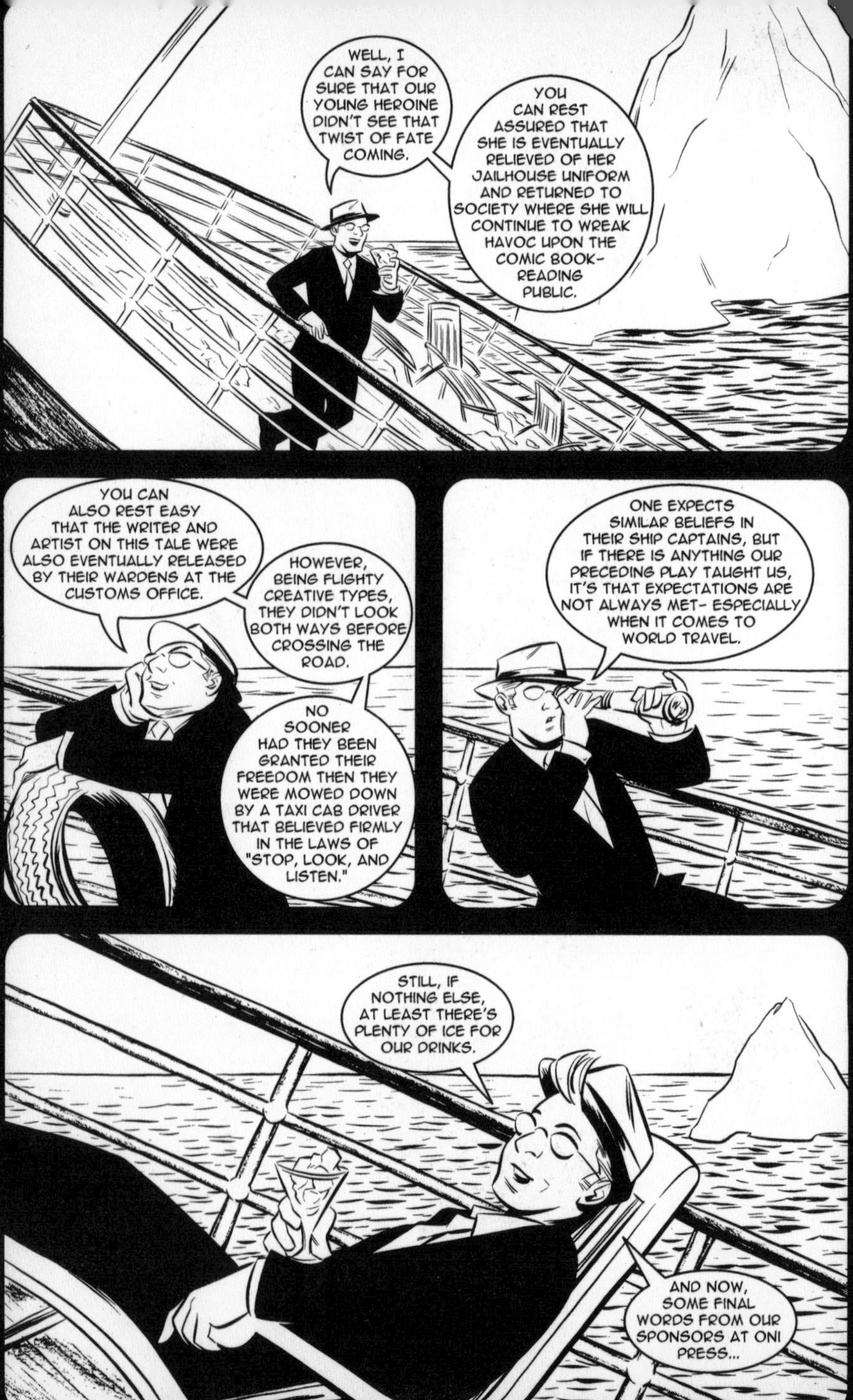
WELL, I CAN SAY FOR SURE THAT OUR YOUNG HEROINE DIDN'T SEE THAT TWIST OF FATE COMING.
YOU CAN REST ASSURED THAT SHE IS EVENTUALLY RELIEVED OF HER JAILHOUSE UNIFORM AND RETURNED TO SOCIETY WHERE SHE WILL CONTINUE TO WREAK HAVOC UPON THE COMIC BOOK-READING PUBLIC.
YOU CAN ALSO REST EASY THAT THE WRITER AND ARTIST ON THIS TALE WERE ALSO EVENTUALLY RELEASED BY THEIR WARDENS AT THE CUSTOMS OFFICE.
HOWEVER, BEING FLIGHTY CREATIVE TYPES, THEY DIDN'T LOOK BOTH WAYS BEFORE CROSSING THE ROAD.
NO SOONER HAD THEY BEEN GRANTED THEIR FREEDOM THEN THEY WERE MOWED DOWN BY A TAXI CAB DRIVER THAT BELIEVED FIRMLY IN THE LAWS OF "STOP, LOOK, AND LISTEN."
ONE EXPECTS SIMILAR BELIEFS IN THEIR SHIP CAPTAINS, BUT IF THERE IS ANYTHING OUR PRECEDING PLAY TAUGHT US, IT'S THAT EXPECTATIONS ARE NOT ALWAYS MET- ESPECIALLY WHEN IT COMES TO WORLD TRAVEL.
STILL, IF NOTHING ELSE, AT LEAST THERE'S PLENTY OF ICE FOR OUR DRINKS.
AND NOW, SOME FINAL WORDS FROM OUR SPONSORS AT ONI PRESS...

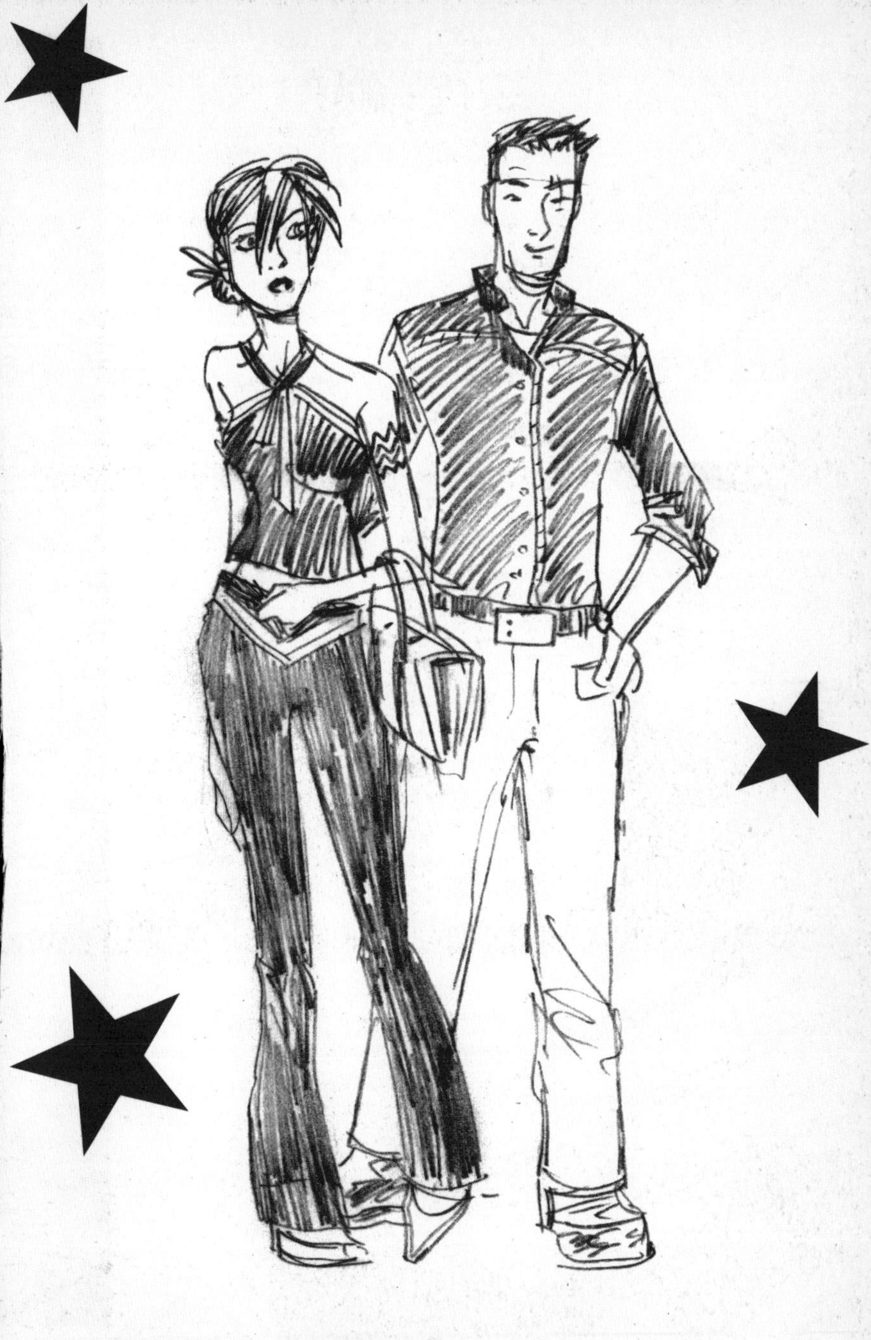

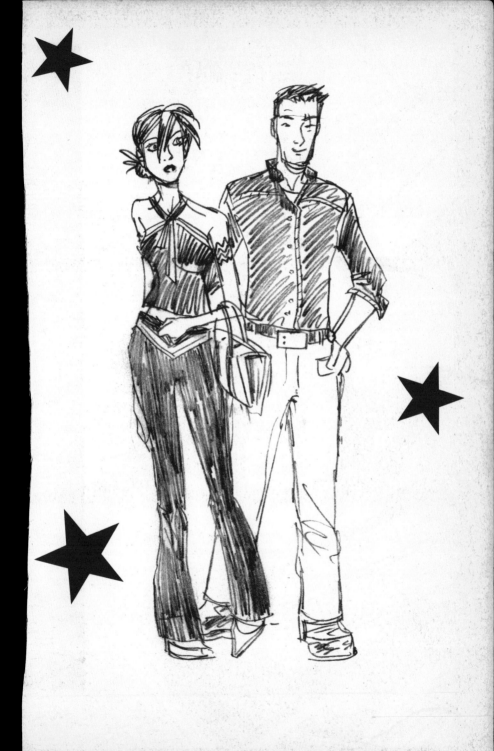

Jen Van Meter made her comic book debut alongside *Buffy the Vampire Slayer*, scripting that character's first-ever comic book story for *Dark Horse Presents Annual 1998*. She followed it up with a collaboration with Frank Quietly in Vertigo's horror anthology *Flinch*, a script for DC's *Gotham Knights*, a segment of Marvel's *Captain America #50*, and the licensed comic book tie-in *The Blair Witch Project*, the best selling issue in Oni Press' history. *Hopeless Savages* is her first creator-owned work (if you don't count her son, Elliot), and its first series was nominated for an Eisner in 2002. Her most recent releases include the *Batman Elseworlds* book for DC, *Golden Streets of Gotham*, and the mini-series *Cinnamon: El Ciclo*. She currently lives in Portland, Oregon with her husband and two children.

Born in West Germany, Christine Norrie has lived in many places but fondly claims St. Louis as her hometown, the place she grew to love comics. She moved to New York in the late nineties, worked in the business end of comic publishing for DC Comics, and later became a freelance illustrator. Since the debut of the first *Hopeless Savages* series, she's been nominated for many awards including the prestigious Eisner Award, the Russ Manning Award, and was a recipient for the New York City Comic Book Museum's Award for Breakout Artist of 2002. Christine Norrie is the comic artist for Redbook magazine's *Q&A with John Gray: You and Him* and *Spy Kids* for Disney, as well as the graphic novel, *Cheat*. Her most recent project has been her lovely daughter, Josephine. She is helped in this endeavor by a menagerie of animals, her dog Orwell, and her husband Andrew.

Ross Campbell is a recluse who currently lives in Savannah, Georgia. He made his comic debut drawing the flashback sequences in this series, *Too Much Hopeless Savages*. By issue 4, he was doing all of the interior art. He also illustrated and lettered *Spooked*, an original graphic novel written by Antony Johnston and published by Oni Press. His first solo creation, *Wet Moon*, is scheduled for publication later this year. He loves cats and giant monsters.

Chynna Clugston-Major is the talented cartoonist behind the award-nominated series, *Blue Monday*- available in three trade paperbacks, *The Kids are Alright*, *Absolute Beginners*, and *Inbetween Days*. She is currently working on the fourth installment of the series entitled *Blue Monday: Painted Moon*. Chynna has also recently completed the six-issue mini-series, *Scooter Girl*, now available in a single volume.

OTHER BOOKS FROM THE CREATORS OF HOPELESS SAVAGES AND ONI PRESS...

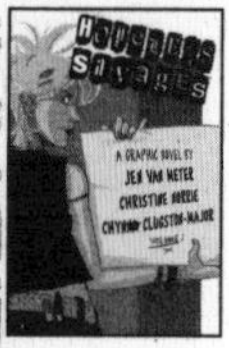
Hopeless Savages

HOPELESS SAVAGES™
VOL. 1
By Jen Van Meter, Christine Norrie, & Chynna Clugston-Major
136 pages, black-and-white interiors
$11.95 US
ISBN 1-929998-75-9

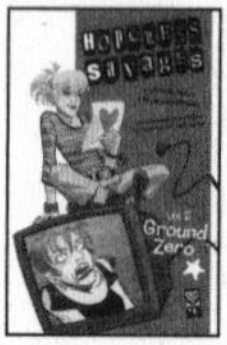
Hopeless Savages
Ground Zero

HOPELESS SAVAGES™
VOL. 2: GROUND ZERO
By Jen Van Meter & Bryan-Lee O'Malley w/ Chynna Clugston-Major, Christine Norrie, & Andi Watson
128 pages, black-and-white interiors
$11.95 US
ISBN 1-929998-99-6

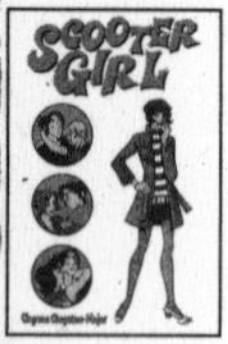
Scooter Girl

SCOOTER GIRL™
By Chynna Clugston-Major
168 pages, black-and-white interiors
$14.95 US
ISBN 1-929998-88-0

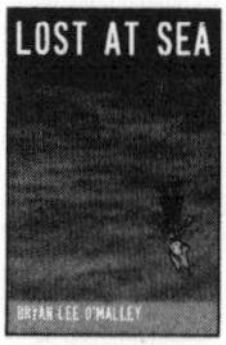
LOST AT SEA
BRYAN LEE O'MALLEY

LOST AT SEA™
By Bryan Lee O'Malley
168 pages, black-and-white interiors
$11.95 US
ISBN 1-929998-71-6

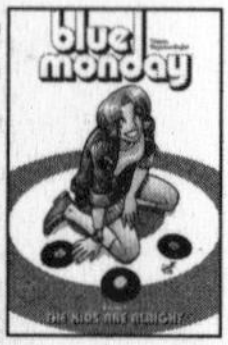
blue monday

BLUE MONDAY™
VOL. 1: THE KIDS ARE ALRIGHT
By Chynna Clugston-Major
136 pages, black-and-white interiors
$10.95 US
ISBN 1-929998-62-7

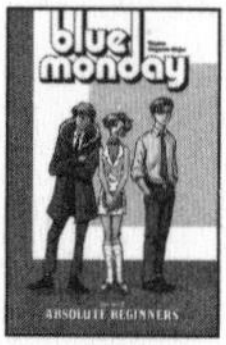
blue monday
ABSOLUTE BEGINNERS

BLUE MONDAY™
VOL. 2: ABSOLUTE BEGINNERS
By Chynna Clugston-Major
128 pages, black-and-white interiors
$11.95 US
ISBN 1-929998-17-1

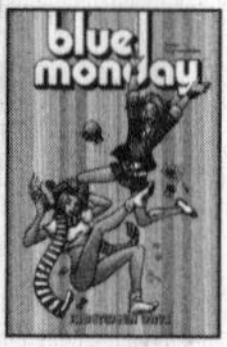
blue monday

BLUE MONDAY™
VOL. 3: INBETWEEN DAYS
By Chynna Clugston-Major
120 pages, black-and-white interiors
$9.95 US
ISBN 1-929998-66-x

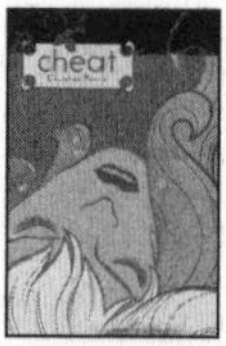
cheat

CHEAT™
By Christine Norrie
72 pages, black-and-white interiors
$5.95 US
ISBN 1-929998-47-3

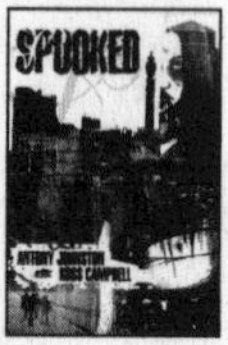
SPOOKED

SPOOKED™
By Antony Johnston & Ross Campbell
168 pages, black-and-white interiors
$14.95 US
ISBN 1-929998-79-1

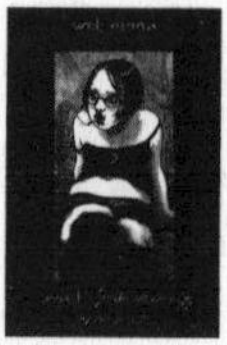

WET MOON™
By Ross Campbell
184 pages, black-and-white interiors
$14.95 US
ISBN 1-932664-07-6

Oni Press graphic novels are available at finer comics shops everywhere. For a comics store near you, call 1-888-COMIC-BOOK, or visit www.the-master-list.com.